ANNE BAXTER

Portrait still from *Chase A Crooked Shadow*. Courtesy of Don Eckhart.

ANNE BAXTER

A Bio-Bibliography

Karin J. Fowler

Bio-Bibliographies in the Performing Arts, Number 20

GREENWOOD PRESS
New York • Westport, Connecticut • London

Library of Congress Cataloging-in-Publication Data

Fowler, Karin J.
   Anne Baxter : a bio-bibliography / Karin J. Fowler.
     p.   cm.—(Bio-bibliographies in the performing arts, ISSN
0892-5550 ; no. 20)
   Includes bibliographical references and index.
   ISBN 0-313-27543-2 (alk. paper)
   1. Baxter, Anne. 2. Baxter, Anne—Bibliography. 3. Actors—
United States—Biography.   I. Title.   II. Series.
PN2287.B39F6   1991
791.43'028'092—dc20   91-22264
 [B]

British Library Cataloguing in Publication Data is available.

Library of Congress Catalog Card Number: 91-22264
ISBN: 0-313-27543-2
ISSN: 0892-5550

First published in 1991

Greenwood Press, 88 Post Road West, Westport, CT 06881
An imprint of Greenwood Publishing Group, Inc.

Printed in the United States of America

The paper used in this book complies with the
Permanent Paper Standard issued by the National
Information Standards Organization (Z39.48-1984).

10 9 8 7 6 5 4 3 2 1

This book is dedicated to Frieda Fowler. I love you, Mama.

Contents

Preface

Anne Baxter's acting career spanned nearly fifty years. At age thirteen, she made her first stage appearance and within a few short years established a film career than won her accolades and awards. Many of her more than eighty films became classics. She starred in almost as many guest roles on television, again winning the admiration of her peers, as well as her audiences. Always willing to take risks, she left her acting life to live in a foreign country with her second husband, an experience which she later wrote about. This writing endeavor earned her critical acclaim, as well. After her four-year break in her profession, Anne returned to acting, to which she brought her special brand of character and authority. Small of stature but grand of spirit, Anne Baxter left an indelible mark on her audiences.

This book is divided into six main sections:

1. A biography of Anne Baxter's life and career.

2. A chronological listing of her life achievements.

3. Listings of her productions: movies are preceded by the mnemonic "F"; television series and movie appearances are preceded by the mnemonic "T"; radio guest roles and dramatic appearances are preceded by the mnemonic "R"; recorded soundtracks are preceded by the mnemonic "M"; and stage appearances are preceded by the mnemonic "S". Cross-references are provided.

4. A bibliography of writings about Anne Baxter: annotate
sources, including books, periodicals, and newspapers,
are preceded by the mnemonic "B." Unannotated sources
in books, periodicals, and newspapers are preceded
by the mnemonic "UB." Cross-references are provided.

5. Awards conferred to Anne Baxter and the films in which
she appeared are preceded by the mnemonic "A."

6. An index of personal names and titles (access is to
entry codes).

Acknowledgments

My thanks go to those who have assisted or contributed in the completion of this book:

Mary Blair and Marilyn Brownstein, Greenwood Press, for their guidance.

James Robert Parish, for his kindness, selflessness, and encouragement in this new endeavor.

Michael R. Pitts, Tom Bourgeois, Jerry Roberts, Barry Rivadue, Art Pierce, Sandy Webber, and Jeff Carrier, Vincent Terrace, Milton Moore, and Edwin Matthias, for their help in my research efforts.

Doug McClelland, for his reflections on his interview with Miss Baxter.

John Doherty (whose uncle, the late Eddie Doherty, wrote the screenplay of <u>The Fighting Sullivans</u>), for sharing his remembrances.

Don Eckhart, for providing wonderful photographs.

Margie Schultz has my special thanks for her friendship and thoughtful exchange of information.

My friends and family, for their continued support.

Biography

A movie star's life was the goal of many young men and
women in the heyday of Hollywood and its nurturing studios.
Although attaining the hope of success and stardom did not
guarantee the actual existence of either, the few who knew they
had the talent and fortitude were willing to put their
aspirations to the test. One such young lady was Anne Baxter.

Beginnings

Anne Baxter was born in Michigan City, Indiana, on
May 7, 1923. Her father was Kenneth Stuart Baxter, who would
become a top executive of Seagram's Distilleries. Her mother,
Catherine Wright, was a daughter of the dean of American
architects, Frank Lloyd Wright, who brought modern architecture
"out of a period of Wall Street Parthenons and Spanish
haciendas." Wright instilled into his children a love of the
arts. Each child was required to specialize in a talent.
Catherine's was music. Her daughter, Anne, was destined to
also have a talent.

The Baxter family moved from Michigan City to White Plains
to Chappaqua to the Bronx in New York City. "I was brought
up right," she said, maintaining that her childhood was loving
yet unspoiled. Strict Presbyterians, her parents instilled
in her the desire to work hard and never accept "the cushion
of her birth."

Even as a prepubescent, Anne achieved a remarkable degree of sophistication. She insisted on knowing the why of everything. She declared her determination to be an actress after seeing a stage production starring Helen Hayes in New York. Her parents and grandfather understood and supported the ten-year-old's desire. Anne's mother encouraged her to attend private schools. Anne attended the Lenox School (1937-1938), then Brearly School (1938-1939).

Anne also attended Theodora Irvine's School of Theatre (1934-1936). This school gave her the solid background to handl the emotional problems that often plagued child actors as they grew older. While attending the school, she made her Broadway debut, at age 13. The Henry Miller Theater production of Seen But Not Heard (S1) garnered Anne very good reviews. Variety described her as "a cute kidlet." The New York Evening Journal interviewed a very mature Anne who said, "There is no stopping my ambition. I always like to dramatize things in my life. Acting is not merely fun, it is an earnest career." Anne's role continued through the run's 60 performances.

Miss Baxter was invited to study with the prestigious, strong-willed acting teacher, actress Maria Ouspenskaya (1936-1940). Miss Ouspenskaya used the method of acting called Stanislavsky, named for the Russian whose ideas started the latter-day "method acting." He insisted that it wasn't enough to walk on stage and say, "Dinner is served." One had to be aware of why it was served and what the cook's grandmother had said in 1894 when the grandfather came home raging drunk on vodka! Maria could not afford a theater to try this on stage, so she kept her students busy backstage doing Stanislavsky exercises. Anne did not always agree with the imperious Russian actress, and they frequently clashed.

Anne's next acting venture on stage was in There's Always a Breeze (S2), which debuted in March, 1938. In October, 1938, she appeared in Madame Capet (S3), with the illustrious actress Eva Le Gallienne. Her summers of 1938 and 1939 were spent at Dennis, Massachusetts, where she appeared in Susan and God (S4) and Spring Meeting (S5) with the Cape Playhouse Stock Company.

Soon thereafter, Anne auditioned for a role in the Broadway production of The Philadelphia Story. She was to play the younger sister of Katharine Hepburn. Miss Hepburn nixed her for the role and accused Anne of overacting, using too many grand gestures and missing her comedy cues. Anne's mentor prove to be Shirley Booth, who took Anne aside and advised her not to give up.

Anne, however, had other aspirations. She had been preparing to travel to Hollywood and try her luck in films. At age 14, she was called by David O. Selznick to test for a role in Tom Sawyer opposite Montgomery Clift. The test was never made, because Clift had acne so bad that Selznick took one look at the clip and sent them both back to New York.

Kay Brown, an agent of Selznick's, thought Anne would be perfect for the lead role in his upcoming film Rebecca. Anne told J. Bawden, of Films in Review, "This time I actually tested in a scene from Dorothy Vernon of Haddon Hall. Then Selznick looked in my mouth and examined my teeth, and I felt like I was a prize racing horse. Hitchcock then filmed me in several scenes from the film and said I was his choice. But Selznick thought I photographed too young next to Laurence Olivier."

Darryl F. Zanuck saw her test and was impressed enough to sign her to a standard seven-year contract, starting at $350 per week. He was unhappy to learn that she was under-age and tried to delay the contract. But Anne had already made plans to remain in Hollywood. Zanuck had no work for her, since she lost out for the role in Rebecca, which went to Joan Fontaine. Anne was instead loaned to M-G-M for the ingenue role in Twenty Mule Team (F1, 1940). Again, Anne was accused of overacting by director Dick Thorpe. Co-star Marjorie Rambeau instructed her to act slowly to gain more effect. During filming, Anne boarded with Nigel and Bonnie Bruce until her mother could join her.

Anne returned to 20th Century-Fox, where she was the ingenue in The Great Profile (F2, 1940), starring John Barrymore in a thinly-veiled caricature performance of himself. "He was very courtly around me," said Anne, "and did not use foul words reserved for the valet. There was a distance in his eyes as if he were sleepwalking, but at times his voice took on another timbre and he could quote long passages from Shakespeare." She felt he was "highly competitive," because Barrymore complained to the director, "Does she have to swim?" in her first scene where she wildly flailed her arms.

Charley's Aunt (F3, 1941), starring Jack Benny, was Anne's next film, where she had a small role. She also was up for the role in Chad Hanna but lost out to Zanuck's favorite star at the time, Linda Darnell. Instead, Anne was given the part of Julie in Jean Renoir's first American film, Swamp Water (F4, 1941), starring Walter Brennan, Walter Huston, and Dana Andrews. In the movie, filmed in the Okefenokee Swamp of Florida, she played the daughter of a hunted but innocent murderer. According to Philip Hartung of Commonweal, Anne's performance was beautifully in keeping with the spirit of bayou folk and well acted.

The 20th Century-Fox Studio publicity department trained its worldwide guns on Anne's exposure. Although she loved working on the stage, she knew that film was the acme of exposure. In the portrait gallery, brown-eyed, brown-haired Anne Baxter was initially treated to the Hollywood makeover. She had grown to her full height of 5'3" but had not yet shed the baby fat of her round cheeks that photographed so much younger. One of her pictures was featured on the cover of True Romances magazine, where she was "stuffed into a jersey outfit" that was intended to make her look sophisticated. All it did was make her feel "looted."

When Orson Welles was casting his movie The Magnificent Ambersons (F5, 1942), one of his most-used actors had an idea. Joseph Cotten had remembered Anne Baxter from her try-out in The Philadelphia Story and suggested they use her for the role of Lucy Morgan. "The film had the most magnificent sets of any film I've been on," she said. Welles had one studio floor excavated so he could film on three levels. He preferred to improvise scenes and even shot the winter scenes in an abandoned ice house. "The film in rough cut was an utter masterpiece. The released version was cut down and was not," Anne later noted Welles had lost interest and started producing Journey into Fear, then left for South America. Howard Barnes, critic for the New York Herald Tribune, praised Anne's work as "a forthrigh portrayal of the young heroine." The story of the Amberson family's decline from the world of the wealthy would become a classic and seemed to secure Welles's place in cinematic importance.

After completing The Magnificent Ambersons, Anne was slated to appear in The Pied Piper (F6, 1942). The sinister-looking Otto Preminger presided over the bunch of child actors in the film. Anne found him to be "utterly charming." According to Time magazine, Anne affected a fine French accent as the young woman who helps Monty Woolley and a group of orphaned children escape the Nazi invasion of Paris to a safe haven in England.

Following The Pied Piper, Billy Wilder borrowed Anne for a prominent role in The Five Graves to Cairo (F8, 1943). He liked her French accent in the previous film and decided she would suit the new role. According to Anne, director Billy Wilder did not realize she would get advice from co-star Erich Von Stroheim. "Erich would take me aside to coach me," said Anne," and I appreciated it until I realized he wanted the scene to go his way." It made for many tense moments on the set.

It was later announced that Anne was to star in the lead role in The Song of Bernadette. However, producer David O. Selznick had other ideas. He wanted his current successor to Linda Darnell, Miss Jennifer Jones, for the role. Jones won an Academy Award for Best Actress for the part and ended up marrying Selznick.

Anne's next few movie roles continued to be in the ingenue genre. World War II was under way and many patriotic war films were being made. Anne's contribution saw her starring in mainly wholesome, girl-next-door, secondary roles. She replaced a pregnant Teresa Wright and again co-starred with Erich Von Stroheim in North Star (F9, 1943), a slightly different war story about a Russian village overtaken by the Nazis. Philip Hartung, of Commonweal, felt Anne was fine in her role of a young freedom-fighter in the fictional Russian town of North Star.

In Crash Dive (F7, 1943), Anne was the love interest of two rival Navy officers, who put aside their personal differences to fight the enemy in a submarine. David Lardner, of the New Yorker, felt it wasn't easy to put your finger on the good it did for Anne Baxter and her co-stars Tyrone Power and Dana Andrews to appear in the film!

The Eve of St. Mark (F10, 1944) was another picture featuring Anne as the love interest of a young man going off to war. Commonweal's movie critic, Philip Hartung, said of Anne's performance, "Anne plays her so honestly and simply that she seems like the girl next door."

Following this film, Anne appeared in The Fighting Sullivans (later known as The Sullivans) (F11, 1944), the true tale of a war-torn family who lost all five sons in a battle in the Pacific. Anne portrayed the wife of one of the sons. Critics noted the film's realism and simplicity.

Anne next appeared in Sunday Dinner for a Soldier (F12, 1945), a pleasant little film about a bayou family who invited a soldier home for his last meal before leaving for the war. David Lardner, of the New Yorker, felt Anne was "natural and effective." Newsweek remarked that this was a "charming little World War II film."

According to a popular screen magazine article at the time titled "Annotations on Anne," one of her favorite guests at her home was John Hodiak, her co-star in Sunday Dinner for a Soldier. John Hodiak was born on April 16, 1914, the son of proud Ukrainian immigrants, from Pittsburgh, Pennsylvania.

He was a child performer in amateur foreign-language plays.
His family moved to Detroit, Michigan, when he was eight years
old. After graduating high school, Hodiak considered joining
the priesthood but ended up joining his father at a Chevrolet
auto factory. With no training, he auditioned at a radio station
and became its announcer. He moved to Chicago and began acting;
his first role on radio was as the lead in Li'l Abner. He
attended Northwestern University and left to sign with M-G-M.
He refused to change his name and brought his parents to live
in a house he purchased for them in Tarzana, California.

Earlier in New York, Hodiak had assisted black actor Canada
Lee in his screen test. Alfred Hitchcock saw it and hired them
both. Hodiak appeared in several films before being cast as
Major Victor Joppolo in A Bell for Adano. His distinctive,
deep voice, his square-jawed good looks and strong build made
him a star in Hitchcock's film Lifeboat, co-starring Tallulah
Bankhead. He was loaned to 20th Century-Fox Studios for Sunday
Dinner for a Soldier, where he met Anne Baxter. The two young
actors began dating during filming and scuttlebutt had it that
the two would be wed following his return from the service.
According to the magazine article, Anne's reply to what she
wanted in a husband was, "He'll be intelligent, tall,
good-natured, humorous and fascinated by books and music. He'll
also like to walk."

After a two-year courtship, on July 7, 1946, John Hodiak
and Anne Baxter were married in a garden ceremony at her parents'
home in Burlingame, California. On July 9, 1951, Anne gave
birth to their only child, Katrina.

Anne and husband John Hodiak were complete opposites in
background and temperament (he was poor and unruffled and self-
effacing; she, rich and "often ruffled as an old-fashioned
petticoat"). Anne loved him deeply, but their two careers
created "professional murder" for their marriage from the very
beginning.

Anne preferred to be buried in her work at this point in
her life. Her next film was a departure from her rather demure
roles to date. She played against type in A Guest in the House
(F13, 1945), opposite Ralph Bellamy and Ruth Warrick. She is
a seemingly nice girl who tries to infect the household with
her malice. Critics agreed that she did her best work in the
film. Commonweal's film critic said Anne's performance "is
played with disarming simplicity and full understanding of evil
implications of her actions." The critic for Theatre Arts
magazine said, Guest in the House provides Anne Baxter with
a role to challenge her fine acting talents."

Her last released movie in 1945 featured Anne as a lady
in waiting to the Russian czarina Catherine the Great in A Royal
Scandal (F14), co-starring Tallulah Bankhead. Anne's
grandfather, Frank Lloyd Wright, visited the set when Anne and
Tallulah were shooting a scene together. He said quite loudly,
"Not bad for an old dame." Being very self-conscious about
her age, Tallulah bristled with anger. "The next take required
her to lightly tap me," said Anne, "but she responded with an
uppercut that sent me reeling. Then she smiled sweetly and
retired to her dressing room." She also did everything she
could to steal scenes from the much-younger actress.

Smoky (F15, 1946) was Anne's next celluloid feature. It
co-starred Fred MacMurray as a loner who befriends a horse doomed
to be destroyed. Anne's role was relatively small in this remake
of the children's classic. The New York Times film critic felt
the movie was as "pretty as a picture card, although not as
satisfactory a horse romance" as the earlier filmed versions.

Her following film was Angel on My Shoulder (F16, 1946),
co-starring Paul Muni and Claude Rains. The subject matter
dealt with a dead "hood" who is given another chance at life
on earth by the devil. His trade-off is to besmirch the new
body he inherits. He falls in love with a young woman who
doesn't know of his predicament, and he refuses to honor the
contract. The New York Times film critic Bosley Crowther felt
the movie was "pretty good -- although hokey."

Tyrone Power was slated to appear in his first post-war
film, The Razor's Edge (F17, 1946). He had previously appeared
with Anne Baxter in Crash Dive, and would now co-star with her
in the filmed version of W. Somerset Maugham's story of the
war veteran who returns home to a disillusioned life. He travels
to far reaches of the world to find peace and, upon his return,
wants to impart his knowledge and experience to those who had
known and loved him before the war. Gene Tierney is the woman
he loved who has turned into a conniving shrew following her
marriage to someone else, for she still covets Power. He tries
to help his young friend, Sophie MacDonald (Anne Baxter), who
has become a dope-taking, drunken prostitute following the deaths
of her husband and son.

The role of Sophie was offered to Susan Hayward, Betty
Grable, Judy Garland and Annabelle Shaw. Grable and Garland
bowed out because of the depressing subject matter. Betty Grable
realized that the part would not suit her, since her specialty
was musical comedy. She felt her audience would not accept
her in that role. Bonita Granville did a screen test and was
about to be cast by Darryl F. Zanuck when Anne asked to try

out for the role. Zanuck had said of Anne, "She's a cold potato," when asked about considering her for the role of Sophie. Anne treated her screen test as an improvisation, because she felt she wouldn't get the part. However, director Edmund Goulding liked the test and gave Anne the job. Some critics felt that most of the parts were miscast in the film, except for Anne's. Eileen Creelman, of the New York Sun, said, "As the drunken, hopeless Sophie, Miss Baxter is again a tragic, appealing figure. Sophie may not be the central character. She is still the one you'll remember."

Anne Baxter was well-rewarded for her work in The Razor's Edge. She won the Golden Apple and Golden Globe Awards. On February 10, 1947, the Academy Award nominations were announced. Anne was nominated for Best Supporting Actress in the company of Ethel Barrymore (The Spiral Staircase), Lillian Gish (Duel in the Sun), Flora Robson (Saratoga Trunk), and Gale Sondergaard (Anna and the King of Siam). The ceremony took place on March 13, 1947, at the Shrine Auditorium, emceed by Jack Benny. A very young and extremely happy Anne Baxter won the Academy Award that year.

Following her success in The Razor's Edge, Anne was scheduled to star in Blaze of Noon (F18, 1947). She played the wife of one of four aviator brothers who brave storms to establish an air mail service. Her role wasn't very important or unusual for her, considering she was another romantic interest of two rivals, this time brothers. According to Time magazine, "As the romance builds in Blaze of Noon, Anne plays a waiting game, and the story falls apart."

Anne's last film released in 1947 was Mother Wore Tights (F19), in which only her voice is used. The film won warm reviews for its stars Dan Dailey and Betty Grable.

Homecoming (F20, 1948) featured Anne in a supporting role to Clark Gable and Lana Turner. She is the long-suffering, nice wife of Army surgeon Gable, who is cold and heartless to his family and patients. While closely working with nurse Turner, he comes to realize that he must change his ways and that it is okay to show his true feelings. He returns to his wife after the untimely death of Turner. John Hodiak also had a supporting role. The film was quickly forgotten by critics and audiences alike. Gable was still in deep mourning for his wife, Carole Lombard, who had died tragically in a plane crash while on tour selling war bonds. The three stars could not save the quick demise at the box office.

After being loaned to M-G-M for Homecoming, Anne returned to 20th Century-Fox Studios, where she was relegated to playing "librarian-type" roles and replacing other actresses, such as Gene Tierney in The Walls of Jericho (F21, 1948). Anne played a young lawyer in love with a married man whose life is made miserable by his wife (Linda Darnell). Anne liked her role in the film and earned generally favorable reviews. Bosley Crowther, of the New York Times, felt she was forceful and appealing.

Anne again co-starred with Tyrone Power in her next film, The Luck of the Irish (F22, 1948), a Chauncey Olcott-type of Irish comedy about a newspaper journalist whose values are compromised by a young woman (Jayne Meadows) who wants him to leave his girl (Anne Baxter) to work for her rich tycoon father. With the help of leprechaun Cecil Kellaway, he makes the right decision. Newsweek said of her performance, "...Anne Baxter is fortified with an appealing brogue."

Yellow Sky (F23, 1949) co-starred Anne with Gregory Peck in Death Valley. She replaced Paulette Goddard. Anne loved working with William Wellman on the salt flats of Death Valley, because she got to work hard and have fun, too. On a shopping excursion, it was rumored that she had "stolen" several pairs of Levis! According to the New York Herald Tribune, Anne "gives a touch of sincerity and compunction to conventional material."

Dan Dailey appeared with Anne in her next film, You're My Everything (F24, 1949). Dailey and Baxter are entertainer parents of a talented, precocious daughter (similar to Shirley Temple). Successful stage performers, they try their luck in the "flickers," and each attains a new success. Anne's character becomes another "It Girl" of the movies. When their style of acting becomes passe, they settle down and have a happy life together. Anne was able to show off her dancing ability and projected great fun in her portrayal. Time magazine's review mentions that the film is a perfect family movie. Commonweal said that Anne's impersonation of a "hot-cha" girl provides some of the most brilliant satire on film.

Anne's next film set for release in 1950 was A Ticket to Tomahawk (F25). Richard Sales and his wife, Mary Loos (sister of writer Anita Loos), co-wrote the screenplay of this adventure movie, again co-starring Anne Baxter and Dan Dailey. Comic overtones heighten the enjoyable performances, with Dailey the only paying fare on a train. Along the way, the track is destroyed and Anne Baxter comes to the rescue, in order for the train to arrive by deadline. Anne proves her mettle and must be reckoned with. A very young Marilyn Monroe appeared

in the film but was rarely seen during filming in the Rockies
town of Durango, Colorado. The location was most uncomfortable
and tacky. Anne became known as the Elsa Maxwell of Durango,
where she fixed up what needed to be fixed. Rory Calhoun and
his hot-blooded wife, actress Lita Baron, entertained the troupe
with their lovers' quarrels. The New York Times felt that "Anne
Baxter is fair and more than middling" as the marshal's daughter
The New Yorker said Anne was comely and innocent but dangerous
with a knife or gun. The audiences agreed with the critics.

   Anne's next feature film at Fox had her replace a pregnant
Jeanne Crain, whom Joseph Mankiewicz hoped to cast in the story
Command Performance, which was to co-star Claudette Colbert.
Several days later, Colbert injured her back and had to bow
out. She was replaced by Bette Davis. With its title changed,
the film was set to be released in 1950.

A Classic in the Making

   "It was a charmed script we were handed," said Anne Baxter.
She would have the pivotal role of the scheming Eve Harrington,
who insinuates herself into the life of aging Broadway star
Margo Channing (Bette Davis). All About Eve (F26, 1950) would
take Anne out of supporting roles. One movie magazine dubbed
her the "Bop Girl of 1949" (the counterpart of the "It Girl"
of the 1920s) and had her pose in cheesecake shots. Her
unconventional prettiness was better suited to her new role.

   Eve Harrington plotted to become the understudy of Margo.
Anne based her interpretation of the role on a personal
experience. "I patterned my performance after my first
understudy on Broadway at 13, who was nice to everybody but
me and would always be in the wings watching me like a hawk.
In the movie, I tried to follow Bette around with my eyes to
get that feeling across," she told J. Bawden of Films in Review.
According to other sources, the story was actually based on
an event in the career of stage actress Elizabeth Bergner.

   Anne considered All About Eve the perfect experience.
At the onset of filming, none of the production staff, cast,
or crew knew they were making a film classic. It was a pleasure
for the entire company to work together. Anne particularly
liked working with Walter Huston and Mankiewicz, because they
really liked women. She felt she had a formidable challenge
in the person of George Sanders, a rather laconic actor. The
only dissension in the production was an outburst from Celeste

Holm, whose portable dressing room was placed outdoors of Stage 9. Because Mankiewicz wanted a cordial set, he, Celeste's agent, and several emissaries made apologies that soothed Holm's ruffled feathers. Of her role in the film, <u>New York Herald Tribune</u> critic Otis Guernsey said, "Anne Baxter gives a tip top performance."

For their roles, Anne Baxter and Bette Davis were both nominated for an Academy Award for Best Actress of 1950. Other nominees included Judy Holliday (<u>Born Yesterday</u>), Eleanor Parker (<u>Caged</u>), and Gloria Swanson (<u>Sunset Boulevard</u>). The nominations were announced on February 12, 1951. The ceremony took place at the RKO Pantages Theatre on March 29, 1951, hosted by Fred Astaire. Anne was considered a dark-horse and many thought that Davis and Baxter canceled each other out of the running. Actually, Bette Davis and the studio had wanted Anne to accept the nomination for Best Supporting Actress for the role, but Anne refused. She said, "The film, after all, was about how different people saw Eve." <u>All About Eve</u> won Oscars for Joseph Mankiewicz and George Sanders. But the Best Actress Academy Award went to Judy Holliday that year. Joseph Mankiewicz had two large plastic kewpie dolls glued to his script lectern to represent the Oscars he'd won for the film.

The Fox Studio was set to cast <u>How to Marry a Millionaire</u>. Included was a role that Anne coveted, which eventually went to Betty Grable. Although Anne had just worked with Marilyn Monroe, she was not too impressed with the young actress. It was well-known in Hollywood that Miss Monroe's tardiness was a problem. Anne considered Monroe's behavior to be unprofessional. She resented this and considered leaving Fox Studios.

<u>Follow the Sun</u> (F27, 1951) was Anne's next film. Sports heroes provided story lines for many movies. Golf's first real hero was Ben Hogan. In February, 1949, he was involved in a near-fatal automobile accident that left him unsure of ever walking again let alone enjoying his beloved sport. With his wife, Valerie, at his side, he made his slow but permanent recuperation. He went on to win the U.S. Open Golf tournament twice, an unheard of feat at the time. Glenn Ford portrayed Ben Hogan, with Anne Baxter as Valerie. Both actors gave performances that warmed the heart and provided inspiration without maudlin sentimentality. <u>Newsweek</u> said she gave a steadily paced, convincing portrayal. The <u>Library Journal</u> said <u>Follow the Sun</u> "illustrates the long struggle for excellence which goes into the making of champions."

Bret Harte's novel The Outcasts of Poker Flat was set to be filmed, with slight changes to characters from the novel. Anne was cast as Cal, originally Mother Shipton in the book. Cal is married to a robber (Cameron Mitchell), whom she hasn't seen for quite some time. She becomes stranded at a cabin with several other people after a blinding snowstorm. Somehow her cruel and sadistic husband and his cronies find the group and try to collect his wife and the loot he stashed at the cabin. Time mentioned that Anne's character is transformed into a good girl for the purpose of providing a romantic story line. Photoplay felt the movie was an "optic symphony." Commonweal thought Anne was excellent as Cal.

In a change of pace, Anne's next film was My Wife's Best Friend, a comedy co-starring Macdonald Carey. In the film, Carey and Baxter are a young married couple who are aboard a plane when they hit a turbulent storm. Thinking they are about to die, they each reveal indiscretions from their pasts. After they survive the storm, their lives take on a different timbre. She will not let him live down his confession. Using many psychological ploys on him, she tortures him by becoming forgiving, patient, noble, and vampish -- this she does when the mood strikes her! In one scene, Anne is dressed in a scanty outfit, sporting a jewel in her navel. According to Time magazine, Anne preferred to be thought of as a glamour girl following that scene. The Spectator's review said Anne had a wonderful time in a creditable performance.

Anne's next film for 20th Century-Fox was a melodramatic tale written by O. Henry titled "The Last Leaf" (F30, 1952). The film was titled O. Henry's Full House when it was released along with three other stories. "The Last Leaf" featured Gregory Ratoff, with whom Anne had previously worked. Anne was a young woman who's lost her love and is so despondent that she can't leave her tiny apartment. She has lost the will to live and believes that when the last leaf falls from the tree outside her window she, too, will die. Across the courtyard is an artist (Ratoff) who befriends her. Through his kindness, patience, and willingness to help her see that she has much to live for, she regains her passion for life. The Spectator review said, "She manages beautifully to make her sweet role palatable." However, Robert Kass, of Catholic World magazine, said the film was "sticky in a way which O. Henry never intended."

Warner Bros. signed Anne to a two-picture contract. The first was I Confess (F32, 1953), which was to be filmed in Quebec, Canada. It was one of the first times a movie was filmed completely on location. Anne was the studio-designated substitute for Norwegian actress Anita Bjork, who was director

Alfred Hitchcock's, as well as co-star Montgomery Clift's, original choice for the role. The film proved to be very tense and unfriendly. Although Clift and Anne had known each other since their teens and had even dated (with approval of his doting mother), she found him to be very reclusive and distant. He had not been completely well since a car crash nearly ended his life while he was shooting Raintree County. His handsome face had sustained injuries that changed his looks, and he began to drink heavily. It was also intimated that Clift began taking drugs to combat the pain he experienced.

Alfred Hitchcock had a penchant for blonde actresses in his films. He asked Anne to bleach her brown hair for the role of the young priest's (Clift) old girlfriend, now married and involved in what turns out to be a murder that he is accused of. Anne's husband is killed and she goes to the priest, not knowing that the real killer has already confessed to the priest. Karl Malden is the police investigator who thinks there is something going on between Baxter and Clift, for he knows of their young teenaged love. Because Clift will not divulge who the killer is, he is accused. Eventually, the killer's wife confessed to the police that they have the wrong person. The killer ends up committing suicide.

During filming of I Confess, Alfred Hitchcock made his famous statement, often quoted, that "all actors are cattle." However, in a chapter of From Where I Sit, Merv Griffin's Book of People, by Peter Barsocchini, Hitch restated the quote: "All actors should be treated like cattle."

I Confess was considered a good, workmanlike thriller, although "fair-to-middling Hitchcock" according to Time magazine. Christian Century magazine found the film to be strangely unsuspenseful. Commonweal thought Anne's portrayal in the based-on-fact movie was hard and brassy.

Anne's second film under contract to Warner Bros. was the Blue Gardenia (F31, 1953), directed by Fritz Lang. Shot in 21 days, it included fine directorial touches but was largely considered a "B" movie. In it, Anne plays a telephone operator who unwittingly believes she has committed a murder while drunk in the dead man's apartment. Ann Sothern and Jeff Donnell provide support. One of them proves to be the real murderer, who killed Raymond Burr with a fireplace poker. Groverman Blake, of the Chicago Sun Times, felt Anne handled her chores more than capably, never becoming typecast. Time said she was a thoroughly attractive murder suspect. Both the National Parent-Teacher magazine and the Green Sheet felt that Anne's inebriation scene was much too long and embarrassing. Neither publication

could recommend it in their critiques. It was agreed that Anne
looked very attractive with her light blonde hairdo.

Anne's private life took a turn for the worse. Citing
extreme cruelty, Anne divorced John Hodiak on January 28, 1953.
She received child support plus alimony. She never seemed to
run out of work, though. She began to appear in guest spots
on radio variety shows, as well as in plays specifically written
for radio. She also longed to return to the stage.

She joined the touring company of John Brown's Body (S6,
1953), in the role originally done by Judith Anderson. She
co-starred with Raymond Massey, Tyrone Power, and ex-husband
John Hodiak. Charles Laughton produced, directed, and staged
the epic poem by Stephen Vincent Benet. Benet used different
meters that rendered it very pleasing to the audience in its
variety of cadences. The staging was complex and venturesome,
for it had to be staged at any kind of meeting place. Laughton
staged it somberly yet informally. Power and Massey divided
the two "Robert E. Lee" passages. The actress in the production
took the descriptive portions of the "Harper's Ferry Raid and
Trial." Massey also played the "John Brown Soliloquy" and
"Lincoln" sequence, with all three sharing the narrative. A
chorus provided chanting and sang old-time songs, mimicked the
sounds of marching and battle, a banjo being strummed, rebel
yells, violin strains, bird calls, and many other "American"
sounds.

The play opened at the Santa Barbara Lobero Theatre on
November 1, 1952, for a run of 80 performances in its first
of two tours. (The play eventually went to New York's Broadway.
Brooks Atkinson epitomized the plot by saying, "John Brown's
Body is a work of art not only in print but on the stage. It
refreshes the whole conception of theater." The second leg
of the tour of 80 performances began in the fall of 1953. Anne
Baxter took over the Judith Anderson role at that time. Raymond
Massey compared the two in his book by saying, "Both these ladie
are actresses of great accomplishment and of high though
differing talents. Charles's direction accommodated each
performance to its greatest effectiveness." The second tour
ended after successfully being staged throughout the United
States and Canada.

Anne's next work saw her traveling to Munich, Germany,
for the film Carnival Story (F33, 1954). Her co-stars were
Lyle Bettger, Steve Cochran, and George Nader. She very much
enjoyed making the film, playing Willi, a vagrant German girl,
who becomes the American carnival's high diver after being taken
in and protected by the high diving star (Bettger) and the

troupe.   Cochran played Anne's lover, who comes in and out of
her life to make trouble for her and the carnival.   George Nader
played a fictional _Life_ magazine reporter who, in essence,
rescues her from Cochran after he comes back into her life
following the death of Bettger.   Anne felt Cochran was a handsome
and talented star, but undisciplined.   His drinking was a problem
for the whole cast.   Anne mothered him or fought him off,
depending on his mood.   He was perfectly typecast for the film.
Lyle Bettger was easy to work with, but he hated wearing the
costume in the high diving scenes.   Mac Tince, of the _Chicago_
Daily Tribune, felt Anne and the other cast members could not
manage to wring anything out of the obvious and awkward script.

Anne was still blonde when she was cast to star in
Bedevilled (F34, 1955), as a nightclub singer fleeing from the
police.   Again affecting a French accent, she was involved in
a murder mystery.   Her co-star was Steve Forrest, as a young
priest in Paris, seeking the right decisions in his life.   He
tries to assist Anne's character, but her luck runs out.   _Time_
magazine called the film an "ecclesiastical striptease that
comes repulsively close to 'priestitution.'"   _Commonweal_ felt
the film had a "definite Catholic slant."   _Catholic World_ cited
Anne's performance as "most believable as the girl gone wrong,"
in a film of thought and substance.

A romantic western was on tap for the busy actress.   Rock
Hudson was slated to co-star with Anne, as Tacey Cromwell, in
One Desire (F35, 1955).   Her character is in love with Hudson.
She takes in his orphaned little brother, while Hudson makes
his mark in the world by establishing himself in business.
Tacey's house of gambling and ill repute is also successful,
and she tries to get him to come back to her.   He has other
ideas after becoming involved with the rich daughter of the
town's most influential man.   Tacey leaves town and tries to
become respectable, taking the young boy and adopting another
orphaned teenager (Natalie Wood).   Hudson's character marries
his rich fiancee and finds that she is a horribly jealous and
hateful woman.   Things go from bad to worse for him in his
personal life.   In a fit of rage, his wife sets fire to their
beautiful home and dies in the inferno.   It is then that Tacey
comes back into his life and he finds he still loves her.   The
Library Journal review said, "Anne Baxter is fine in a meaty
role."

The ever-busy actress was next scheduled to appear in the
fourth filming of _The Spoilers_ (F36, 1955), with Jeff Chandler
and Rory Calhoun.   Adapted from the novel by Rex Beach, this
rather tepid western was set in the gold rush days in the Alaskan
Territory.   Swindlers try to take over the richest mine co-owned

by Chandler. Anne is the owner of a saloon that caters to the
men, as well as their pocketbooks. Calhoun again co-starred
with Anne, as a bogus gold commissioner who, together with a
phony judge, also succeeds in the swindle before Chandler
recognizes the ruse and acts upon the situation. The New York
Times felt this familiar tale was nothing out of the ordinary
in story line or the cast's acting abilities.

Next Anne was cast as a murderess in The Come On (F37,
1956). She co-starred with John Hoyt, a fellow blackmailer.
They meet Sterling Hayden, who is criminally-minded as well.
Hayden decides that Hoyt is not needed and he is killed. Anne
and Hayden plan a heist that backfires and they end up being
killed for their efforts. The film was considered sub-par,
although the critics felt Anne looked marvelous in her bathing
suits and costumes designed by Edith Head.

On October 19, 1955, Anne's ex-husband, John Hodiak, died
of a heart attack at the age of 38. They had remained friendly
since their separation, and his death was devastating to Anne.
She was saddened that their marriage had not succeeded.

Anne again buried herself in work. Her new film was
reportedly to be one of the major film endeavors of all time.
Cecil B. DeMille was refilming his classic The Ten Commandments
(F38, 1956).

Cecil DeMille built the most elaborate set and hired the
most extras and celebrated cast for his new movie. The first
day on the set, Anne was called to do a love scene with Charlton
Heston, who played Moses. Anne was Princess Nefretiri, daughter
of the pharaoh. Anne was to kneel at Heston's leg, clutching
him. All of a sudden Heston disappeared. He came back an hour
later and surprised the entire crew by being literally bare-
chested (his hirsute chest was not photogenic in the eyes of
Cecil B. DeMille!). Anne's beautiful gowns were designed by
Edith Head, and she wore a red, page-boy styled wig. DeMille
wanted to show off as much of his star, Anne Baxter, as the
censors would allow. He had Anne tested in see-through costumes
wearing a gold G-string. She felt the photographic stills were
shocking and learned that some of them circulated for several
years thereafter. "I thought I should wear a nose-guard because
I looked so Irish," she told J. Bawden, "but DeMille said no."
She was haunted by one of the ridiculous lines she had to utter
to Heston: "Oh, Moses, Moses, you stubborn, splendid, adorable
fool!" However silly the dialogue, the movie would become
another screen classic and would go on to win several Academy
Awards.

Still freelancing, Anne decided to branch out into television, since her movie roles were not of the caliber she preferred. She also returned to the stage, as the naive divorcee Mollie Lovejoy in The Square Root of Wonderful (S7, 1957). She falls in love with a new suitor, which causes much concern for her ex-husband, ex-in-laws, and her young son. Variety said, "Miss Baxter isn't able to do much with the role of the muddled heroine. In any case, it gives her little opportunity to be either a dazzling vision or a stunning actress." The play closed after 45 performances.

Anne's next adventure on stage was in England. She flew there to appear on the London stage in The Joshua Tree, which ran for five months.

Anne returned to the United States following her London stage debut to appear again with Charlton Heston in Three Violent People (F39, 1956). Cast as his reformed dance hall girl-turned-respectable wife, she is the focus of unsettled passions when his brother (Tom Tryon) takes a liking to his sister-in-law. The two brothers (Heston as a returning Confederate soldier) almost lose their Texas ranch to carpetbaggers. Together they outwit them, and romance again blossoms for the young married couple. Time magazine said Anne was probably the most relentless camera-hugger in the business! In Charlton Heston's autobiographical journal, he mentions that their on-screen and off-screen relationship was initially very tenuous. He kept his distance in order to work off the negative feelings he had to use in his portrayal of the betrayed husband. But he believed Anne was a lady and a thorough professional, remembering her fondly. He even admitted in his journal that he was "smart-alecky" in his actions.

Immediately following release of Three Violent People, Anne flew to England to star in Chase a Crooked Shadow (F40, 1958). This story featured Anne as a rich widow recuperating from her grief at a beautiful island estate. Richard Todd enters her life and mysteriously announces that he is her supposedly long-dead brother. However, his deviousness reveals his true identity. Time magazine called her a "powder-blue beauty" (for she was again blonde), "writhing in poor-little-rich-girl loneliness. The film was competently directed and later retold in television movie One of My Wives if Missing.

Chase a Crooked Shadow was filmed at Cliveden, the famous country house belonging to the Astor family. The estate was originally built in Buckinghamshire in 1666. It had been rebuilt three times in its history: it burned down twice, then was permanently rebuilt in 1851. Cliveden was also the setting for the coming-out gala of Daphne Fairbanks, the 18-year-old daughter of Mary Lee and Douglas Fairbanks, Jr. Anne was invited, escorted by Billy Wallace, the current beau of Princess Margaret. Also attending were Stavros Niarchos and his wife, Merle Oberon, Princess Margaret, Prince Philip, Lady Elizabeth Clyde, wife of the executive producer of the film, and Queen Elizabeth II. Anne was surprised by the Queen's charming ability to make her feel comfortable. She was equally surprised by Queen Elizabeth's physical attractiveness -- no photograph did her justice.

Anne Baxter's life was about to take her away from the film industry. She was ready for the change.

New Frontiers

Anne was 37 years old when she met Randolph Galt at a dinner party in late 1959. The Clift Hotel in San Francisco, was sponsoring the dinner party following Anne's hosting of a PBS television memorial program about her famous grandfather, Frank Lloyd Wright. Wright had designed the Tokyo Imperial Hotel in 1923, the world's first earthquake-safe building (he had also designed a theater for Anne when she was three years old). Although Anne had not been dating anyone in particular at that time, she found herself attracted to Galt.

Randolph Galt was born in Honolulu, Hawaii, in 1929, to well-do-do parents who made their residence there. An adventure by nature, Galt was involved in several projects when they met. Anne fell in love with him on their third date, she told reporters.

Their six-year age difference played no part in deterring their mutual admiration. She called him "Ran" or "Ranny," while he called her "Banana." She was, at 5'3-3/4" in height, a foot shorter than the new man in her life. He proposed weeks later, giving her an emerald engagement ring. She accepted without hesitation.

Galt raised Santa Gertrude-breed cattle on a 37,000-acre ranch near Riverina in Australia. Called Galt Rancho, Giro Station, it was located approximately 150 miles north of Sydney. Their prospective married life would have its inception in this far-away continent.

Anne's parents felt she was making a big mistake in forsaking her career and wanting to leave the country. His

parents were friendly but reserved when Anne visited them at
their home in Hawaii. But they seemed to take to their future
daughter-in-law.

While Anne was still in Los Angeles, Edith Head helped
her to choose selections for her $3,000 wedding trousseau.
Juel Park provided Dietrich-like sexy undergarments and sleepwear
for the bride-to-be. The press got wind of her impending
wedding.

As soon as the news was leaked that Anne would soon be
changing her marital status, an emotionally unstable man began
sending threatening letters and calling her personal telephone
number. Apparently, Anne had given him her autograph several
years before. In his demented capacity, he wired Hedda Hopper
and Louella Parsons that he would stop the wedding. He sent
a photograph of himself and a baby to her parents stating, "Has
she told you about us?" When he brandished a gun at her agent,
Arthur Park, he was finally stopped in his tracks by the
Los Angeles Police Department.

Although Anne's parents did like Randolph Galt, they could
not accept her wanting to live in Australia. They did not attend
her wedding to Galt, held at his parents' home in Kahala, Hawaii.

Famed Hollywood photographer John Engstead took wedding
portraits of Anne and Galt. Daughter Katrina Hodiak was her
flower girl. Ran's sister was Anne's matron of honor, with
his brother-in-law acting as Ran's best man. J. Watson Webb,
Jr., stood in for Anne's father, giving her away on
February 18, 1960. The only other attendant on Anne's behalf
was her long-time secretary, Helen Freeman.

Soon thereafter, the couple journeyed to Giro Station.
(Later they sent for Katrina). Their nearest neighbor lived
ten miles away. They generated their own electricity an average
of five hours per day. They were lucky to get fuel for their
stove, for most bush cooks had to use coal or wood. At Giro,
they were able to "keep" their rations of meat and milk in a
cold room. Anne lived the life of a "frontier wife" in the
Australian outback. The experience became her Everest, complete
with frogs in the toilet bowl and sludge on the floors.

It was very expensive to run a ranch of that size. Home
utilities were very costly, since supplies were limited in their
remote location. Because of this and the fact that Ran was
often away on business, she was eager to act again.

Cimarron (F41, 1960) was based on a popular novel by Edna Ferber, which had been filmed previously in 1931. This new version was beautifully photographed, but something got lost in this translation to celluloid. Glenn Ford co-starred with Anne, although her role was in a supporting capacity. She play another saloon owner with a heart of gold. Ford tries to minister to settlers following the great land rush in Oklahoma. Along the way, he gets himself involved with other people's problems. His training in law had him battle racial bigotry that was hurled against Indians and blacks, to the detriment of his wife (Maria Schell) and family. Commonweal felt the film had many good actors who were saddled with rather skimpy roles. Arthur Knight, of Saturday Review, felt Anne's work brought a spot of life and color to the film. The New Yorker film critic felt none of the admirable performers would be remembered for their work in this filmed version of the bestseller. Newsweek believed the cast uniformly overacted.

Anne also appeared in several television series as guest star. "Goodbye, My Love," on G.E. Theater (T10, 1960), saw her appear opposite the show's host, Ronald Reagan. The episod was directed by Ida Lupino.

She then co-starred with Dean Stockwell in Dance Man (T9, 1960), about a lonely woman and a poisonous con man who runs a ballroom dance studio. She felt Stockwell was excellent to work with, both sensitive and very private. At the time, he was married to Millie Perkins, who had just played Anne in the film version of The Diary of Anne Frank. Anne also was a guest on Checkmate (T8, 1960), a one-season western that starred Sebastian Cabot, Anthony George, and Doug McClure as doctor and crime investigators, respectively.

Upon Anne's return to Australia, she learned she was pregnant. Only several weeks into the pregnancy, she lost the baby at home. The next day, she tried to do laundry chores, washing clothes by hand and carrying the heavy loads to be hung on clotheslines outside. She began to hemorrhage. Hours later when Ran returned from his work on the ranch, she was rushed to Sydney Hospital, where she underwent surgery. Unknowingly, she was given a shot of morphine for pain. She immediately went into a life-threatening, allergic reaction to the drug.

The press found out about her predicament. Hounded, Ran and Anne "escaped" by sneaking out of the hospital. Anne's car ride home was on the floor of the back seat. She recuperate at Ran's apartment in Sydney. Anne's courage and fortitude earned her the label "American owner's wife" from the local citizens -- quite an accomplishment.

Life toiled on at the ranch. Anne sanded floors, painted walls, milked cows, planted a garden, and tried to generally improve the status of the aging farm house. She worked from dawn to dusk.

Eight-year-old daughter Katrina found life pretty uncomfortable and lonely on the remote ranch. Adjusting to a new stepfather and being home-tutored part of the time proved exhausting to both Katrina and Anne. Anne was grateful for the hard work ethic she brought to this new phase of her life. She tried to keep up her looks, which was quite a feat considering water was a scarce commodity.

Anne learned that she was pregnant again. Not wanting to risk her health, she decided to fly back to Los Angeles. She and Katrina set up household and Anne began to look for movie roles. Earning income was high on her list of priorities.

Soon she was offered the role of Teresina in A Walk on the Wild Side (F43, 1962). Anne played the owner of a cafe-style diner in a lazy southern town. Laurence Harvey played a drifter who returns to town to find Capucine, an old girlfriend living at an establishment owned and operated by Barbara Stanwyck. Jane Fonda played a young girl who becomes Harvey's traveling companion and whom he uses to make Capucine jealous.

The film was not a very pleasant experience for Anne. There was much dissension felt by the cast and crew alike. It was felt that Harvey held court. Some members of the cast were rumored to be jealous of Capucine. Mrs. Harry Cohn threw a dinner party for the cast. She later married Harvey.

The critics and audiences were not impressed with A Walk on the Wild Side. The only favorable reviews were garnered by Anne Baxter, Joanna Moore, and Juanita Moore.

Following filming of A Walk on the Wild Side, Anne returned to Australia to film A Season of Passion (F42, 1962), which was also titled Summer of the Seventeenth Doll. Glad to be home for a few months and still able to ply her craft, she thoroughly enjoyed making the film, which turned out to be a sleeper hit. It co-starred American actor Ernest Borgnine as her long-time boyfriend, a sugar cane cutter. He and his pal, John Mills, work in the cane fields several months of the year. When it is time to return to civilization, they get themselves spruced up and buy dolls for their girlfriends. This sixteenth summer, however, things have changed for them all. Angela Lansbury is Mills's new girlfriend. Although she is readily accepted by the others, things are different. They realize that they have to grow up and change with the times. Anne's character finds it harder than the others to alter her life-style, for the doll each year represented his love for her, and she was afraid his feelings had changed. Newsweek considere the film to be honest, compassionate, and enlightening. Howard Thompson, of The New York Times, felt Anne's performance in this tender comedy was "first-rate, but a bit strident, although sterling."

After completing A Season of Passion, Anne accepted a role that took her back to England. Mix Me a Person (F44, 1962) was a film in which Anne played a psychotherapist who treats a young man (British pop singer Adam Faith) who has been framed for a murder he did not commit and now faces execution. Through Anne's therapy and intervention, justice is served. This British-production had only minor distribution in United States theaters. The film, however, did elevate Faith's popularity on the British music charts.

Anne was grateful to have completed filming of these three films in short duration (they were to be released in 1962). Because of the precariousness of her advancing pregnancy, it was decided that Anne would have her baby in Los Angeles. Docto Red Krohn delivered Anne of another daughter, Melissa Ann, on an unseasonably warm October 4, 1960. Anne later learned that actress Joanne Woodward gave birth to her daughter, Melissa, and left the same hospital the day Anne entered to give birth. They shared the name of their babies, as well as the fancy stitchery of Dr. Krohn.

The Santa Ana winds brought devastating fires to the Bel Air estates near Hollywood. In an eerie stroke of luck, Anne's home was the only one to remain standing on their street. Her agent, Arthur Park, and his wife lost everything, although they were in Mexico at the time of the fire.

When Anne returned to Giro Station, things had not changed. Now she had a baby to deal with, as well as maintaining the household as she had done in the past. She had very little help from the absent Ranny.

Two more years slowly passed by for the wilderness family. When Anne became pregnant again, she packed up the children and they returned to the United States. Her parents were extremely happy to see her again. On March 11, 1964, the 44th wedding anniversary of Kenneth and Catherine Baxter, Anne delivered her third daughter, Maginel. The new baby was named after the youngest artist sister of Frank Lloyd Wright.

After four years of struggling in Australia, Anne realized her marriage to Galt was beginning to crumble. They decided to salvage what they could of the marriage. Working the huge ranch put a sizable hole in their finances as well. They decided to permanently relocate to the United States. The Galts moved to an abandoned mining camp in New Mexico. Ran seemed to be in his element, enjoying the rustic ambience immensely. Anne found it to be boring and her life totally unfulfilling.

On February 9, 1967, Anne separated from Randolph Galt. She decided to try and recapture her successful career in film. During her stays in Los Angeles following the births of her two younger daughters, she had appeared on several television series as a guest. She decided to return to this medium.

When asked by the press what it was like during her life in Australia, Anne explained, "In the outback, even the government worried about you. In the bush, they couldn't care less." Anne lived in the bush. However, she did not regret the hard work and deprivations she and her family endured. She felt they provided personal growth and education. She decided to put her experiences in writing. Her journal became a catharsis.

Later, Louise Bernikow, of the New York Times Book Review, summed up Anne's life experiences in Australia. "She learned making do with less, unspoiling herself. First she felt purified and triumphant, then caged, then restless." Anne's own words were, "It was terribly hard work, and I was terribly lonely. The nearest town was an hour and a half away by jeep. I had two babies and lost a third out there in the country. I cooked, took care of the children and a 26-room house, learned a little about cattle and rode horses whenever I wasn't pregnant." One of the reasons she decided to return to acting upon the breakup of her marriage was, "I neglected to face the fact that my work had provided vital airings for explosives inside."

Return to First Love

Anne accepted a cameo role in Jerry Lewis's film The Family Jewels (F45, 1965). Jerry Lewis aficionados were the only ones thrilled with this lame comedy. Anne's role was forgettable as well.

She flew to Spain to appear in the western The Tall Women (F46, 1967). The movie, about seven women making their way

through perilous Indian country, was poorly acted, poorly dubbed
and poorly edited. It went completely unnoticed by the audience
and critics. Its distribution was so meager that it disappeared
Only die-hard, late-night movie addicts are likely to ever see
it.

Anne returned to Los Angeles to appear in a cameo bit in
The Busy Body (F47, 1967), a mob-filled black comedy. Popular
comedians of the day joined character actor Robert Ryan in trying
to locate a missing suit that hides a stash of money wanted
by the mob. Richard Pryor made his film debut in The Busy Body
Sid Caesar and Dom DeLuise kept the action lively and hilarious
Anne was seen as an actress in a movie scene which was being
watched by passengers on an airplane.

Realizing that films were changing and good roles were
getting very hard to find, Miss Baxter decided to sign with
Universal Studios "as a stock company of one," using her strong
maturity to great advantage.

She starred in a television movie, Stranger on the Run
(T18, 1967). Her co-star was Hollywood leading man and stalwart
performer, Henry Fonda, who was also making his television movie
debut. Michael Parks had the third leading role in this
intelligent, adult western. Fonda is a fugitive who is preyed
upon by a sadistic sheriff (Parks). Anne gives him shelter
and tries to help him escape the clutches of the posse that
has been sent to hunt him down and kill him. The telefilm earned
favorable reviews for all the major stars.

Companions in Nightmare (T29, 1968) was Anne's next
television movie appearance. This film marked the debut of
honored actor Melvyn Douglas in this particular medium. Douglas
is a psychiatrist who conducts group therapy sessions with
important professional people. As the therapy progresses, it
is learned that one member of the group is a murderer. It was
a standard mystery but well-acted. This telefilm was a sequel
to Ritual of Evil, which had starred Louis Jourdan.

In a pilot for the television series Marcus Welby, M.D.,
Anne guest-starred as the love interest of an aging doctor
(Robert Young). Following a heart attack, he must hire someone
younger to take over his practice. He acquires the services
of Dr. Steven Kiley (James Brolin). In the story, Anne is a
deeply caring woman who also is concerned about a young woman
who is destroying her life. (The pilot was rebroadcast in two
separate episodes, on November 3, 1975, and January 26, 1976,
under the title Robert Young, Family Doctor. Anne was offered
a co-starring role, but she emphatically turned it down.

Anne found plenty of work as a guest star in many television series, often appearing more than once in a particular series. She guest-starred in two different episodes of Ironside, starring her co-star from The Blue Gardenia, Raymond Burr, as a wheelchair-bound police detective (T27 and T34). She reprised her role as Olga (then Zelda) in several episodes of the popular, campy series Batman, starring Adam West and Robin Ward. Vincent Price and Anne created much havoc for the Dynamic Duo!

By now, Anne had been separated from Randolph Galt for several years. She received her final divorce decree from him on January 29, 1970.

The Name of the Game was a popular television fixture from 1968 to 1971. The intelligent series focused on an investigative newspaper that exposed those involved in crime and other subversive activities. Each week's story involved one of the leading characters -- Robert Stack, Gene Barry, and Anthony Franciosa (T28, T32, T36, and T40). Anne Baxter starred in four story lines that were quite diverse. Her guest appearance in the episode titled The Bobby Currier Story (T32) won her an Emmy nomination for Outstanding Single Performance by an Actress in a Leading Role. In the episode, she plays the mother of a troubled youth. She and her husband are very worried when they learn their son has committed the heinous crime of kidnapping the local sheriff's daughter then taking her on a cross-country killing spree (loosely based on real-life fugitives Charles Starkweather and Caril Fugate in the 1950s). The episode was considered by most to be almost too realistic in theme and enactment.

Anne's performance was noteworthy, but she lost the award to Geraldine Page, who won for her role in the warm Truman Capote autobiographical memoir The Thanksgiving Visitor. Lee Grant was also nominated for her role in an episode of the series Judd for the Defense.

In 1971, Anne returned to the stage. She was asked to replace Lauren Bacall, as Margo Channing, in the Broadway musical Applause (S9), based on the film 1950 All About Eve. It had been rumored that Bette Davis would take over the role, but that did not materialize. Instead, Anne was asked to take the part on July 19, 1971. Lauren Bacall had won wonderful reviews for her enthusiastic performance. Anne was eager to try her wings. From the onset, Anne won over the audiences the critics. On August 4, 1971, Variety said, "Neither of the actresses is much of a singer, and while Miss Baxter may not be as strong a dancer as Miss Bacall, her acting seems to have slightly more range and depth." Anne told Jerry Tallmer of the New York Post

on August 7, 1971, "I turned this down twice. I'm a non-dancer.
I'm not athletic." David Thomson mentioned that her appearance
in Applause was "one of life's braver attempts at wit."
Audiences and critics found her portrayal of Margo Channing
intriguing. Her contract for the musical ran through April
26, 1972.

Anne and Bette Davis were supposed to be feuding. A rumor
had spread rampantly when the two stars appeared in the original
film in 1950. Nothing could have been further from the truth.
As a matter of fact, Bette was the first to congratulate Anne
backstage after her first appearance. Davis exclaimed, "You
were Margo!" Their paths were destined to cross again.

Anne starred in several more episodic television series.
She was chosen to star in The Late Liz (F48, 1971), which was
based on an autobiographical novel by Elizabeth Burns (real
name Gert Behanna). Anne is the daughter of a doting millionaire
who feels she must please him. Unable to fit the image he
demands she adopt, she becomes an alcoholic. She marries three
times and produces two sons. After an attempted suicide, she
is "rescued" by a newfound belief and faith in God (at age of
53 in 1947). With the help of friends and her minister, she
gets the strength to leave her third husband (Steve Forrest),
a plastic surgeon who coldly uses her to get closer to her rich
acquaintances and influential people. She joins Alcoholics
Anonymous and, through her new philosophy, she learns to depend
on herself and God.

Marquita Ross, of Christianity Today, felt the film was
a worthwhile endeavor, delivering a message without preaching.
Ross mentions that honey blonde Anne Baxter never looked better,
even though her scenes of inebriation were reminiscent of those
of Susan Hayward in Smash-Up! and I'll Cry Tomorrow.

Another film effort released in 1971 was her small role
in Jimmy Stewart's Fool's Parade (F49), in which she is the
blowzy, patriotic madam of a riverboat, whose ambition is to
become a member of the Daughters of the American Revolution.
Stewart is a long-time convict released on parole during the
Depression with a cache of money owed to him by the state.
However, a prison guard (George Kennedy) and ex-cons who know
of his "wealth" decide to follow him and confiscate his
settlement. Anne had no trouble remembering how to interpret
her role. But it was generally agreed by the critics that the
film "belongs to James Stewart."

The third film featuring Anne Baxter in a starring capacity
in 1971 was the television movie If Tomorrow Comes (T41). This

film was loosely based on a true incident involving a teenaged Caucasian girl (Patty Duke) who eloped with a Japanese-American youth at the beginning of World War II, just after Japan's attack on Pearl Harbor on December 7, 1941. Anne is a high school teacher who knows of the young couple's plight and sympathizes with them when the couple's parents and neighbors are intent on breaking up their relationship.

Taking a much-needed respite from film work, Anne devoted more time to her journal. Her daughters were growing up quickly and would soon be going out on their own.

Anne's only appearance on film in 1972 was in the television movie pilot <u>The Catcher</u> (T42). She had a small role in the mediocre, unsold crime drama, starring Michael Witney as a missing persons investigator who gets mixed up in a murder mystery.

In 1973, Anne portrayed the mother of a mentally ill daughter in <u>Lisa, Bright and Dark</u> (T47), a television <u>Hallmark Hall of Fame</u> presentation. In the movie, which was based on a true story fictionalized by John Neufield, Lisa tries to overcome her problems with the help of group therapy sessions conducted by two of her teenaged girlfriends. Stories of this sort were very popular in the 1970s, since many series were featuring themes that dealt with teenage trauma from stress, drugs, etc.

Anne was very interested in sponsoring the arts, for she loved classical music. In early 1973, she was selected as the new president of the Chamber Symphony Society of California. She was introduced at an office-warming cocktail party following a concert at Royce Hall in Los Angeles. On the first Sunday of February, 1973, the group's board of trustees attended a party in honor of the event at the recreation center of the University of California, Los Angeles.

Anxious to return to the stage after a long absence, Anne was eager to appear with co-stars Hume Cronyn and his wife, Jessica Tandy, in <u>Noel Coward's in Two Keys</u> (S10, 1974). Originally published in three vignettes, Coward's stage production included two "plays" with the same cast members in each (including Thom Christopher).

The first play was "Come into the Garden, Maude," in which a rich couple (Cronyn and Tandy) travel to Europe. Anne is a European princess, who is no longer married and looking for a new marital prospect. Cronyn's ill-tempered wife drives him into the arms of the princess. The second play, "A Song

of Twilight," was a longer play in which Cronyn was a recently
knighted, aging author whose homosexuality was revealed. Anne
played a one-time actress who wants to include him in her memoir
and expose his sexual proclivity. Coward based this vignette
on an actual incident in the life of W. Somerset Maugham, his
one-time friend.

The play began production at the Ethel Barrymore Theater
in New York City, on February 17, 1974. It ran for 140
performances, closing on June 29, 1974. It reopened at the
Playhouse in Wilmington, Delaware, on February 17, 1975, closing
August 2, 1975.

Dan Sullivan, of the Los Angeles Times, reported that Anne'
throaty voice and well-preserved, handsome beauty assisted in
the performances of the entire cast. Another critic from the
Los Angeles Times felt Anne softened her European accent in
the first playlet so as not to "put on the dog."

Arthur Hailey's "The Moneychangers" (T49, 1976), also billed
as The Moneychangers, introduced Anne's first appearance in
a television mini-series. It also starred Kirk Douglas, with
whom she previously starred in The Walls of Jericho. This mini-
series was based on Hailey's bestselling novel about corruption
in the banking industry. Anne played Edwina Dorsay, manager
of a large branch bank. She called this acting project "an
octopus." She added, "I'm a cable. I go right through the
story."

In the Write Words

Anne took every opportunity to put the final touches on
her manuscript. She had shown a copy to old friend Bennett
Cerf. He urged her to polish it and consider having it
published.

She asked playwright friend Robert Anderson for advice
on writing her memoirs. "Write a letter," he told her. "It's
that simple." That's exactly what she did. With bulldog
determination, she took the task in hand. Her dear friend Edith
Head and her husband, Bill Ihnens, graciously lent Anne the
key to their home when they were away, so she could pour herself
into rewriting the book. Her agent, Kay Brown, agreed with
Bennett Cerf's initial response. She referred it to John Dodds
of G. P. Putnam's Sons publishing house. Anne credited Dodds
with shaping the book "with a cold machete."

She told an interviewer, "What a learning experience. What's left out makes what's left in important."

Her journal materialized into Intermission: A True Story, which was published by G. P. Putnam's Sons in December, 1976. It sold for $10.00 hardback. Intermission: A True Story met with great success and garnered Baxter rave reviews. Some critics, such as Craig Fisher of the Los Angeles Times, felt Anne omitted certain indiscretions that would have made the story more complete. Fisher acknowledged, however, that her writing style -- short chapters -- made the book ideal for light reading. Stanley Eichelbaum, of the San Francisco Chronicle, interviewed a humble Anne Baxter, who seemed genuinely embarrassed about the good reviews. Playgirl magazine was actually the first to review the book, heralding it as an extraordinary work. The New York Times book critic called the author of Intermission: A True Story "another Doris Lessing."

Dinah Shore interviewed Anne on her syndicated talk show Dinah! on April 12, 1977. Several weeks later, Anne appeared on The Mike Douglas Show.

Anne told Stanley Eichelbaum that working on the book "was traumatic going back to straighten out all those beads. I wanted to be accurate. Fortunately, I have an excellent memory. What actor doesn't? It's a tool of our trade."

In October, 1977, in an interview with J. Bawden, of Films in Review, she said, "I like to think of myself as a dieter who has been very good for a long time. Now it's time for dessert and I want to gorge on a hot-fudge sundae. I'm one of the survivors and I've got the emotional battle scars to prove it. But I'm convinced my best acting is still to come."

A Fine Romance

Ever since her divorce from Randolph Galt in 1970, Anne had put her personal romantic life on hold. She focused on her career and caring for her three daughters, to whom she was extremely devoted. She was determined to provide for them comfortably.

While in New York on a book signing tour, she met Wall Street financier David Klee. Several years her senior, he was eager to please the fun-loving, industrious actress with whom he developed an immediate rapport. Without fanfare and little publicity, Anne and David Klee were married in February, 1977.

David convinced Anne to settle in the east. They chose to live in the beautifully quaint town of Easton, Connecticut. There they built a honeymoon home which was comfortable, cozy, and inviting. The happy couple entertained friends and family. Tragically, their happiness was not to last. Just prior to their first wedding anniversary, David Klee succumbed to a heart attack. Her twin jobs of motherhood and acting, especially acting, kept her going through her grief.

Anne refused to relinquish her estate in Easton, Connecticut. She also maintained a home in Brentwood, California, where she was active in community efforts. One of her most important concerns was keeping San Vicente Boulevard's median strip green. She was also a founding member of The Group, originally part of the Otis Art Institute.

She prided herself on being a positive person. Not wanting to wallow in grief, she returned to work in another fact-based television movie. Anne played the strong, supportive mother of Maureen Connolly, in Little Mo (T50, 1978). Glynnis O'Connor was Maureen, the first American tennis player to win the Grand Slam twice. Sadly, Maureen Connolly died of cancer at age 34. Anne's performance elevated the ratings that season.

On January 29, 1979, Anne learned of the death of her beloved mother, Catherine Wright Baxter, at age 85 (several years earlier, she was preceded in death by her husband). Catherine Baxter had become known in her own right as a painter of Christmas scenes and later as an interior decorator. She died in a convalescent hospital in Laguna Hills, California.

Later on that year, Anne accepted a role in Cause Celebre, a play presented at the Ahmanson Theatre in Los Angeles. The play opened on December 12, 1979, and closed May 31, 1980. Co-starring with Dorothy McGuire, Anne received good reviews for her role as a middle-aged woman who is accused of killing her impotent husband with the assistance of her teenaged lover. Critics agreed that Anne looked wonderful in the costumes.

Nero Wolfe (T51, 1979) was a pilot for a prospective television series, based on the Rex Stout novel The Doorbell Rang. In it, Anne plays a woman tycoon who contacts the famed orchid-tending Wolfe to find out why she's being investigated by the F.B.I. The original actor in the title role (Thayer David) was replaced by William Conrad. The series only lasted one season.

Anne also appeared on the small screen in another mini-series based on John Steinbeck's bestselling classic novel East

of Eden, (T52, 1980). East of Eden had been filmed in 1955,
starring James Dean (in his movie debut). The television remake
was filmed on location in the beautiful central California
countryside. The story was an emotional drama of two brothers'
rivalry for the love of their father. Their mother, Cathy (Jane
Seymour), is an emotionally abusive, neglectful woman who uses
her beauty to get her way. In order to leave the boring life
she has grown to hate, she abandons her sons to their father
and runs off to the seaside of Monterey, where she finds haven
with an aging bordello madam (Anne Baxter). The sadistic Cathy
ends up causing the alcohol-poisoning death of the madam, but
not before making the older woman sign away her home and property
to her. In the end, Cathy's body ages and betrays her. However,
her cruelty has not waned, even when her sons finally find her.
Anne's scenes were powerful, and she wasn't afraid to enact
a slovenly, hopelessly drunken woman who is easily duped.

     In 1980, Anne starred in her last feature film. Jane Austen
in Manhattan was a fictional account of an acting teacher's
discovery of an unpublished play written by Jane Austen. She
and a former student of hers, who is now a drama coach himself
(Robert Powell), become rivals when each tries to stage the
play in entirely different styles. The play had been purchased
at a Sotheby Parke auction in the Art Theater, bringing in a
fee of $55,000 for the very rich beneficiaries. Powell's
charismatic character wants to use the play for existential
experiments to lure beautiful young students to him. Anne is
adamant in her desire to use the same group of students in a
conventional, operatic version of the play. Anne used her long-
time screen authority to launch her theatrical arguments.

     Stage scenes of Jane Austen in Manhattan (F50, 1981) were
actually filmed at the Great Jones Street Building, owned by
La Mama Experimental Theatre Club. Scenes were also filmed
at Roseland, at the Bistro Bar in SoHo, in a communal loft near
Fulton Street, at Sotheby Parke Bernet, and in a townhouse.
The film was originally broadcast on British television and
enjoyed a short run in American theaters.

     In actuality, the play written by the very young Jane Austen
was adapted from Samuel Richardson's novel, Sir Charles
Grandison, or the Happy Man, a Comedy. It was bought at auction
in New York by one of Miss Austen's descendants. In 1977, the
manuscript was fought over by rival producers , who were anxious
to stage it on and off Broadway.

     Anne's 28-year-old singer-songwriter daughter, Katrina
Hodiak (Vonditter), appeared with her in the 90-minute film.
Anne mentioned her daughter's talents to director James Ivory,

since the role called for someone who could sing. In an
interview with Richard Shepard, of the New York Times, Anne
said, "I find it peculiar working with her. There is nothing
in my experience I can draw from. I felt awkward from the first
day and I have stayed away from her. I'm the farthest thing
from a stage mother you can find. A cameraman who didn't know
her told me he sensed there was something between us and wanted
to know what it was. 'I'm her mother,' I said."

Autumn Leaves

     In 1982, Anne made her final stage appearance. She was
asked to play Queen Gertrude, mother of the Danish prince, in
the American Shakespeare Theatre's production of Hamlet (S12,
1982), staged in Stratford, Connecticut, starting on
August 3, 1982. Hamlet is a troubled young man who learns from
his father's ghost that his uncle killed him. His mother marrie
his uncle, which infuriates Hamlet. He is anguished because
he wants to obey his father's ghost by avenging his death.
He also knows that his religious beliefs denounce killing.
In a sword fight, his uncle is killed, and Hamlet dies from
the poisonous pierce of his uncle's sword as well.

     Several days before she was to make her Shakespearean
theater debut, Anne fell at her home in Easton, breaking her
ankle. For the duration of the play's run, she appeared in
a walking cast.

     Anne's deep voice and somewhat exaggerated acting style
seemed suited for the play, even though the role called for
her to be a dependent sort. The New York Times stage critic
said, "Her queen is completely independent."

     Anne told Helen Dudar, of the New York Times, on
August 1, 1982, that "to be the fulcrum -- the Freudian fulcrum,
anyway -- of the play and have so little to say" was an
acknowledged, unusual problem for her. The full-length play
gives the queen only 157 lines out of 4,042. No matter how
many lines Peter Coe may have cut in his staging of Hamlet,
Anne's participation was full-scale, straight-backed, and in
a nicotine-darkened vocal range.

     The following year, Bette Davis was scheduled to star in
the new 1983 prime-time television series Hotel (T54), as the
proprietress of the St. Gregory, a fashionable San Francisco
landmark. Miss Davis had been in ill health. She suffered
a stroke following a mastectomy. On January 9, while

recuperating at her home, Bette fell and broke her hip. She was unable to report to work on the set of Hotel by the February 15 deadline. Ironically, Anne visited Bette at her home just days before.

The producers called Anne and asked her to fill in for the ailing Davis. Miss Davis did appear in the pilot for the series, which aired on September 21, 1983. When Anne first appeared in the recurring role of Victoria Cabot, manager of the hotel and sister-in-law to Davis's character (in the episode of September 28, 1983), Davis's absence is explained away with the excuse that she is opening another hotel in South America.

"What I'm hoping," Anne told Roderick Mann in a Los Angeles Times interview on August 30, 1983, "is that now that Bette is out of the hospital, we will actually have some episodes together. I'd love to work with her again."

The role allowed Anne to have romantic moments along with her demanding duties as manager. Anne thoroughly enjoyed her stint on Hotel. "What's funny," she said to Mann, "is that Melissa, one of my three daughters, is taking a course in hotel management at Cornell. And in the next episode, I have a niece who is an intern from a hotel school, and who proves to be such a little bitch that I fire her. I can't wait for Melissa to see that show!"

In 1984, Anne also managed to appear on a Dean Martin Celebrity Roast (T53) and on a segment of Hollywood Screen Stars' Screen Tests (T55). In 1985, she also made a guest appearance on The Night of a 100 Stars II (T56).

Anne decided not to sell her home in Easton, Connecticut. She began commuting to Los Angeles every other weekend during her tenure with the series Hotel. She worked a high-pressured schedule that would have taxed a woman half her age with less energy. She was a firm believer that people should put themselves and their careers at risk every year or so. She surely practiced what she preached! "I guess I do take chances," she said. "But then I have a large appetite for life -- I want to experience everything. I look at young people today talking about being 'cool' and think how much they're missing. Staying cool, as they call it, leeches the life and enthusiasm out of you." She gardened and took long walks to keep fit. She exercised and ate moderately. She looked at least ten years younger than her age.

In her office above a florist shop in Easton, Anne sat each evening, writing on legal-sized yellow tablets in longhand.

Her project was a book about her family, especially her beloved grandfather, Frank Lloyd Wright. "I remember him vividly," she recalled. "I've looked at all the home movies my father had taken when I was a little girl. There's a lovely shot of my grandfather with his beret and his gabardine outfit." While brewing her favorite tea in a little Herrend pot and using her favorite Iowa brand of honey, she wrote of his effect on people. "It has to do with a meteor in a Victorian pond, which my grandfather was. I had a marvelous relationship with him. It was absolutely flawless and unscarred," she said. Wright's six children could hardly make the same claim. Anne was willing to examine old wounds and her family's patterns of dealing with them.

Anne was also working on negotiating a movie based on her autobiography, Intermission: A True Story. In the spring of 1985, she visited Australian producer-impresarios Harry Miller and Michael Edgley to make plans for putting her story on film. The screenplay was to be written by Stephen Maclean. In an interview with Miller, he said, "When she came back to Australia she wanted to revisit the place where she had lived. And 20 years after she had left Australia and the wilderness, she sounded as though she could finally look back and smile about that part of her life."

Anne later revealed, "I had to shake hands with a lot of old ghosts. Of course, I was nervous -- that place is laced with so much emotion for me. I couldn't quite call it a homecoming. I did try to make it a home, but I couldn't."

She kept in touch with Miller by telephone. He said, "Anne could joke and laugh. When she was talking with the director and screenwriter for the Intermission movie, she had them in stitches with stories about her time on the ranch."

"Everyone wants to know who'll play me," she said. "But I'm not involved in any of that -- I'm staying well away. But I do think it should be an American actress."

Over the Thanksgiving holidays, Anne was at home in Connecticut. On December 3, 1985, she went to New York to do Christmas shopping and visit friends. That evening, they dined at Tout Va Bien in Manhattan, her favorite restaurant. The next morning she was scheduled for a 10:30 appointment with her favorite hairdresser, Leslie Blanchard. On a busy Madison Avenue street, she hailed a taxi and was seen collapsing on the sidewalk. Someone called an ambulance. They took her to Lenox Hill Hospital, less than two blocks away.

Anne was admitted under the name "Anne B. Klee." One of the attendants feverishly working to save her finally realized to whom they were administering life support. In a deep coma, she was transferred to the 8th floor intensive care unit. She remained there for nine days. On December 12, 1985, with her three daughters at her bedside, Anne died from the effects of a massive stroke.

Anne Baxter was survived by her daughters, Katrina Hodiak Vonditter, Melissa Galt, and Maginel Galt. At the family's request, no funeral services were conducted. However, memorials were scheduled to be conducted at a later date. The family requested that donations, in lieu of flowers, be made to the Frank Lloyd Wright Home and Studio Foundation in Oak Park, Illinois.

The producers of Hotel commissioned a portrait of Anne Baxter to be hung in the lobby of the St. Gregory Hotel, to honor and remember her. "The painting will hang as long as Hotel is on the air," said an insider to TV Guide.

The cast and crew of Hotel were shocked and deeply saddened, for their love for her was reciprocated. Because she had become almost like a mother to co-star James Brolin, he was the last to be told. He was devastated by the news.

"Shall we have one last waltz?" was the last line Anne Baxter spoke on the series Hotel. In the episode, she was reunited with an old love (Robert Lansing), who attends a convention at the hotel. He is a police chief who wants her to give up her job at the hotel to be with him. She decides she cannot leave the career and friends she loves. An executive of the series said, "We are probably going to 'freeze' that last dance while a tribute to this great actress flashes on the screen."

It was noted that the producers decided not to replace her. "Later in the season, Victoria Cabot will die." It was later revealed that her character also dies of a stroke. The series remained on the air two more years. Peter (James Brolin) was promoted to fill Victoria's vacancy. Chris (Connie Selleca) was transferred into Peter's old job.

Anne Baxter was a gifted actress who grew more attractive with each year. Earl Wilson described her in 1971 as "a beautiful creature with her weight attractively distributed." In a July 18, 1970, article in the Washington Post, she is said to have "a husky voice, a deep-throated sound that carries a hint of a hidden chuckle." Others knew her as an outspoken,

candid, and articulate person with many interests. She loved
nature, music, and Japanese interior decorating.

Anne Baxter made her childhood dream come true. Although
she never quite attained superstardom, she refused to submerge
her personality, breeding, and professionalism.   These
attributes insured her longevity in the hearts of her friends
and fans, as well as those in the movie industry itself. Anne
maintained her popularity throughout her life. She lived in
the shadow of her favorite motto, bestowed upon her by her famou
grandfather: "See into life -- don't just look at it!"

Chronology

1923   Anne Baxter is born on May 7, in Michigan City, Indiana.

1934-   Anne attends Theodora Irvine's School of Theatre.
1936

1936   Anne makes her debut on Broadway in <u>Seen But Not Heard</u>,
            as Elizabeth Winthrop. She is 13 years old.

1936-
1940   Anne studies acting with renowned actress Maria
            Ouspenskaya.

1937-   Anne attends Lenox School.
1938

1938-   Anne attends Brearly School.
1939

1938   Anne appears in summer theater in <u>There's Always a Breeze</u>
            and <u>Susan and God</u>. She also appears as Rosalie on
            Broadway in <u>Madame Capet</u>.

1939   Anne appears in summer theater in <u>Spring Meeting</u>.

1940   Anne has first movie role as Jean Johnson in <u>Twenty
            Mule Team</u>. She co-stars as Mary Maxwell in <u>The Great
            Profile</u>.

1941   Anne has small role as Amy Spettigue in <u>Charley's Aunt</u>.
            She then co-stars as Julie in <u>Swamp Water</u>. She graduates
            from high school on the lot of 20th Century-Fox Studios.

1942   Anne is cast as Lucy Morgan in <u>The Magnificent Ambersons</u>.
        She next stars as Nicole Rougeron in <u>The Pied Piper</u>.

1943   Anne has starring role as Jean Hewlett in <u>Crash Dive</u>.
        She appears as Mouche in her second war film, <u>Five Graves</u>
        <u>to Cairo</u>. In <u>North Star</u>, Anne has a small but
        significant role as Marina.

1944   Anne stars as Janet Feller in <u>The Eve of St. Mark</u>.
        She also stars as Katherine Mary in <u>The Fighting</u>
        <u>Sullivans</u> (later retitled <u>The Sullivans</u>).

1945   Anne stars as Tessa Osborne in <u>Sunday Dinner for a</u>
        <u>Soldier</u>. During filming, she and co-star John Hodiak
        begin dating. Anne has the role of Countess Anna
        Jaschikoff in <u>A Royal Scandal</u>. She appears on radio
        shows <u>The Comedy Theatre</u>, <u>The Edgar Bergen Show</u>,
        <u>Cavalcade of America</u>, <u>Bill Stern Sports</u>, <u>Adelaide Hawley</u>
        <u>Theater of Romance</u>, and <u>The Charlie McCarthy Show</u>.

1946   Anne co-stars as Julie Richards in <u>Smoky</u>. She appears
        as Barbara Foster in <u>Angel on My Shoulder</u>. She wins
        the role of Sophie MacDonald in <u>The Razor's Edge</u>. She
        appears on radio shows <u>The Charlie McCarthy Show</u> and
        <u>The Drene Show</u>. She marries John Hodiak on July 8,
        1946. Only married a few months, she suffers an attack
        of appendicitis on September 16, 1946.

1947   Anne stars as Lucille Stewart in <u>Blaze of Noon</u>. She
        provides the voice of the mother in <u>Mother Wore Tights</u>.
        She is a guest on radio shows <u>The Kraft Music Hall</u>,
        <u>Screen Guild Theatre</u>, <u>The Charlie McCarthy Show</u>, and
        <u>Cavalcade of America</u>. On February 10, 1947, Anne is
        nominated for an Academy Award for Best Supporting
        Actress for her role as Sophie MacDonald in <u>The Razor's</u>
        <u>Edge</u>. On March 13, 1947, Anne wins the Oscar.

1948   Anne co-stars as Penny Johnson in <u>Homecoming</u>. She also
        appears as Julie Norman in <u>The Walls of Jericho</u>. Her
        third film released is <u>The Luck of the Irish</u>, where
        appears as Nora. She is a guest on radio shows <u>Truth</u>
        <u>or Consequences</u> and <u>Dewey-Warren Bandwagon</u>.

1949   Anne stars as Mike in <u>Yellow Sky</u>. She next has the
        role of Hannah Adams in <u>You're My Everything</u>.

1950   Anne has a major role as Kit Dodge, Jr., in <u>A Ticket</u>
        <u>to Tomahawk</u>. She wins coveted role of Eve Harrington
        in <u>All About Eve</u>. She appears on radio shows <u>Camel</u>

Screen Guild Theatre, Screenwriters Guild Annual Award Show, The Anacin Hollywood Star Theatre, and Lux Radio Theatre of the Air.

1951   Anne stars as Valerie Hogan in Follow the Sun. She is a guest star on radio shows Theatre Guild on the Air, Hedda Hopper, Screen Guild Theatre, and Suspense. On February 12, 1951, announcement is made of Anne's nomination for a Best Actress Academy Award for her role in All About Eve. The award goes to Judy Holliday. On July 9, 1951, Anne gives birth to daughter Katrina Hodiak.

1952   Anne is Cal in The Outcasts of Poker Flat. She is next seen as Virginia Mason in My Wife's Best Friend. Anne is Joanna in her third release this year, "The Last Leaf," in O. Henry's Full House. She stars on radio show Suspense. Anne files for divorce from John Hodiak on December 22, 1952, citing extreme cruelty, and wins custody of Katrina.

1953   Anne appears as Norah Larkin in The Blue Gardenia. She then stars as Ruth Grandfort in I Confess. Her radio shows appearances are in The Theater Guild on the Air, The Oscar Awards, The Bob Hope Show, the Martin and Lewis Show, and American Red Cross. In the fall, she takes over for Judith Anderson in the national stage tour of John Brown's Body. On January 27, 1953, she wins final divorce from John Hodiak.

1954   Anne's only film role this year is as Willi in Carnival Story, filmed entirely on location outside of Munich, Germany.

1955   Anne stars in three films this year: as Monica Johnson in Bedevilled; as Tacey Cromwell in One Desire; and as Cherry Malotte in the remake of The Spoilers. John Hodiak dies on October 19, 1955.

1956   This year Anne stars as Rita Kendrick in The Come On. She then appears as Princess Nefretiri in the remake of The Ten Commandments. In Three Violent People, she plays Lorna Hunter Saunders and again co-stars with Charlton Heston (who was Moses in The Ten Commandments).

1957   Anne returns to the stage as Mollie Lovejoy in The Square Root of Wonderful. She also makes her television debut in the General Electric (G.E.) Theater, as a guest star with show's host Ronald Reagan.

1958   Anne stars as Kimberley in Chase a Crooked Shadow.
        She stars on TV series Playhouse 90, G.E. Theater, and
        The Lux Video Theater. She appears as Louise Schaeffer
        on the London stage in The Joshua Tree, which ran for
        five months.

1959   Anne has roles in TV series Wagon Train, Riverboat,
        and Zane Grey Theater. Anne's beloved grandfather,
        Frank Lloyd Wright, dies on April 5, 1959, after an
        abdominal obstruction. She meets 31-year-old Randolph
        Galt at the Clift Hotel in San Francisco, following
        Anne's hosting of a PBS memorial program about Frank
        Lloyd Wright.

1960   Anne appears on TV series Checkmate, The June Allyson
        Show, and G.E. Theater. She also has a radio promotional
        interview for Cimarron, now filming. On February 18,
        1960, she marries Randolph Galt in Kahala, Hawaii.
        They begin their married life at Giro Station, some
        150 miles north of Sydney, Australia. She suffers a
        miscarriage. She later gives birth to daughter Melissa
        Ann, on October 4, 1960.

1961   Anne stars as Dixie in Cimarron. She also has a role
        in TV series The U.S. Steel Hour.

1962   Anne is Olive in Season of Passion (later titled Summer
        of the Seventeenth Doll), filmed in her adopted homeland
        of Australia. She next stars as Teresina Vidaverri
        in A Walk on the Wild Side. Her final movie released
        this year stars Anne as Dr. Anne Dyson in Mix Me a
        Person.

1963   Anne stars in the suspense TV thriller Alfred Hitchcock
        Presents.

1964   Anne has guest-starring role in popular TV series Dr.
        Kildare. On March 11, 1964, she gives birth to third
        daughter, Maginel, who is named after the sister of
        Frank Lloyd Wright. The family returns to the United
        States and settles in New Mexico.

1965   Anne's only screen appearance (a cameo) is in the Jerry
        Lewis film The Family Jewels.

1966   Anne's television work continues in two episodes of
        Batman.

1967   Anne returns to film as Mary Ann in the Spanish-made
The Tall Women. She has the role of Margo Foster in
The Busy Body. She again co-stars in four episodes
of TV series Batman. She also appears on TV series
Cowboy in Africa and My Three Sons. She makes her
television movie debut in Stranger on the Run. On
February 9, 1967, Anne separates from Randolph Galt.

1968   Anne is a guest star on TV series The Danny Thomas Show,
The F.B.I., Run for Your Life, Get Smart, Ironside,
The Name of the Game, and The Virginian. She also has
a starring role in TV movie Companions in Nightmare.

1969   Anne stars on TV series The Big Valley, The Name of
the Game, and Ironside. She has a role in TV pilot
for proposed series Marcus Welby, M.D. For her role
in the Name of the Game episode titled "The Bobby Currier
Story," Anne wins an Emmy nomination for Best Actress
in a Drama, Single Performance. Geraldine Page wins
the Emmy.

1970   Anne appears on TV series Paris 7000. She also appears
in two different story episodes of The Name of the Game.
She then stars in Bracken's World. She also has roles
in TV movies The Challengers and Ritual of Evil. Anne
receives her final divorce decree from Randolph Galt
on January 29, 1970. She is honorary mayor of University
City, California.

1971   Anne returns to the stage, replacing Lauren Bacall as
Margo Channing in the musical remake of All About Eve,
titled Applause. Bette Davis was Margo in the original
film. She also stars as Liz Addams Hatch in the
fictionalized autobiography of Elizabeth Burns in The
Late Liz. She has a small role as Cleo in Fool's Parade.
Her next role is in TV movie If Tomorrow Comes.

1972   Anne has important guest role in TV pilot movie The
Catcher, which did not become a series.

1973   Anne stars in TV series Lisa, Bright and Dark. She
also appears in TV series Columbo, Cannon, Mannix,
Banacek, and Love Story. In February, Anne is named
new president of the Chamber Symphony Society of
California.

1974   Anne has role on stage in Noel Coward's In Two Keys.
On Armed Forces Radio in Europe, Anne is heard in the
Playhouse 25 production of "Swamp Water."

1975   Anne is busy working on her journal she is turning into
        book form. She is heard on Armed Forces Radio in the
        Playhouse 25 production of "The Plow and the Candle."

1976   Anne is a bank manager in TV mini-series Arthur Hailey's
        "The Moneychangers," (later titled The Moneychangers).
        Anne's book Intermission: A True Story is published
        in December, by G. P. Putnam's Sons; it is an immediate
        success. Anne meets David Klee.

1977   Anne marries Wall Street banking financier David Klee
        in a private ceremony in February. They move to a new
        home in Easton, Connecticut. Ten months later, David
        Klee dies after suffering a heart attack.

1978   Anne is the mother of Little Mo, a TV movie about tennis
        star Maureen Connolly.

1979   Anne returns to the stage as Alma in Cause Celebre.
        She stars in TV pilot movie for proposed series Nero
        Wolfe. Anne's beloved mother, Catherine Wright Baxter,
        dies at age 85, on January 29.

1980   Anne co-stars as Lilianna with singer-songwriter daughte
        Katrina Hodiak in Jane Austen in Manhattan. (This film
        was released in the United States in 1981.) Anne has
        a small role in TV mini-series John Steinbeck's "East
        of Eden" (later titled East of Eden).

1982   Anne appears in her last stage play, as Queen Gertrude,
        in Hamlet, at the American Shakespeare Theatre, in
        Stratford, Connecticut.

1983   Anne is offered the role of Victoria Cabot on the TV
        series Hotel, after Bette Davis must bow out due to
        poor health. The series debuts September 28, 1983.
        It runs for two more seasons with Anne at the helm.

1984   Anne appears as guest on TV specials The Dean Martin
        Celebrity Roast and Hollywood Stars' Screen Tests.

1985   Anne appears on TV special Night of 100 Stars II. Anne
        visits Sydney, Australia, to negotiate a deal on filming
        her autobiography, Intermission: A True Story. She
        is also working on a book about her family that focuses
        on her beloved grandfather, Frank Lloyd Wright. On
        December 3, she suffers a stroke in New York while
        hailing a cab. After remaining in coma for eight days,
        Anne Baxter dies on December 12, 1985.

Filmography

This chapter consists of Anne Baxter's motion picture credits. Included in the filmography are release dates, casts and credits, synopses, and reviews.

F1   TWENTY MULE TEAM (M-G-M, released 5.9.40)
       BW   84 Minutes

Producer: J. Walter Ruben. Director: Richard Thorpe. Screenplay: Cyril Hume, E. E. Paramore, and Richard Mailbaum. Photography: Clyde De Vinna. Editor: Frank Sullivan. Based on a story by Robert C. Du Soe and Owen Atkinson.

CAST: Wallace Beery (Skinner Bill Bragg), Leo Carrillo (Piute
          Pete), Marjorie Rambeau (Josie Johnson), Anne Baxter
          (Jean Johnson), Douglas Fowley (Stag Roper), Noah Beery,
          Jr. (Mitch), Burton Churchill (Jackass Brown), Arthur
          Hohl (Seiters), Clem Bevans (Chuckawalla), Charles Halton
          (Adams), Minor Watson (Marshal), Oscar O'Shea
          (Conductor), Lloyd Ingraham (Stockholder), with Ivan
          Miller, Lew Kelly, and Sam Appel.

SYNOPSIS: Furnace Flat, outside of Death Valley, is the setting for this western, starring Beery as a blackmailer trying to find the location of a mountain of pure borax that is as desirable to own as gold. Anne Baxter is the daughter of the local tavern owner (Rambeau). She is attracted to Roper, who ends up getting killed by Bragg. Bragg leaves town when the posse pursues him. Later he finds out that he has been pardoned.

REVIEWS: New York Times, 4/7.40, p. 4
           Variety, 5.1.40
           New York Times, 5.10.40, p. 26

<u>Variety</u>, 5.1.40: "Marjorie Rambeau runs a desert saloon and fights to prevent her young daughter (Baxter) from eloping with the heavy Fowley." The director "carries the ideas of the writers by tossing in all the familiar ingredients to retain, nevertheless, plenty of action, gun-popping, and wild rides."

<u>New York Times</u>, 5.10.40: "Anne Baxter is an attractive little desert flower."

NOTES: The print was processed with sepia to provide greater idea appeal. Noah Beery, Jr., is the nephew of Wallace Beery.

See: B419, B469

F2   THE GREAT PROFILE (20th Century-Fox, released 10.17.40)
          BW   82 Minutes

Producer: Raymond Griffith. Director: Walter Lang. Screenplay: Milton Sperling and Hilary Lynn. Photography: Ernest Palmer. Music: Cyril J. Mockridge. Editor: Francis D. Lyon.

CAST: John Barrymore (Evans Garrick), Mary Beth Hughes (Sylvia), Gregory Ratoff (Boris Mefoofsky), John Payne (Richard Lansing), Anne Baxter (Mary Maxwell), Lionel Atwill (Dr. Bruce), Edward Brophy (Sylvester), Willie Fund (Confucious), Joan Valerie (Understudy), Charles Lane (Director), Marc Lawrence (Tony), Cecil Cunningham (Miss Perkins), Hal K. Dawson (Ticket Seller), William Pawley (Electrician), Eddie Dunn (Furniture Man), James Flavin (Detective), and Dorothy Dearing (Debutante).

SYNOPSIS: Actor Evans Garrick is a long-past-good-reviews ham whose once sterling work on the stage dissipates into lechery and drunkenness. He disgraces his family by becoming an acrobat. Anne Baxter is a young woman who tries to reform the eccentric, amorous actor.

REVIEWS: <u>New York Times</u>, 6.16.40, p. 3
          <u>New York Times</u>, 10.18.40, p. 25
          <u>Newsweek</u>, 9.2.40, p. 49
          <u>Photoplay</u>, 11.40, p. 68
          <u>Variety</u>, 8.21.40, p. 6

<u>Variety</u>, 8.21.40: "Mary Beth Hughes is okay as the thespian's wife, while Anne Baxter and John Payne are authoress and show backer, respectively."

NOTES: The film is considered a modified account of true events
        which took place in Barrymore's dressing room at the
        Belasco Theater the previous year. It was generally
        felt that he overacted horribly and made a pathetic
        spectacle of himself.

See: B105, B299

F3   CHARLEY'S AUNT (20th Century-Fox, released 8.1.41)
        BW   81 Minutes

Producer: William Perlberg. Director: Archie Mayo. Screenplay:
George Seaton. Photography: Peverell Marley. Music: Alfred
Newman. Based on the play by Brandon Thomas. Available on
video cassette.

CAST: Jack Benny (Lord Fancourt Babberly, also known as Babbi),
        Kay Francis (Donna Lucia), James Ellison (Jack Chesney),
        Anne Baxter (Amy Spettigue), Edmund Gwenn (Stephen
        Spettigue), Reginald Owen (Mr. Radcliffe), Laird Cregar
        (Sir Francis Chesney), Arleen Whelan (Kitty Verdun),
        Richard Haydn (Charley Stafford), Lionel Pape (Babberly),
        Will Stanton (Messenger), Montague Shaw (Elderly Man),
        Claud Allister and William Austin (Spectators), and
        Maurice Cass (Octogenarian).

SYNOPSIS: Lord Fancourt Babberly is a young Oxford student
who agrees to get his pal out of the sentimental doldrums by
impersonating his aunt. He becomes very popular, and the other
young students get caught up in the hilarity of the situation.

REVIEWS: Commonweal, 8.29.41, p. 448
           Film Daily, 7.23.41, p. 6
           Hollywood Reporter, 7.23.41, p. 3
           Motion Picture Herald Product Digest (MPHPD),
             7.26.41, p. 262
           New York Times, 8.2.41, p. 18
           Newsweek, 8.11.41, p. 60
           Time, 8.18.41, p. 71
           Variety, 7.23.41, p. 8

Variety, 7.23.41: "Supporting players are selected for maximum
results from their respective portrayals. Ellison and Haydn
are the two undergraduates who get Benny into the predicament;
Anne Baxter and Arleen Whelan are the coy maidens whose hands
are sought by Ellison and Haydn."

New York Times, 8.2.41: "Arleen Whelan and Anne Baxter bustle about in twittering feminine apprehension."

NOTES: Charley's Aunt was first performed in London in 1892. It grossed millions of dollars in royalties for Brandon Thomas and his heirs. It has been translated into 18 languages, including Esperanto. It cost 20th Century-Fox Studios $125,000 to film Charley's Aunt. It was later remade as the musical Where's Charley? in 1952, starring Ray Bolger, Allyn McLerie, and Robert Shackelton.

See: B57, B220, B464, B470

F4   SWAMP WATER (20th Century-Fox, released 11.16.41)
         BW   90 Minutes

Producer: Irving Pichel. Director: Jean Renoir. Screenplay: Dudley Nicholas. Photography: Peverell Marley. Music: David Buttolph. Based on the story by Vereen Bell.

CAST.   Walter Brennan (Tom Keefer), Walter Huston (Thursday Regan), Anne Baxter (Julie), Dana Andrews (Ben), Virgini Gilmore (Mabel MacKenzie), John Carradine (Jesse Wick), Mary Howard (Hannah), Eugene Pallette (Sheriff Jeb McKane), Ward Bond (Tim Dorson), Quinn Williams (Bud Dorson), Russell Simpson (Marty McCord), Joseph Sawyer (Hardy Hagan), Paul Burns (Tulie MacKenzie), Dave Morris (Barber), Frank Austin (Fred Ulm), and Matt Willis (Mile Tonkin).

SYNOPSIS: A young man wanders into the Okefenokee Swamp to find his dog. Instead, he meets up with a guiltless fugitive (Brennan). The family who lives in the swamp has harbored the fugitive for years by the time Ben picks up his trail. Keefer threatens to kill him, but Ben is convinced of the man's innocence. They enter into a fur-trapping partnership and Ben gives his share to Brennan's daughter (Baxter). She finds out the true story and gives away his secret. Ben refuses to divulg Keefer's whereabouts and forces the real killer to confess (the killer is his own father, Regan). Eventually, Keefer is brought out of the swamp and freed.

REVIEWS: Commonweal, 11.28.41, p. 144
              Film Daily, 10.20.41, p. 8
              Hollywood Reporter, 10.20.41, p. 3
              MPHPD, 10.18.42, p. 318
              New Republic, 12.8.41, p. 763

New York Times, 11.2.41, p. 5
New York Times, 11.17.41, p. 15
Newsweek, 11.24.41, p. 72
Scholastic, 12.8.41, p. 30
Variety, 10.22.41, p. 8

Variety, 10.22.41: "All of the players, both bit and featured, do exceptionally well, with the three women particularly standing out despite unflattering makeup and costumes."

New York Times, 11.17.41: "The performances of such capable folk as Walter Huston, Walter Brennan, John Carradine, Dana Andrews and Anne Baxter are perilously close to silly."

NOTES: This film was Jean Renoir's first endeavor in an English-language market. He attempts a "Faulkneresque" study of folk living in the Okefenokee Swamp, where the movie was filmed.

See: B221, B471, R37

F5   THE MAGNIFICENT AMBERSONS (RKO-Mercury, released
          8.13.42)   BW   88 Minutes

Producer: Orson Welles. Director: Orson Welles. Screenplay: Orson Welles. Photography: Stanley Cortez. Music: Bernard Herrmann. Editor: Robert Wise. Art Direction: Mark-Lee Kirk. From the novel by Booth Tarkington. Available on video cassette.

CAST: Joseph Cotten (Eugene Morgan), Dolores Costello (Isabel Amberson), Anne Baxter (Lucy Morgan), Tim Holt (George Amberson Minafer), Agnes Moorehead (Fanny Minafer), Ray Collins (Jack Amberson), Richard Bennett (Major Amberson), Donald Dillaway (Wilbur Minafer), and Erskine Sanford (Bronson).

SYNOPSIS: In an Orson Welles voice-over, we are introduced to the characters and their story, an expose of the decline of American aristocracy in the late 1870s. Isabel Amberson marries the stuffy, socially acceptable Wilbur Minafer and they produce a handsome, spoiled and devilish son, George. Isabel had originally been in love with Eugene Morgan, who leaves town, marries another, becomes widowed and returns with daughter Lucy. Morgan, now a wealthy auto inventor, realizes he still loves Isabel, who is also now widowed. George has his eye on Lucy, but he's terribly jealous of his mother's interest in Morgan. Together with his equally jealous Aunt Fanny, George steps in to break up the relationship. Because of his lazy, haughty

attitude, George loses Lucy when she insists that he choose
a career other than that of an idle gentleman. Morgan's car
factory prospers and the Ambersons' wealth melts away -- the
deserved come-uppance to George Amberson Minafer.

REVIEWS: American Cinematographer, 11.76, p. 123
            American Film, 3.76, p. 22
            Commonweal, 8.21.42, p. 423
            Film Comment, Summer, 1971, p. 48
            Film Daily, 7.3.42, p. 5
            Film Quarterly, Summer, 1974, p. 196
            Hollywood Reporter, 7.1.42, p. 3
            London Times, 3.5.43, p. 6
            MPHPD, 7.4.42, p. 749
            New Republic, 8.10.42, p. 173
            New York Times, 11.16.41, p. 5
            New York Times, 8.14.42, p. 13
            New York Times, 8.16.42, p. 3
            New Yorker, 8.15.42, p. 53
            Newsweek, 7.20.42, p. 56
            Photoplay, 4.42, p. 44
            Rob Wagner's Script, 7.4.42, p. 24
            Time, 7.20.42, p. 42
            Variety, 7.1.42, p. 8

Variety, 7.1.42: "Miss Baxter, a cute, personable and fine
little actress, is another on the more cheerful side."

New York Times, 8.8.42: "Anne Baxter gives a fine performance,"
in the "exceptionally well-made film dealing with a subject
scarcely worth the attention which has been lavished upon it."

NOTES: With this film, Orson Welles demonstrated beyond a
          reasonable doubt that the screen is his medium, whether
          or not he appears on it.

See: B36, B57, B198, B222, B251, B281, B286, B304, B310,
          B320, B323, B325, B382, B384, B460, B464, B480, B514,
          B525

F6   THE PIED PIPER (20th Century-Fox, released 8.12.42)
          Color   87 Minutes

Producer: Nunnally Johnson. Director: Irving Pichel.
Screenplay: Nunnally Johnson. Photography: Edward Cronjager.
Music: Alfred Newman. Art Direction: Richard Day and Maurice
Ransford. Set Decoration: Thomas Little. Costumes: Dolly Tree.
Editor: Allen McNeil. Sound: E. Clayton Ward and Roger Herman.

Based on the novel by Nevil Shute which appeared in Collier's magazine.

CAST: Monty Woolley (Howard), Roddy McDowall (Ronnie
        Cavanaugh), Anne Baxter (Nicole Rougeron), Otto Preminger
        (Major Diessen), J. Carroll Naish (Aristide Rougeron),
        Lester Matthews (Mr. Cavanaugh), Jill Esmond
        (Mrs. Cavanaugh), Ferike Boros (Madame), Peggy Ann Garner
        (Sheila Cavanaugh), Maurice Tanzin (Pierre), Fleurette
        Zama (Rose), William Edmunds (Frenchman), Marcel Dalio
        (Foquet), Marcelle Corday (Madame Bonnie), Edward Ashley
        (Charendon), Norton Lowry (Roger Dickinson), Odette
        Myrtil (Madame Rougeron), Jean Del Val (Railroad
        Official), George Davis (Barman), Robert O. Davis
        (Lieutenant), Henry Rowland (Military Policeman), Helmut
        Dantine (Aide), Otto Reichow and Henry Guttman (German
        Soldiers), Hans Von Morhart and Hans Von Twardowski
        (Sergeants), William Yetter (Officer at Road), Adrienne
        d'Ambricourt (Servant), Mici Goty (Proprietress), Jean
        De Briac (Fisherman), Ernest Hansman (Soldier), Julika
        (Anna), Wilson Benge (Waiter), Brandon Hurst (Major
        Domo), and Thomas Louden (Medford).

SYNOPSIS: During World War II, an old Englishman (Woolley)
vacationing in Paris leads an increasing brood of street urchins
in his care to a safe haven in England. When they are
intercepted by a Nazi sweep of Paris, he unknowingly picks
up a French maid (Baxter) at a chaotic railroad station. She
helps them find their escape route. She also reveals to the
pig-headed old man that she once loved his dead son. Roddy
McDowall is the leader of the children, and Otto Preminger is
the arrogant Nazi officer.

REVIEWS: Commonweal, 8.21.42, p. 424
            Film Daily, 7.8.42, p. 7
            Life, 8.10.42, p. 47
            London Times, 11.28.42, p. 6
            New York Times, 8.13.42, p. 15
            New York Times, 8.23.42, p. 4
            New Yorker, 8.15.42, p. 53
            Newsweek, 7.27.42, p. 69
            Photoplay, 9.42, p. 24
            Scholastic, 9.14.42, p. 35
            Theatre Arts, 10.42, p. 637
            Time, 8.10.42, p. 86
            Variety, 7.8.42, p. 8

Variety, 7.8.42: "Anne Baxter is an attractive French heroine
and J. Carroll Naish is believable as the cautious Breton."

New York Times, 8.13.42: "Anne Baxter, as the young French girl who reveals in the darkened railway carriage that she once loved Howard's dead son, is direct and simple."

NOTES: The producers had the good judgment not to let the harsh savagery of Nazism overwhelm the story.

See: B72, B223, B351, B362, B464, B472, B525

F7   CRASH DIVE (20th Century-Fox, released 4.28.43)
          Color   105 Minutes

Producer: Milton Sperling. Director: Archie Mayo. Screenplay: Jo Swerling. Photography: Leon Shamroy. Special Effects: Fred Sersen. Editor: Walter Thompson. Music: Emil Newman and David Buttolph. Based on a story by W. R. Burnett.

CAST: Tyrone Power (Lt. Ward Stewart), Anne Baxter (Jean
         Hewlitt), Dana Andrews (Lt. Cdr. Dewey Connors), James
         Gleason (McDonnell), Charles Grapewin (Pop), Dame May
         Whitty (Grandmother), Henry Morgan (Brownie), Ben Carter
         (Oliver Cromwell Jones), Charles Tannen (Hammond), Frank
         Conroy (Capt. Bryson), Florence Lake (Doris), John Archer
         (Curley), George Holmes (Crew Member), Frank Dawson
         (Butler), Minor Watson (Admiral), Edward McWade (Crony),
         Kathleen Howard (Miss Bromley), David Bacon (Lieutenant)
         and Stanley Andrews (Captain).

SYNOPSIS: Stewart is transferred from a P.T. mosquito boat to a submarine. On the way to his new duty, he meets a New London teacher (Baxter), who is taking a group of her students on a trip to Washington, D.C. Stewart and the teacher get off on the wrong foot, but he eventually wins her over. He then learns that she is the fiancee of his superior officer (Andrews). The two officers must put aside their romantic rivalry as they go to war. Their submarine leaves to raid a secret land base of the Nazis.

REVIEWS: Commonweal, 5.14.43, p. 100
            Film Daily, 4.22.43, p. 7
            Hollywood Reporter, 4.21.43, p. 3
            MPHPD, 7.11.42, p. 965
            New York Times, 4.29.43, p. 25
            New York Times, 5.2.43, p. 3
            New Yorker, 5.1.43, p. 36
            Time, 5.10.43, p. 98
            Variety, 4.21.43, p. 8

<u>Variety</u>, 4.21.43: "Power is expertly cast both in the romantic role and as the sub officer. Andrews also turns in a top performance, as does Anne Baxter."

<u>New York Times</u>, 4.29.43: "The picture is romance and thriller of the most fictitious sort. It leaves one wondering blankly whether Hollywood knows we're at war. Anne Baxter is the little lady over whom there is so much to do."

NOTES: This film won an Academy Award for Special Effects. Archie Mayo was honored in his ability to stage the underwater war scenes. When the U.S.S. <u>Corsair</u> hits the high seas, the film becomes educational as well as entertaining. <u>Crash Dive</u> scenes were filmed at the U.S. Naval Substation at New London, Connecticut.

See: B24, B33, B73, B106, B211, B224, B305, B357, B406, B408, B494

F8   FIVE GRAVES TO CAIRO (Paramount, released 5.26.43)
         BW   96 Minutes

Producer: Charles Brackett. Director: Billy Wilder. Screenplay: Charles Brackett and Billy Wilder. Photography: John Seitz. Music: Miklos Rozsa. Editor: Doane Harrison. Based on the play by Lajos Biro.

CAST: Franchot Tone (Cpl. John J. Bramble), Anne Baxter (Mouche), Akim Tamiroff (Farid), Erich Von Stroheim (Field Marshal Rommel), Peter Van Eyck (Lt. Schwegler), Fortunio Bonanova (Gen. Sebastiano), Konstantin Shayne (Maj. Von Bulow), Fred Nurney (Maj. Lamprecht), Miles Mander (British Colonel), Leslie Denison (British Captain), and Ian Keith (British Captain).

SYNOPSIS: A British corporal gets left behind in Sidi Halfaya and poses as a loyal German agent at the seedy hotel where General Rommel and his staff are billeted. He learns Rommel's secrets and escapes to the British lines to let them know where the supply depots are hidden in the Egyptian desert. Anne Baxter is the maid at the hotel, who has a romance with a young Nazi officer (Van Eyck).

REVIEWS: <u>Commonweal</u>, 6.11.43, p. 203
           <u>Film Daily</u>, 5.4.43, p. 8
           <u>Hollywood Reporter</u>, 5.4.43, p. 3
           <u>Life</u>, 6.14.43, p. 47

MPHPD, 5.8.43, p. 1301
New York Times, 5.27.43, p. 21
New York Times, 5.30.43, p. 3
New Yorker, 6.5.43, p. 48
Newsweek, 5.31.43, p. 87
Rob Wagner's Script, 6.12.43, p. 14
Time, 5.24.43, p. 98
Variety, 5.5.43, p. 8

Variety, 5.5.43: "All the key actors turn in trim performances Anne Baxter's French maid bespeaks a bright future for this comely miss."

New York Times, 5.27.43: "There is a little side issue between Peter Van Eyck as a Nazi officer and Anne Baxter as an ex-patriate French maid," in this film that is "probably the most conglomerate war film to date."

NOTES: This movie is a remake of 1939's Hotel Imperial, starring Ray Milland, Isa Miranda, Albert Dekker, Reginald Owen, and Gene Lockhart. Charles Brackett and Billy Wilder dressed up this World War II film by using shenanigans that made it easy to believe that this was not a real story about the Desert Fox (Rommel). They borrowed Anne Baxter because she affected a French accent so well.

See: B29, B57, B74, B107, B225, B307, B324, B356, B371, B418, B460, B464, R2

F9   NORTH STAR (RKO, released 11.4.43)
      BW   105 Minutes

Producer: Samuel Goldwyn. Director: Lewis Milestone. Associate Producer: William Cameron Menzies. Screenplay: Lillian Hellmann Photography: James Wong Howe. Music: Aaron Copeland. Songs by Aaron Copeland and Ira Gershwin. Available on video cassette

CAST: Anne Baxter (Marina), Dana Andrews (Kolya), Walter Huston (Dr. Kurin), Walter Brennan (Karp), Ann Harding (Sophia) Jane Withers (Claudia), Farley Granger (Damian), Erich Von Stroheim (Dr. Von Harden), Dean Jagger (Bodion), Eric Roberts (Grisha), Carl Benton Reid (Boris), Ann Carter (Olga), Esther Dale (Anna), Ruth Nelson (Nadya), Paul Guilfoyle (Iskin), Martin Kosleck (Dr. Richter), Tonio Selwart (German Captain), Peter Pohlens (German Lieutenant), Robert Lowery (Russian Pilot), Gene

O'Donnell (Russian Gunner), Frank Wilcox (Petrov), Loudie
Claar (Woman on Hospital Cot), Lynn Winthrop (Guerrilla
Girl), and Charles Bates (Petya).

SYNOPSIS: North Star is a Russian border village on a collective
farm. When the Nazis invade them, the men become guerrillas.
The children, women, and village doctor (Huston) remain behind.
As they burn their village, the Nazis put out the fires and
one Nazi-hating German doctor (Von Stroheim) accompanying the
troops bleeds the children. A group of older children, including
Anne Baxter, run arms to the guerrillas. The German doctor
is killed by Dr. Kurin.

REVIEWS: Commonweal, 11.19.43, p. 117
            Film Daily, 10.13.43, p. 11
            Hollywood Reporter, 10.12.43, p. 3
            Life, 11.1.43, p. 118
            MPHPD, 10.10.43, p. 1585
            Nation, 10.30.43, p. 509
            New Republic, 11.8.43, p. 653
            New York Times, 11.5.43, p. 23
            New York Times, 11.7.43, p. 3
            New York Times Magazine, 10.10.43, p. 16
            Newsweek, 11.8.43, p. 86
            Photoplay, 1.44, p. 6
            Scholastic, 11.29.43, p. 26
            Theatre Arts, 12.43, p. 716
            Time, 11.8.43, p. 54
            Variety, 10.13.43, p. 10

Variety, 10.13.43: "The cast is excellent. Anne Baxter, Dana
Andrews, Walter Huston, Walter Brennan, Ann Harding, Jane
Withers, Farley Granger, Erich Von Stroheim, Dean Jagger all
contribute fine performances."

New York Times, 11.15.43: "Anne Baxter, Dana Andrews, Jane
Withers, and Farley Granger are conventionally spirited as young
folk."

NOTES: North Star was the first attempt by a major United
          States producer to present the Russians as defending
          their homes in World War II, showing the decisive role
          in which the guerrillas defeated the Germans. It was
          the first to depict the sickening Nazi atrocity of
          bleeding children. The film was later edited to de-
          emphasize the good Russians and retitled Armored Attack
          (also shown in computer-colorized version).

Songs: "No Village Like Mine"
          "Younger Generation"
          "Song of the Guerrillas"

See: B4, B42, B108, B226, B281, B284, B309, B322, B350, B357,
     B363, B407, B464

F10   THE EVE OF ST. MARK (20th Century-Fox, released 5.30.44)
      BW   95 Minutes

Producer: William Perlberg. Director: John M. Stahl.
Screenplay: George Seaton. Photography: Joseph La Shelle.
Editor: Louis Sackin. Music: Cyril J. Mockridge. Music
Direction: Emil Newman. Based on the play by Maxwell Anderson.

CAST: Anne Baxter (Janet Feller), William Eythe (Pvt. Quizzy
          West), Michael O'Shea (Pvt. Thomas Mulveroy), Vincent
          Price (Pvt. Francis Marion), Ruth Nelson (Nell West),
          Ray Collins (Deckman West), Stanley Prager (Pvt.
          Glinka), Henry Morgan (Pvt. Shevlin), Robert Bailey
          (Cpl. Tate), Joann Dolan (Lill Bird), Toni Favor (Sal
          Bird), George Mathews (Sgt. Ruby), John Archer (Pvt.
          Carter), Murray Alpen (Sgt. Kriven), Dickie Moore
          (Zip West), Joven E. Rola (Pepita), Harry Shannon
          (Chaplain), David Essex (Guide), Roger Clark (The
          Captain), and Jimmy Clark (Neil West).

SYNOPSIS: Eythe is a young soldier who goes off to war in the
Pacific, leaving behind his girl (Baxter). The young farm boy
carries on a telepathic discourse with his mother and sweetheart.
Vincent Price is a young southern aristocrat who quotes Shelley,
Keats, and Shakespeare and contracts malaria.

REVIEWS: Commonweal, 6.16.44, p. 205
          Film Daily, 5.22.44, p. 6
          Hollywood Reporter, 5.17.44, p. 3
          Nation, 6.3.44, p. 661
          New Republic, 6.19.44, p. 816
          New York Times, 5.31.44, p. 22
          New York Times, 6.4.44, p. 3
          New Yorker, 6.3.44, p. 61
          Newsweek, 6.12.44, p. 72
          Variety, 5.17.44, p. 10

Variety, 5.17.44: "It is a picture of superlative performances.
William Eythe, as the farmboy inductee, has his biggest part
to date, and does much with it. He and Anne Baxter share the

romance, and she, too, gives a fine characterization, as does, notably, Michael O'Shea, in the same role he created in the Broadway stage version, when he was known as Eddie O'Shea."

New York Times, 5.31.44: "Anne Baxter is rather dreamy in the role of the farmboy's girl."

NOTES: John M. Stahl directed this film in a variety of cinematic styles. It is the filming of the moving 1942 Broadway hit of the same name, starring William Prince, Mary Rolfe, James Monks, Aline MacMahon, and Michael O'Shea. The producer's purpose in filming the story was to give hope to friends and relatives of missing in action American servicemen who were defending the Philippines.

See: B5, B54, B109, B164, B228, B284, B306, B410, B464

F11   THE FIGHTING SULLIVANS (20th Century-Fox, released 2.8.44)
      BW   111 Minutes

Producer: Sam Jaffe. Director: Lloyd Bacon. Screenplay: Mary C. McCall, Jr. Photography: Lucien Andriot. Music: Cryil J. Mockridge and Alfred Newman. Editor: Louis Loeffler. From the story by Edward Doherty and Jules Schermer.

CAST: Anne Baxter (Katherine Mary), Thomas Mitchell (Mr. Sullivan), Selena Royle (Mrs. Sullivan), Edward Ryan (Al), Trudy Marshall (Genevieve), John Campbell (Frank), James Cardwell (George), John Alvin (Matt), George Offerman, Jr. (Joe), Roy Roberts (Father Francis), Ward Bond (Lieutenant), Mary McCarty (Gladys), Bobby Driscoll (Al as a Child), Nancy June Robinson (Genevieve as a Child), Marvin Davis (Frank as a Child), Buddy Swan (George as a Child), Billy Cummings (Matt as a Child), Johnny Calkins (Joe as a Child), Jorn Nesbitt (Admiral), Selmer Jackson (Damage Control Officer), Harry Shannon (CPO), Barbara Brown (Nurse), Larry Thompson (Yeoman), and Addison Richards (Naval Captain).

SYNOPSIS: This is the real-life story of five brothers from Waterloo, Iowa, who were lost together in the sinking of the Juneau off the Solomon Islands during World War II. Thomas Mitchell and Selena Royle are the parents of the five lost sons. Anne Baxter is Al's wife.

REVIEWS: *Commonweal*, 2.25.44, p. 470
            Cosmopolitan, 4.44, p. 112
            Film Daily, 2.3.44, p. 9
            Musician, 5.44, p. 96
            Nation, 3.11.44, p. 316
            New York Times, 10.24.43, p. 3
            New York Times, 2.10.44, p. 19
            New York Times, 2.13.44, p. 3
            Newsweek, 2.21.44, p. 91
            Scholastic, 4.10.44, p. 31
            Scribner's Commentator, 4.10.44, p. 4
            Variety, 2.9.44, p. 12

Variety, 2.9.44: "Miss Baxter is the refreshing, attractive little-town belle who fits in admirably with the surroundings and the faithful production backgrounds furnished by Sam Jaffe.'

NOTES: "I don't see how it could have been any more
            realistic," said Mrs. Sullivan at the movie's premiere
            at the Roxy Theater in New York City, also attended
            by husband, Thomas. They had seen the movie being
            made, but it was when they first saw the actors in
            uniform "that it really got me," she said. The
            Sullivans sold war bonds in the lobby of the theater.
            The five brothers were all posthumously awarded Purple
            Hearts and were honored by the christening of a
            battleship named after them. The movie was also known
            as *The Sullivans*.

See: B227, B284-285, B357, B464

F12   SUNDAY DINNER FOR A SOLDIER (20th Century-Fox, released
       1.24.45)   BW   86 Minutes

Producer: Walter Morosco. Director: Lloyd Bacon. Screenplay:
Wanda Tuchock and Melvin Levy. Photography: Joe MacDonald.
Editor: J. Watson Webb. Music: Alfred Newman. Based on a story
by Martha Cheavens.

CAST: Anne Baxter (Tessa Osborne), John Hodiak (Eric Moore),
           Charles Winninger (Grandfather), Anne Revere (Agatha),
           Connie Marshall (Mary), Chill Wills (Mr. York), Robert
           Bailey (Kenneth Normand), Bobby Driscoll (Jeeb), Jane
           Darwell (Mrs. Dobson), Billy Cummings (Michael),
           Marietta Canty (Samanthy), Barbara Sears (WAC
           Lieutenant), Larry Thompson and Bernie Sell (Military
           Policemen), and Chester Conklin (Photographer).

SYNOPSIS: On a Sunday afternoon, an impoverished, parentless brood hope to entertain a serviceman (Hodiak) in their ramshackle houseboat just as the more prosperous townspeople would. The family consists of the adult sister (Baxter), three moppets, and a shiftless grandfather. Before the soldier leaves for duty, romance buds for him and the young lady of the house.

REVIEWS: Commonweal, 3.23.45, p. 566
            Nation, 2.3.45, p. 136
            New Republic, 2.12.45, p. 227
            New York Times, 1.25.45, p. 1
            New Yorker, 1.27.45, p. 65
            Newsweek, 2.5.45, p. 96
            Time, 2.5.45, p. 91
            Variety, 12.6.44, p. 6

Variety, 12.6.44: "Anne Baxter, as the older sister, as always, gives a plausible performance."

New York Times, 1.25.45: "Anne Baxter is appealing as Tessa."

NOTES: While filming, Anne Baxter and John Hodiak admitted to becoming closer as they steadily dated. They eventually announced their plans to marry. Ironically, in the movie, he does not appear on the screen until an hour into the story. Some critics felt that this somehow misfired in the buildup to the short screen romance between Hodiak and Baxter.

See: B7, B76, B110, B230, B308, B357, B386

F13   GUEST IN THE HOUSE (United Artists, released, 2.15.45)
      BW   121 Minutes

Producer: Hunt Stromberg. Director: John Brahm. Screenplay: Ketti Frings. Photography: Lee Garmes. Editing: James Newcom and Walter Hanneman. Music: Alfred Newman. Based on a play by Hagar Wilde and Dale Eunson. Available on video cassette.

CAST: Anne Baxter (Evelyn Heath), Ralph Bellamy (Douglas Proctor), Aline MacMahon (Aunt Martha), Ruth Warrick (Ann Proctor), Scott McKay (Dan Proctor), Jerome Cowan (Mr. Hackett), Marie McDonald (Miriam), Percy Kilbride (John), Margaret Hamilton (Hilda), and Connie Laird (Lee Proctor).

SYNOPSIS: By pretending to be sickly and helpless, an odd youn
woman (Baxter) insinuates herself into the lives of a happy
family and proceeds to wreak havoc by trying to drive them mad
with her evil conniving. However, she stops when Aunt Martha
realizes what will end Evelyn's horrible deeds. Evelyn is
literally scared to death when shown an empty birdcage.

REVIEWS: Commonweal, 2.2.45, p. 398
            Nation, 1.27.45, p. 110
            New York Times, 2.16.45, p. 19
            New York Times, 2.18.45, p. 1
            New Yorker, 2.24.45, p. 71
            Newsweek, 1.1.45, p. 66
            Theatre Arts, 1.45, p. 40
            Time, 1.29.45, p. 94
            Variety, 12.6.44, p. 6
            Woman's Home Companion, 11.44, p. 11

Variety, 12.6.44: "Miss Baxter, Ruth Warrick, as the older
brother's wife, Bellamy and Marie McDonald, a blonde looker,
handle the more important roles and provide substantial marquee
value."

New York Times, 2.18.45: "Anne Baxter plays the wrecker with
so much coyness that anyone, shy of a blind man, could see that
she was up to tricks."

NOTES: The play had a moderate theater run.

See: B6, B43, B48, B54, B75, B112, B134, B162, B174, B229, B369
     B452, S12

F14 ROYAL SCANDAL (20th Century-Fox, released 4.11.45)
     BW   94 Minutes

Producer: Ernst Lubitsch. Directors: Otto Preminger and Ernst
Lubitsch. Screenplay: Edwin Justus Mayer. Photography: Arthur
Miller. Editor: Dorothy Spencer. Music: Alfred Newman. Adapt
by Bruno Frank from the play by Lajos Biro and Melchior Langyel

CAST: Tallulah Bankhead (Czarina Catherine -- Catherine
           the Great), Charles Coburn (Chancellor), Anne Baxter
           (Countess Anna Jaschikoff), William Eythe (Alexei),
           Vincent Price (Marquis de Fleury), Mischa Auer (Capta.
           Sukov), Sig Ruman (General Ronsky), Vladimir Sokoloff
           (Malskoff), Mikhail Rasumny (Drunken Guard), Grady

Sutton (Boris), Don Douglas (Variatinsky), Egon Brecher
(Wassillikov), and Eva Gabor (Countess Demidow).

SYNOPSIS: This film tells of one of Catherine the Great's
amorous adventures with a handsome young captain of the guards
(Eythe). She finds him immensely attractive after he rides
for three days and nights to tell her of one of the conspiracies
against her life. However, his jealous fiancee (Anne Baxter),
handmaiden to the czarina, puts a stop to the philandering in
this ficitonalized account of a true escapade.

REVIEWS: New York Times, 4.11.45, p. 16
          Newsweek, 4.16.45, p. 70

Newsweek, 4.16.45: "Anne Baxter is the constant rider's true
love who has other plans for the energies of Catherine the
Great's new interest."

NOTES: The film was started by Lubitsch but finished by
          Preminger. It was based on a stage play titled The
          Czarina. The story was also previously filmed by
          Ernst Lubitsch in 1924, under the title Forbidden
          Paradise.

See: B49, B54, B77, B111, B135, B231, B410, B464

F15 SMOKY (20th Century-Fox, released 6.26.46)
     Color   87 Minutes

Producer: Robert Bassler. Director: Louis King. Screenplay:
Lillie Hayward, Dwight Cummings, and Dorothy Yost. Photography:
Charles Clarke. Special Effects: Fred Sersen. Music: David
Raskin and Emil Newman. Editor: Nick De Maggio. Based on the
novel by Will James.

CAST: Fred MacMurray (Clint Barkley), Anne Baxter (Julie
          Richards), Burl Ives (Bill), Bruce Cabot (Frank
          Denton), Esther Dale (Gram), Roy Roberts (Jeff Nicks),
          J. Farrell MacDonald (Jim), Victor Killian (Junkman),
          Max Wagner (Bart), Guy Beach (Sheriff), Howard Negley
          (Nelson), Bud Geary (Peters), Harry Carter (Bud),
          Bob Adler (Scrubby), and Herbert Heywood (Livery Stable
          Proprietor).

SYNOPSIS: Cowpuncher MacMurray and the beautiful stallion,
Smoky, are two untamed, indomitable characters who have
occasional differences yet understand each other implicitly.

They first meet when Clint is hired to saddle break the horse.
After Clint earns Smoky's complete trust, the horse is horribly
treated by another cowpoke, whom Smoky ends up trampling to
death because of the abuse. Smoky returns to the wild and is
hunted, to be eventually sold to the rodeo. Clint finds him
and nurses him back to health at the ranch owned by Anne Baxter
who learns to love them both.

REVIEWS: Commonweal, 7.26.46, p. 360
            Film Daily, 6.14.46, p. 8
            Hollywood Reporter, 6.13.46, p. 3
            MPHPD, 6.15.46, p. 3041
            New York Times, 6.23.46, p. 3
            New York Times, 6.27.46, p. 29
            New Yorker, 7.6.46, p. 43
            Time, 7.8.46, p. 98
            Variety, 6.19.46, p. 8
            Woman's Home Companion, 8.46, p. 10

Variety, 6.19.46: "Anne Baxter, operator of a Utah horse and
cattle ranch, rings true with no attempt at glamour."

New York Times, 6.27.46: "The scenarists have worked in a slig
romance with Anne Baxter playing the role of the attractive
ranch owner." "Here is a picture for the whole family."

NOTES: Smoky is an elaborate remake of the 1933 version.
            Jack Lindell, equine supervisor, scouted 38 states
            to find the perfect horse for the role. The horse
            chosen won a seven-year contract and a beginning sala
            of $300 a week even before a screen test was done.
            They cast more than 40 horses to emote on screen
            without tricks. During filming in the hot Utah
            location, bleach spots on Smoky's black hide were
            touched up with walnut stain makeup. The story was
            later filmed in 1966, starring Fess Parker, Diana
            Hyland, Katy Jurado, Hoyt Axton, and Chuck Roberson.

See: B27, B58, B78, B232, B272, B344, B419

F16 ANGEL ON MY SHOULDER (United Artists, released 10.20.46)
     BW   101 Minutes

Producer: Charles R. Rogers. Director: Archie Mayo. Screenpla
Harry Segall and Roland Kibbee. Photography: James Van Trees.
Editor: Asa Clark. Special Effects: Howard Anderson. Music:
Dimitri Tiomkin. From the original story by Harry Segall.

Available on video cassette.

CAST: Paul Muni (Eddie Kagle), Anne Baxter (Barbara Foster),
           Claude Rains (Nick), Onslow Stevens (Dr. Higgins),
           Hardie Albright (Smiley), James Flavin (Bellamy),
           Erskine Sanford (Minister), Marion Martin
           (Mrs. Bentley), Jonathan Hale (Chairman), Murray Alpen
           (Jim), Fritz Leiber (Scientist), Kurt Katch (Warden),
           Sarah Padden (Agatha), Maurice Cass (Lucius), Addison
           Richards (Big Harry), Ben Welden (Shaggsy), Joel
           Freidkin (Malvola), George Meeker (Mr. Bentley), and
           Chester Clute (Kramer).

SYNOPSIS: Paul Muni is a gangster who is killed then transported
to a temporary life on earth after making a pact with the devil
(Rains). He is anxious to get revenge on the welcher who killed
him, while the devil wants him to take over and disgrace the
body of a good judge Muni now inhabits. The gangster finds
out that the jurist has a high-minded girlfriend (Anne Baxter)
with whom he also falls in love. He refuses to defame the
judge's life, which leads him to the ultimate sacrificial climax.

REVIEWS: Film Daily, 9.18.46, p. 8
           Hollywood Reporter, 9.16.46, p. 3
           MPHPD, 9.21.46, p. 3210
           New York Times, 10.21.46, p. 27
           New Yorker, 10.19.46, p. 114
           Newsweek, 11.4.46, p. 92
           Scholastic, 11.4.46, p. 37
           Time, 10.46, p. 104
           Variety, 9.18.46, p. 16

Variety, 9.18.46: "Anne Baxter is excellent as the troubled
fiancee."

New York Times, 10.21.46: "Anne Baxter is appealing as the
girl who twists the devil's tail."

NOTES: Once again Claude Rains plays an "ectoplasmic" fellow
           who guides a spirit back to earth. In Here Comes
           Mr. Jordan, he was an angel of good will. In Angel
           on My Shoulder, he is the personification of evil.
           The story was remade as a television movie in 1980,
           starring Peter Strauss, Richard Kiley, Barbara Hershey
           (in Anne Baxter's role), Janis Paige, Seymour Cassel,
           Scott Colomby, and Murray Matheson.

See: B43, B57, B113, B147, B216, B260, B438

F17 THE RAZOR'S EDGE (20th Century-Fox, released 11.19.46)
     BW   146 Minutes

Producer: Darryl F. Zanuck. Director: Edmund Goulding.
Screenplay: Lamar Trotti. Photography: Arthur Miller. Editor:
J. Watson Webb. Special Effects: Fred Sersen. Music: Alfred
Newman. Dances: Larry Pilcey. From the philosophical novel
by W. Somerset Maugham. Available on video cassette.

CAST: Tyrone Power (Larry Darrell), Gene Tierney (Isabel
           Bradley), John Payne (Gary Maturin), Anne Baxter
           (Sophie MacDonald), Clifton Webb (Elliot Templeton),
           Herbert Marshall (W. Somerset Maugham), Lucille Watson
           (Mrs. Louise Bradley), Frank Latimore (Bob MacDonald),
           Elsa Lanchester (Miss Keith), Fritz Kortner (Kosti),
           John Wengraf (Joseph), Cobina Wright, Sr. (Princess
           Novemali), Albert Petit (Albert), Noel Cravat (Russian
           Singer), and Henry Lefondal (Police Inspector).

SYNOPSIS: Marshall plays Maugham and narrates the film about
a young war pilot who looks for spiritual peace and harmony
after World War II, while his friends wallow in greed and luxury.
He travels to the Far East then returns to spread his spiritual
enlightenment to his vain, selfish old flame (Tierney). He
tries to aid a young friend (Anne Baxter), who has become an
inebriated prostitute after the deaths of her husband and child;
she later drowns in an apparent suicide.

REVIEWS: Commonweal, 12.13.46, p. 230
           Cosmopolitan, 12.46, p. 65
           Film Daily, 11.20.46, p. 12
           Fortnight, 12.30.46, p. 41
           Good Housekeeping, 2.47, p. 13
           Hollywood Reporter, 11.20.46, p. 3
           Library Journal, 11.15.46, p. 1613
           Life, 8.12.46, p. 75
           Life, 11.18.46, p. 97
           MPHPD, 11.30.46, p. 3334
           New Republic, 12.9.46, p. 764
           New York Times, 7.28.46, p. 1
           New York Times, 11.10.46, p. 5
           New York Times, 11.17.46, p. 5
           New York Times, 11.20.46, p. 42
           New York Times, 12.8.46, p. 9
           New Yorker, 11.30.46, p. 86
           Newsweek, 12.2.46, p. 109
           Photoplay, 2.47, p. 4
           Rob Wagner's Script, 1.4.47, p. 13
           Scholastic, 1.6.47, p. 34

Theatre Arts, 1.47, p. 41
Time, 12.9.46, p. 101
Variety, 11.20.46, p. 22
Woman's Home Companion, 2.47, p. 11

New York Times, 11.20.46: "Anne Baxter, as the wretched fallen woman, fairly wallows in debauchery and pathos."

Variety, 11.20.46: "Miss Baxter walks off with perhaps the film's personal hit as the dipso, rivaled only by Webb's effete characterization."

NOTES: Although Maugham is portrayed, the account is fictional. The story was remade in 1984, starring Bill Murray, Catherine Hicks, and Theresa Russell (in the Anne Baxter role). Anne won an Academy Award for Best Supporting Actress. She also won the Golden Apple and Golden Globe Awards for the role.

See: B8, B24, B33, B57, B67, B71, B79, B104, B114, B136, B166, B175, B180, B182, B233, B269, B288, B302, B323, B340, B351, B364, B372, B387, B397, B408, B411, B413, B417, B460, B464, B473, B482, B486, B488, B509, B510, B519

F18   BLAZE OF NOON (Paramount, released 3.4.47)
       BW   91 Minutes

Producer: Robert Fellows. Director: John Farrow. Screenplay: Frank Wead and Arthur Sheekman. Photography: Thomas Tutwiler. Special Effects: Gordon and Devereaux Jennings. Editor: Sally Forrest. Music: Adolph Deutsch. Based on the novel by Ernest K. Gann.

CAST: Anne Baxter (Lucille Stewart), William Holden (Colin McDonald), William Bendix (Porkie), Sonny Tufts (Roland McDonald), Sterling Hayden (Tad McDonald), Howard da Silva (Gafferty), Johnny Sands (Keith McDonald), Jean Wallace (Poppy), Edith King (Mrs. Murphy), Floyd Corrigan (Rev. Polly), Dick Hogan (Sydney), and Will Wright (Mr. Thomas).

SYNOPSIS: A young "crate jockey" (Holden) marries just before he and his three brothers start flying the early airmail. He gets lost in a night storm while his young wife (Baxter) nervously but patiently waits -- not an easy task considering a couple of brothers were killed earlier while flying.

REVIEWS: <u>Commonweal</u>, 3.21.47, p. 567
            <u>Flying</u>, 4.47, p. 48
            <u>Nation</u>, 3.22.47, p. 340
            <u>New Republic</u>, 3.24.47, p. 41
            <u>New York Times</u>, 3.5.47, p. 31
            <u>New Yorker</u>, 3.15.47, p. 68
            <u>Newsweek</u>, 3.17.47, p. 103
            <u>Time</u>, 3.24.47, p. 100
            <u>Variety</u>, 3.5.47, p. 6

<u>New York Times</u>, 3.5.47: "The film is well performed by William
Holden, Sonny Tufts, and William Bendix, notably -- and by Anne
Baxter, Howard da Silva, and Sterling Hayden in a lesser degree

<u>Variety</u>, 3.5.47: "Miss Baxter does a strong job as the wife,
adding much to the general interest of the story."

NOTES: This film is very close in subject matter to the 1933
           film <u>Night Flight</u>, with Helen Hayes and Clark Gable.

See: B80, B116, B165, B234, B335, B373, B422

F19 MOTHER WORE TIGHTS (20th Century-Fox, released 8.21.47)
     Color   109 Minutes

Producer: Lamar Trotti. Director: Walter Lang. Screenplay:
Lamar Trotti. Photography: Harry Jackson. Editor: J. Watson
Webb. Songs and Music: Mack Gordon and Josef Myrow. Music:
Alfred Newman and Charles Henderson. Based on the book by Mari
Young.

CAST: Betty Grable (Myrtle McKinley Burt), Dan Dailey (Fran
           Burt), Mona Freeman (Iris Burt), Connie Marshall (Mik
           Burt), Vanessa Brown (Bessie), Robert Arthur (Bob
           Clarkman), Sara Allgood (Grandmother McKinley), Willi
           Frawley (Mr. Schneider), Ruth Nelson (Miss Ridgeway),
           Annabel Shaw (Alice Slemmerhammer), Michael Dunne
           (Roy Bivins), George Cleveland (Grandfather McKinley)
           Veda Ann Borg (Rosemary Olcott), Sig Ruman (Papa),
           Lee Patrick (Lil), Senior Wences (Specialty), Maude
           Eburne (Mrs. Muggins), Antonio Filauri (Papa Capucci)
           Lotte Stein (Mama), William Forrest (Mr. Clarkman),
           Kathleen Lockhart (Mrs. Clarkman), Chick Chandler
           (Ed), Kenny Williams (Dance Director), Will Wright
           (Withers), and Frank Orth (Stage Doorman). Voice:
           Anne Baxter.

SYNOPSIS: Anne Baxter provides the narration for the mother
in this film which chronicles the steady rise in fame of a loving
vaudeville family.

REVIEWS: Commonweal, 9.19.47, p. 554
            Cosmopolitan, 10.47, p. 55
            Film Daily, 8.19.47, p. 8
            Hollywood Reporter, 8.20.47, p. 3
            MPHPD, 8.2.47, p. 3783
            New York Times, 8.17.47, p. 3
            New York Times, 8.21.47, p. 33
            Newsweek, 9.1.47, p. 77
            Time, 9.8.47, p. 100
            Variety, 8.20.47, p. 16
            Woman's Home Companion, 10.47, p. 10

NOTES: Contains songs by Jack Gordon and Josef Myrow:
            "Rolling down Bowling Green"
            "Kokomo, Indiana"
            "You Do"
            "There's Nothing Like a Song"
            "This is My Favorite City"
            "Fare-Thee-Well, Dear Alma Mater"

See: B8, B264, B324, B447, B464, B479, B511

F20 HOMECOMING (M-G-M, released 4.29.48)
     BW   113 Minutes

Producer: Sidney Franklin. Director: Mervyn LeRoy. Screenplay:
Paul Osborn. Photography: Harold Rosson. Editor: John Dunning.
Music: Bronislau Kaper. Adapted by Jan Lustig from the original
story by Sidney Kingsley.

CAST: Clark Gable (Ulysses Delby Johnson), Lana Turner
            (Lt. Jane "Snapshot" McCall), Anne Baxter (Penny
            Johnson), John Hodiak (Dr. Robert Sunday), Ray Collins
            (Lt. Col. Avery Silver), Gladys Cooper (Mrs. Kirby),
            Cameron Mitchell (Sgt. Monkievicks), and Marshall
            Thompson (Sgt. McKeen).

SYNOPSIS: Clark Gable is an Army surgeon who has a reputation
as a very uncaring, stony person. He is married to the nice
Anne Baxter. He meets Army nurse Snapshot, who initially doesn't
like him any more than he does her. However, after working
closely with her, he begins to see the goodness in life. He
returns to his wife after Snapshot's untimely death.

REVIEWS: Commonweal, 5.28.48, p. 164
            New Republic, 5.17.48, p. 36
            New York Times, 8.11.47, p. 16
            New York Times, 4.30.48, p. 28
            New York Times, 5.23.48, p. 5
            Photoplay, 7.48, p. 22
            Time, 5.10.48, p. 100
            Variety, 4.7.48, p. 4

Variety, 4.7.48: "Miss Baxter does a beautiful smooth job as
the understanding wife."

NOTES: The stars were filmed on sets with scenery faked to
            look like fields of war.

See: B81, B116, B158, B235, B254, B495

F21 THE WALLS OF JERICHO (20th Century-Fox, released 8.4.48)
     BW   111 Minutes

Producer: Lamar Trotti. Director: John M. Stahl. Screenplay:
Lamar Trotti. Photography: Arthur Miller. Editor: James B.
Clark. Music: Cyril Mockridge. From the novel by Paul Wellman.

CAST: Cornel Wilde (Dave Connors), Linda Darnell (Algeria
            Wedge), Anne Baxter (Julie Norman), Marjorie Rambeau
            (Mrs. Dunham), Kirk Douglas (Tucker Wedge), Ann Dvorak
            (Belle Connors), Colleen Townsend (Marjorie Ransome),
            Henry Hull (Jefferson Norman), Barton MacLane (Gotch
            McCurdy), Art Baker (Peddigrew), Griff Barnett (Judge
            Hutto), Hope Landin (Mrs. Hutto), William Tracy (Cully
            Caxton), Ann Morison (Nellie), Frank Ferguson (Tom
            Ransome), Helen Brown (Mrs. Ferguson), Whitford Kane
            (Judge Foster), and Will Wright (Doctor Patterson).

SYNOPSIS: Dave Connors is a politically inclined attorney from
Kansas who is married to an alcoholic wife (Dvorak). He also
loves a young lawyer (Baxter), whom he cannot marry. Algeria
Wedge is a former love of his, who is now married to the town's
newspaper publisher, who is also his political adversary.
Algeria starts a scandal that ends in a murder trial, where
Julie publicly announces her affection for Connors, causing
the "Walls of Jericho" to crumble.

REVIEWS: New York Times, 8.5.48, p. 16
            Newsweek, 8.9.48, p. 68
            Photoplay, 10.48, p. 13

Time, 8.30.48, p. 72
Variety, 8.4.48, p. 6

Variety, 8.4.48: "As a Portia, Miss Baxter registers in her
courtroom plea to save a girl accused of murder and to clear
her own reputation, fouled through machinations of Miss Darnell.
Her love scenes with Wilde are also good."

New York Times, 8.5.48: "Anne Baxter, as the picture's mentally
harassed Portia, is forceful and appealing, especially in the
final courtroom scene, where she courageously bares her pristine
relationship with Connors."

NOTES: This film is a generally unrewarding study of life
          in a Kansas county seat during the Teddy Roosevelt
          era.

See: B82, B374, B408-409, B448, B488, R26

F22 LUCK OF THE IRISH (20th Century-Fox, released 9.15.48)
     BW   99 Minutes

Producer: Fred Kohlmar. Director: Henry Koster. Screenplay:
Philip Dunne. Photography: Joseph La Shelle. Editor: J. Watson
Webb, Jr. Music: Cyril Mockridge and Lionel Newman. From the
novel There was a Little Man by Constance and Guy Jones.

CAST: Tyrone Power (Stephen Fitzgerald), Anne Baxtger (Nora),
          Cecil Kellaway (Horace), Lee J. Cobb (D. C. Augur),
          James Todd (Bill Clark), Jayne Meadows (Frances),
          J. M. Kerrigan (Taedy), Phil Brown (Higginbotham),
          Bill Swingley (Terrance), Jimmy O'Brien (Singer),
          Charles Irwin (Cornelius), Louise Lorimer (Augur's
          Secretary), Tim Ryan (Clancy), Harry Antrim (Senator
          Ransom), Margaret Wells (Mrs. Augur), John Goldsworthy
          (Butler), Dorothy Neuman (Agency Manager), Ruth
          Clifford (Secretary), Douglas Gerrard (Receptionist),
          Tito Vuojo Greel (Vendor), Tom Stevenson (Gentleman's
          Gentleman), Norman Leavitt (Milkman), Claribel Bressel
          (Bride), Lee MacGregor (Groom), Frank Mitchell (Irish
          Dancer), Albert Morin (Captain of Waiters), Hollis
          Jewell (Cab Driver), Ann Frederick (Hat Check Girl),
          Eddie Parks (Pickpocket), and John Roy (Subway Guard).

SYNOPSIS: Leprechaun Kellaway takes sides in a conflict
involving a set of values: newspaperman Power must choose between
good -- writing for a living and marrying Anne Baxter -- and

evil -- selling out to a New York publishing tycoon (Cobb) and his daughter (Meadows).

REVIEWS: Commonweal, 9.24.48, p. 572
            New York Times, 9.16.48, p. 34
            New York Times, 9.26.48, p. 1
            Newsweek, 9.13.48, p. 94
            Time, 10.4.48, p. 96
            Variety, 9.11.48, p. 8

Variety, 9.11.48: Miss Baxter seems wasted in a role that requires none of the heavy thesping with which she's made her mark. However, she carries off well the part of Power's vis-a-vis, making her Irish brogue sound authentic."

New York Times, 9.16.48: "Jayne Meadows, as the girl he (Power) gives up, is much more beguiling than Anne Baxter, with her quaint charm and her midwest Irish-brogue."

NOTES: This is a modernized version of a Chauncey Olcott-
            type Irish comedy, with the leprechaun similar in
            appearance to Og in Finian's Rainbow.

See: B24, B57, B83, B117, B194, B236, B408

F23 YELLOW SKY (20th Century-Fox, released 2.1.49)
     BW   98 Minutes

Producer: Lamar Trotti. Director: William Wellman. Screenplay: Lamar Trotti. Photography: Joe MacDonald. Editor: Harmon Jones Music: Alfred Newman. Based on the story by W. R. Burnett. Available on video cassette.

CAST: Gregory Peck (Stretch), Anne Baxter (Mike), Richard
            Widmark (Dude), Robert Arthur (Bull Run), John Russell
            (Lengthy), Henry Morgan (Half Pint), James Barton
            (Grandpa), Charles Kemper (Walrus), Robert Adler (Jed)
            Harry Carter (Lieutenant), Victor Killian (Bartender),
            Paul Hurst (Drunk), Hank Worden (Rancher), Jay
            Silverheels (Indian), and William Gould (Banker).

SYNOPSIS: Gregory Peck is a nice farmboy who returns from the Civil War and joins a gang in this western set in 1867. They rob an Arizona bank and head for the Badlands, where they find refuge in a ghost town inhabited by a sharpshooting young woman (Baxter) and her grandfather. They find out that the woman and her grandfather are hiding gold. While Peck's unruly friend

plan to rob them, he realizes that he doesn't want to be involved
in any more criminal activity. He ends up falling in love with
Baxter. The gang turns against him, and Peck and Baxter are
saved by Indians.

REVIEWS: Good Housekeeping, 3.49, p. 10
           Life, 1.10.49, p. 42
           New Republic, 2.21.49, p. 31
           New York Times, 2.2.49, p. 36
           New York Times, 2.13.49, p. 1
           New Yorker, 2.12.49, p. 69
           Newsweek, 10.20.48, p. 78
           Photoplay, 2.49, p. 21
           Rotarian, 4.49, p. 37
           Time, 12.13.48, p. 102
           Variety, 11, 19.48, p. 6

Variety, 11.19.48: "Peck shines as the outlaw leader and
matching dramatic stride for stride with him is Miss Anne Baxter
as the ghost town girl."

New York Times, 2.2.49: "Except for the one alien female, whom
Anne Baxter truculently plays, the actors are male and mangy-
looking, with 5 o'clock shadows to excess."

NOTES: At the end of the film, the Indians and bad guys ride
           out of town without shooting an arrow or lifting a
           scalp, which is unique in western movies.

See: B30, B84, B118, B151, B179, B183, B208, B255, B286, B317,
     B337, B419, B464, B497, B518, R21

F24 YOU'RE MY EVERYTHING (20th Century-Fox, released 7.22.49)
     Color   94 Minutes

Producer: Lamar Trotti. Director: Walter Lang. Screenplay:
Lamar Trotti and Will H. Hayes, Jr. Photography: Arthur E.
Arling. Music: Alfred Newman. Dances: Nick Castle. Song:
Mack Gordon. Based on a story by George Jessel.

CAST: Dan Dailey (Timothy O'Connor), Anne Baxter (Hannah
           Adams), Anne Revere (Aunt Jane), Stanley Ridges
           (Mr. Mercer), Shari Robinson (Jane), Henry O'Neill
           (Prof. Addams), Selena Royle (Mrs. Adams), Alan Mowbray
           (Joe Blanton), Robert Arthur (College Boy), Buster
           Keaton (Butler), Ruth Clifford (Nurse), Phyllis Kennedy
           (Elizabeth), Chester Jones (Butler), Nyas and Warren

Berry (Dancers), John Hiestand (Announcer), Hal K. Dawson (Ticket Seller), Charles Lane (Mr. Phum), Robe Emmett Keane (Architect), Joe Haworth (Doorman), Libb Taylor (Housekeeper), Geraldine Harris (Maid), Vincen Graeff (Newsboy), and Mack Gordon (Himself).

SYNOPSIS: Dan Dailey is a song and dance man married to singer-actress Baxter. Together they have a very talented and precocious daughter (Shari Robinson). As a family, they all try to make it in the "flickers," where each becomes a star. When musicals become passe, they buy a valley ranch and settle down.

REVIEWS: Commonweal, 8.5.49, p. 415
           New Republic, 8.1.49, p. 29
           New York Times, 7.23.49, p. 7
           New York Times, 7.31.49, p. 7
           New Yorker, 7.30.49, p. 63
           Newsweek, 8.1.49, p. 64
           Rotarian, 10.49, p. 39
           Theatre Arts, 10.49, p. 96
           Time, 8.8.49, p. 70
           Variety, 7.6.49, p. 8

Variety, 7.6.49: "Miss Baxter is excellent in the vapid part of the wife, nicely spanning the gap between proper Bostonian and jazz-age Hollywood.

New York Times, 7.23.49: "As the wife, a fair flower of Boston, Anne Baxter is attractive, too, notably in her gay burlesquing of a ha-cha Clara Bow girl."

NOTES: This film is reminiscent of the real-life moppet stars of the thirties, most notably Shirley Temple. Songs included: "You're My Everything," by Harry Warren, Mort Dixon, and Joe Young; "Varsity Drag," by De Sylva Brown, and Henderson; "I May be Wrong," by Harry Ruski and Henry Sullivan; "Chattanooga Choo-Choo," by Harry Warren and Mack Gordon; "Serenade in Blue," by Harry Warren and Mack Gordon; "I Can't Begin to Tell You," by James V. Monaco and Mack Gordon; and "Would You Like to Take a Walk?" by Harry Warren, Mort Dixon, and Billy Rose.

See: B40, B85, B119, B237, B256, B264, B318, B336, B375, B464, B465, B498, B509, R20

F25 A TICKET TO TOMAHAWK (20th Century-Fox, released 5.19.50)
     Color   90 Minutes

Producer: Robert Bassler. Director: Richard Sale. Screenplay:
Mary Loos and Richard Sale. Photography: Harry Jackson. Editor:
Harmon Jones. Music: Cyril Mockridge and Lionel Newman.
Available on video cassette.

CAST: Dan Dailey (Johnny), Anne Baxter (Kit Dodge, Jr.),
           Rory Calhoun (Dakota), Walter Brennan (Terence
           Sweeney), Charles Kemper (Chuckity), Connie Gilchrist
           (Madame Adelaide), Arthur Hunnicutt (Sad Eyes), Will
           Wright (Dodge), Chief Yowlachie (Pawnee), Victor Sen
           Yung (Long Time), Mauritz Hugo (Dawson), Raymond
           Greenleaf (Mayor), Harry Carter (Charley), Harry
           Seymour (Velvet Fingers), Robert Adler (Bat), Lee
           MacGregor (Gilo), Raymond Bond (Station Master),
           Charlie Stevens (Trancos), Chief Thundercloud (Crooked
           Knife), Marion Marshall (Annie), Joyce MacKenzie
           (Ruby), Marilyn Monroe (Clara), Barbara Smith (Julie),
           Jack Elam (Fargo), Paul Harvey (Mr. Bishop), John
           War Eagle (Lone Eagle), Shooting Star (Crazy Dog),
           Herbert Heywood (Old Timer), William Self
           (Telegrapher), Guy Wilkerson (Dr. Brink), Edward Clark
           (Jet), and Olin Howlin (Conductor).

SYNOPSIS: The film recounts the adventures of a narrow-gauge,
ten-wheeler on its first run into the Rockies. It must get
a train into Tomahawk by a deadline, with at least one paying
passenger (Dailey). After a journey beset with obstacles like
hostile Indians and a stagecoach tycoon who tries to thwart
the endeavor, the train is forced to stop when the track ends
40 miles from the specified destination. Strapped to the
locomotive, Dailey, a traveling salesman selling the Saturday
Evening Post, encounters a sharpshooting lady sheriff (Anne
Baxter), who plans to haul the engine by mule.

REVIEWS: BFI Monthly Film Bulletin, 7.50, p. 102
           Christian Century, 5.24.50, p. 663
           Commonweal, 5.19.50, p. 152
           Film Daily, 4.21.50, p. 6
           Hollywood Reporter, 4.17.50, p. 4
           London Times, 7.17.50, p. 6
           MPHPD, 4.22.50, p. 269
           New York Times, 5.20.50, p. 8
           New York Times, 5.21.50, p. 1
           New Yorker, 5.27.50, p. 62
           Newsweek, 5.22.50, p. 90
           Rotarian, 7.50, p. 38

Time, 5.15.50, p. 96
Variety, 4.19.50, p. 8

Variety, 4.19.50: "Dailey does well by his traveling salesman,
and Miss Baxter romps through her spot as the gal able with
a gun but shy on birds-and-bees instruction."

New York Times, 5.20.50: "Anne Baxter is fair and more than
middling as the Marshal's daughter, who escorts the enterprise.
She plays a western hoyden with a burning curiousity about
romance and is a doggone good shot in all departments but she's
not in the championship class (a la Annie Get Your Gun)."

NOTES: The movie was filmed in the Colorado mountains. It
          contained the song, "Oh, What a Forward Young Man,"
          by Mack Gordon and Harry Warren, used as a campfire
          song-and-dance number by Dailey and a quartet of young
          ladies, among them Marilyn Monroe.

See: B8, B120, B167, B238, B338, B376, B419, B427, B432

F26   ALL ABOUT EVE (20th Century-Fox, released 10.13.50)
      BW   138 Minutes

Producer: Darryl F. Zanuck. Director: Joseph L. Mankiewicz.
Screenplay: Joseph L. Mankiewicz. Photography: Milton Krasner.
Editor: Barbara McLean. Music: Alfred Newman. Orchestration:
Edward Powell. Special Effects: Fred Sersen. Based on the
story "The Wisdom of Eve," by Mary Orr. Available on video
cassette.

CAST: Bette Davis (Margo Channing), Anne Baxter (Eve
          Harrington), George Sanders (Addison DeWitt), Celeste
          Holm (Karen), Gary Merrill (Bill Simpson), Hugh Marlow
          (Lloyd Richards), Thelma Ritter (Birdie), Marilyn
          Monroe (Miss Casswell), Gregory Ratoff (Max Fabian),
          Barbara Bates (Phoebe), Walter Hampden (Aged Actor),
          Randy Stuart (Girl), Craig Hill (Leading Man), Leland
          Harris (Doorman), Barbara White (Autograph Seeker),
          Eddie Fisher (Stage Manager), William Pullen (Clerk),
          Claude Stroud (Pianist), Eugene Borden (Frenchman),
          Helen Mowery (Reporter), Steve Geray (Captain of
          Waiters), and Bess Flowers (Well-wisher).

SYNOPSIS: This film is a witheringly witty look at Broadway
life. Davis is an acid-tongued, aging actress who lets an up-
and-coming young actress (Baxter) enter her realm. Seemingly

innocent, Eve plots to take the place of the older actress.
She ingratiates herself into Margo Channing's coterie, but soon
the others discover how devious Eve really is. George Sanders
is a vicious and powerful drama critic. Merrill is a director
with whom Margo is in love. Hugh Marlowe is a brittle, glib
playwright who spars with wife, Celeste Holm. Thelma Ritter
is a wisecracking maid.

REVIEWS: American Cinematographer, 1.51, p. 10
            American Film, July-August, 1983, p. 66
            BFI Monthly Film Bulletin, 1.51, p. 264
            Christian Century, 11.29.50, p. 439
            Commonweal, 10.27.50, p. 16
            Esquire, 12.50, p. 74
            Film Daily, 9.13.56, p. 6
            Films in Review, 12.50, p. 37
            Good Housekeeping, 12.50, p. 16
            Harper's, 1.51, p. 103
            Hollywood Reporter, 9.13.50, p. 3
            Life, 10.30.50, p. 79
            MPHPD, 9.16.50, p. 485
            Nation, 10.28.50, p. 397
            New American Mercury, 1.51, p. 95
            New Republic, 11.6.50, p. 21
            New Statesman and Nation, 12.16.50, p. 624
            New York Times, 5.28.50, p. 4
            New York Times, 10.14.50, p. 13
            New York Times, 10.22.50, p. 1
            New Yorker, 10.21.50, p. 128
            Newsweek, 10.16.50, p. 94
            Rotarian, 1.51, p. 38
            Saturday Review, 10.21.50, p. 31
            Scholastic, 11.29.50, p. 19
            Sight and Sound, 1.51, p. 373
            Spectator, 12.8.50, p. 648
            Theatre Arts, 12.50, p. 8
            Time, 10.16.50, p. 96
            Variety, 9.13.50, p. 6

Variety, 9.13.50: "Miss Baxter gives the proper shading to
her cool and calculating approach in the process of ingratiating
and ultimate opportunities."

New York Times, 10.14.50: "Although the title character --
the self-seeking, ruthless Eve, who would make a black widow
spider look like a lady bug -- is the motivating figure in the
story and is played by Anne Baxter with icy calm; the focal
figure and most intriguing character is the actress whom Bette
Davis plays."

NOTES: Reportedly, this story is based on an actual event.
           The characters are composite prototypes. The film
           won Academy Awards for Best Picture, Director,
           Screenplay, and Supporting Actor (George Sanders).
           It was remade as a Broadway musical, Applause.

See: B3, B8, B10, B13, B35, B39, B52-53, B57, B64-65, B87, B97,
     B100, B122, B127, B143, B162, B168, B180, B191, B193, B201,
     B206, B209, B213, B216-217, B239, B251, B253, B262, B286,
     B288, B301, B3210, B323, B328, B339, B348, B351, B366-367,
     B377, B383, B388, B390, B398, B414, B421, B425, B427-428,
     B432-433, B454, B456-457, B460, B464, B467, B499, B510,
     B514, B517, B519, B521, R27, S9

F27 FOLLOW THE SUN (20th Century-Fox, released 4.25.51)
     BW   93 Minutes

Producer: Samuel G. Engel. Director: Sidney Lanfield.
Screenplay: Frederik Hazlitt Brennan. Photography: Leo Tover.
Editor: Barbara McLean. Music: Cyril Mockridge. Based on an
article by Brennan published in Reader's Digest.

CAST: Glenn Ford (Ben Hogan), Anne Baxter (Valerie Hogan),
           Dennis O'Keefe (Chuck Williams), June Havoc (Norma),
           Larry Keating (Jay Dexter), Roland Winters
           (Dr. Graham), Nana Bryant (Sister Beatrice), Sam Snead
           James Demaret, and Dr. Cary Middlecoff (Themselves),
           Harold Blake (Ben Hogan, age 14), Ann Burr (Valerie,
           age 14), Harmon Stevens (Mrs. Johnson), Louise Lorimer
           (Mrs. Clinton), Esther Somers (Mrs. Edwards), and
           Harry Antrim (Dr. Everett).

SYNOPSIS: Ben Hogan suffered a near-fatal car accident in
February, 1949. This film dramatizes the Texan's story of
courage and inspiration in his successful comeback to be the
first pro golfer to win the national championship twice. Ford
is Hogan and Anne Baxter is his loyal wife, Valerie. Dennis
O'Keefe is a fictitious golf champion, who cheats on his wife,
played by June Havoc.

REVIEWS: BFI Monthly Film Bulletin, 5.51, p. 264
           Christian Century, 7.25.51, p. 879
           Commonweal, 5.11.51, p. 117
           Film Guide, 3.20.51, p. 6
           Hollywood Reporter, 3.19.51, p. 3
           Library Journal, 4.1.51, p. 608
           MPHPD, 3.24.51, p. 765

New York Times, 4.26.51, p. 34
Newsweek, 4.16.51, p. 105
Scholastic, 4.4.51, p. 31
Scribner's Commentator, 4.4.51, p. 617
Time, 4.30.51, p. 106
Variety, 3.21.51, p. 6

Variety, 3.21.51: "Two extremely competent performers carry off the roles of Hogan and his wife -- Glenn Ford and Anne Baxter. In their hands, the parts come alive with a compelling sincerity, reflecting thespian skill, thoughtful writing, and sympathetic direction."

New York Times, 4.26.51: "Anne Baxter, as Mrs. Hogan, gives a warm, vibrant performance of a loyal wife in sorrow and triumph."

NOTES: Although this film is centered around golf, its humanistic drama has a definite appeal to the audience of any backround. Its box-office success was assured as much as the previously released M-G-M film, The Stratton Story, based on the life of baseball player Monty Stratton, who lost a leg.

See: B169, B184, B240, B378, B449, B464

F28   OUTCASTS OF POKER FLAT (20th Century-Fox, released 5.15.52)
      BW   81 Minutes

Producer: Julian Blaustein. Director: Joseph M. Newman.
Screenplay: Edmund H. North. Photography: Joseph La Shelle.
Editor: William Reynolds: Music: Hugo Friedhofer and Lionel Newman. Based on a story by Bret Harte.

CAST: Anne Baxter (Cal), Dale Robertson (John Oakhurst), Miriam Hopkins (Duchess), Cameron Mitchell (Ryker), Craig Hill (Tom Dakin), Barbara Bates (Piney), William Lynn (Jake), Dick Rich (Drunk), Tom Greenway (Townsman), Russ Conway (Vigilante), John Ridgley (Bill Akeley), Harry T. Shannon (Bearded Miner), Harry Harvey, Sr. (George Larabee), with Lee Phelps, Harry Carter, and Billy Lynn.

SYNOPSIS: Mitchell and his henchmen rob an assay office-bank and slay two people. They escape and seek safety in a cabin in the Sierras, where they thought they would not be found. Little did they know that his wife (Baxter) is among a group

of people who have sought shelter at the cabin during a snow
blizzard. The gang holds them hostage. Robertson is the gamble
who outwits their captors.

REVIEWS: BFI Monthly Film Bulletin, 7.52, p. 92
            Christian Century, 7.23.52, p. 863
            Commonweal, 6.6.52, p. 224
            Film Daily, 5.13.52, p. 12
            Hollywood Reporter, 5.5.52, p. 3
            Library Journal, 5.15.52, p. 873
            Literary Digest, 3.27.52, p. 21
            London Times, 1.25.52, p. 7
            MPHPD, 5.10.52, p. 1357
            New York Times, 5.16.52, p. 19
            New Yorker, 5.24.52, p. 129
            Theatre Arts, 7.52, p. 88
            Time, 5.26.52, p. 100
            Variety, 5.7.52, p. 6

Variety, 5.7.52: "Performers respond to the downbeat mood of
the story with good portrayals of their respective characters."

Commonweal, 6.6.52: "Anne Baxter excellently plays Cal."

NOTES: Most reviewers felt that this was not a very well-
          filmed Bret Harte story.

See: B89, B122, B161, B170, B185, B241, B281, B419

F29 MY WIFE'S BEST FRIEND (20th Century-Fox, released 10.11.52)
     BW   87 Minutes

Producer: Robert Bassler. Director: Richard Sale. Assistant
Director: Hal Klein. Screenplay: Isobel Lennart. Photography:
Leo Tover. Editor: Robert Simpson. Music: Leigh Harline and
Lionel Newman. Based on a story by John Briard Harding.

CAST: Anne Baxter (Virginia Mason), Macdonald Carey (George
         Mason), Cecil Kellaway (Rev. Chamberlain), Casey Adams
         (Pete Bentham), Catherine McLeod (Jane Richards),
         Leif Erickson (Nicholas Reed), Frances Bavier
         (Mrs. Chamnberlain), Mary Sullivan (Flossy
         Chamberlain), Martin Milner (Buddy Chamberlain), Billie
         Bird (Katie), Michael Ross (Mike) Morgan Farley
         (Dr. McCarran), Ann Staunton (Hannah), Emmett Vogan
         (Walter Rogers), Wild Red Barry and Henry Kulky (Pugs),
         John Hedloe (Pilot), John McKee (Co-pilot), Phil

Hartman (Cab Driver), Junius Matthews (Dr. Smith),
Joe Haworth (Steward), and Ed Dearing (Police Chief).

SYNOPSIS: Anne Baxter is a shrewish wife who takes full
advantage of her husband (Carey) after they confess their
indiscretions to each other when they think they will be killed
in an airplane crash. They survive and she tortures him by
displaying several personalities in her quest: a tolerant, sweet
woman; an abject slave; and then a sophisticated lady.

REVIEWS: BFI Monthly Film Bulletin, 10.52, p. 144
            Commonweal, 11.7.52, p. 120
            Film Daily, 10.6.52, p. 6
            London Times, 9.29.52, p. 10
            MPHPD, 10.11.52, p. 1558
            New York Times, 10.11.52, p. 17
            Spectator, 9.26.52, p. 393
            Tatler, 10.8.52, p. 84
            Variety, 10.8.52, p. 6

Variety, 10.8.52: "Anne Baxter, better known (and more
impressively) for straight dramatics, switches to comedy with
only fair success as the flighty heroine of this John Briard
Harding story, scripted by Isobel Lennart."

Commonweal, 11.7.52: "This giddy comedy features a tour de
force performance by Anne Baxter."

See: B88, B123, B202, B242, B321

F30 "THE LAST LEAF," O. HENRY'S FULL HOUSE (20th Century-Fox,
      released 10.16.52)   BW   114 Minutes

Producer: Andre Hakim. Directors: Jean Negulesco, Henry Koster,
Henry Hathaway, Howard Hawks, Henry King, and Jasper Blystone.
Screenplay: Ivan Goff, Ben Roberts, Richard Breen, Walter
Bullock, and Lamar Trotti. Photographer: Lloyd Ahern, Lucien
Ballard, Milton Krasner, and Joe MacDonald. Editors: Nick De
Maggio, Barbara McLean, and William B. Murphy. Music: Alfred
Newman. Based on the book by O. Henry. Narrated by John
Steinbeck.

CAST: Anne Baxter (Joanna), Jean Peters (Susan), Gregory
         Ratoff (Behrman), Richard Garrick (Doctor), Steven
         Geray (Radolf), Hal J. Smith (Dandy), Martha Wentworth

(Mrs. O'Brien), Bert Hicks (Sheldon Sidney), and Ruth Warren (Neighbor).

SYNOPSIS: Anne Baxter is a sad young woman who has suicidal thoughts following an ended love affair. She believes that when the last leaf falls from a vine outside her window, she will die. Ratoff is an artist who befriends her and tries to convince her to hang on to life.

REVIEWS: BFI Monthly Film Bulletin, 10.52, p. 138
            Catholic World, 10.52, p. 61
            Christian Century, 11.26.52, p. 1391
            Film Daily, 8.26.52, p. 6
            Films in Review, 10.52, p. 416
            Hollywood Reporter, 8.18.52, p. 3
            Library Journal, 11.15.52, p. 1981
            London Times, 9.22.52, p. 2
            MPHPD, 8.23.52, p. 1501
            Nation, 11.22.52, p. 475
            National Parent-Teacher, 10.52, p. 38
            New Statesman and Nation, 10.11.52, p. 420
            New York Times, 10.17.52, p. 33
            New York Times 10.26.52, p. 1
            Newsweek, 10.6.52, p. 113
            Saturday Review, 9.13.52, p. 34
            Scholastic, 10.1.52, p. 20
            Scribner's Commentator, 9.13.52, p. 20
            Sight and Sound, October-December, 1952, p. 77
            Spectator, 10.3.52, p. 425
            Tatler, 10.15.52, p. 144
            Theatre Arts, 12.52, p. 86
            Time, 9.22.52, p. 102
            Variety, 8.20.52, p. 6

Variety, 8.20.52: "The two femmes are excellent and Ratoff outstanding."

New York Times, 10.17.52: "Anne Baxter, Jean Peters, and Gregor Ratoff do a competent job of handling the wistful dramatics and the broad humors of 'The Last Leaf.'"

NOTES: John Steinbeck gives a brief introduction to O. Henry' story, along with the importance of his work in literature. "The Last Leaf" is part of a compendium of turn-of-the-century tales of New York: "The Cop and the Anthem," with Charles Laughton, Marilyn Monroe and David Wayne; "The Clarion Call," with Dale Robertson, Richard Widmark, Joyce MacKenzie, and Richard Rober; "The Ransom of Red Chief," with Fred

Allen, Oscar Levant, and Lee Aaker; and "The Gift
of the Magi," with Jeanne Crain, Farley Granger, and
Fred Kelsey.

See: B61, B124, B171, B203, B290, B379, B386

F31   THE BLUE GARDENIA (Warner Bros., released 4.27.53)
      BW   90 Minutes

Producer: Alex Gottlieb. Director: Fritz Lang. Screenplay:
Charles Hoffman. Photography: Nicholas Musuraca. Editor: Edward
Mann. Music: Raoul Kraushaar. Songs: Bob Russell and Leter
Lee. From a story by Vera Caspary.

CAST: Anne Baxter (Norah Larkin), Richard Conte (Casey Mayo),
           Ann Sothern (Crystal Carpenter), Raymond Burr (Harry
           Prebble), Jeff Donnell (Sally Ellis), Richard Erdman
           (Al), George Reeves (Haynes), Ruth Storey (Rose),
           Ray Walker (Homer), and Nat "King" Cole (Himself).

SYNOPSIS: Anne Baxter is a telephone operator who hits a drunk
over the head with a poker, then flees to his apartment. Because
her conscience bothers her, she confesses to a newspaperman
(Conte), who promises to get to the bottom of the mystery of
who really killed the drunk. He believes she is innocent.
He discovers that the murder was committed by another girl,
who was hiding in the apartment.

REVIEWS: BFI Monthly Film Bulletin, 12.53, p. 175
           Film Daily, 3.23.53, p. 14
           Hollywood Reporter, 3.12.53, p. 3
           National Parent-Teacher, 5.53, p. 37
           New York Times, 4.28.53, p. 31
           Time, 3.23.53, p. 108
           Variety, 3.18.53, p. 6

Variety, 3.18.53: "Miss Baxter and Conte do what they can but
fight a losing battle with the script."

New York Times, 4.28.53: "Anne is part of a thoroughly
respectable cast in this hackneyed and tedious film. Miss
Baxter, as the poker swinger, has the most to do."

NOTES: Nat "King" Cole sits at a piano and sings the title
           song, "Blue Gardenia," which went on to become a big
           hit on the music charts.

See: B25, B46, B91, B126, B155, B173, B280, B296, B360-361,
     B365, B368, B400, B443-444, B452, B464, B509, B513

F32   I CONFESS (Warner Bros., released 5.22.53)
      BW   94 Minutes

Producer: Alfred Hitchcock. Director: Alfred Hitchcock.
Screenplay: George Tabori and William Archibald. Photography:
Robert Burks. Editor: Rudi Fehr. Music: Dimitri Tiomkin.
From the play by Paul Anthelme. Available on video cassette.

CAST: Montgomery Clift (Michael), Anne Baxter (Ruth
          Grandfort), Karl Malden (Larrue), Brian Aherne
          (Robertson), O. E. Hasse (Keller), Roger Dana
          (Grandfort), Dolly Haas (Mrs. Keller), Charles Andre
          (Father Maillais), Judson Pratt (Murphy), Ovila Legare
          (Villette), and Gilles Pelletier (Father Benoit).

SYNOPSIS: Anne Baxter is a married woman who believes she is
still in love with her childhood boyfriend, who is now a priest
(Clift). They are reunited when a blackmailer threatens to
reveal an old compromising situation. A refugee working in
the church (Hasse) returns one night to the church and kills
the blackmailer, then confesses to Clift. Since the killer
was wearing a priest's robe and Clift is a priest, he immediately
becomes a suspect. Police Inspector Malden learns of the young
romance when Anne confesses to him, hoping to clear Clift.
Instead, the ploy backfires and Clift is brought to trial.
He is subsequently found not guilty, but the crowd turns against
him. The killer, in the meantime, is confronted by his wife,
whom he shoots as she confesses her husband's guilt. Hasse
is revealed as the twittering murderer. He is chased through
town and is shot, dying in Clift's arms.

REVIEWS: America, 3.28.53, p. 717
          American Photographer, 7.53, p. 16
          BFI Monthly Film Bulletin, 5.53, p. 67
          Catholic World, 4.53, p. 63
          Christian Century, 5.15.53, p. 463
          Commonweal, 3.6.53, p. 550
          Film Daily, 2.5.53, p. 6
          Films in Review 3.53, p. 148
          Hollywood Reporter, 2.5.53, p. 3
          Library Journal, 3.1.53, p. 437
          Look, 4.21.53, p. 110
          Nation, 4.11.53, p. 314

National Parent-Teacher, 4.53, p. 40
New York Times, 3.23.53, p. 28
New Yorker, 4.4.53, p. 82
Newsweek, 3.2.53, p. 90
Saturday Review, 2.21.53, p. 33
Sight and Sound, July-September, 1953, p.34
Theatre Arts, 4.53, p. 89
Time, 3.2.53, p. 92
Variety, 2.11.53, p. 6

Variety, 2.11.53: "Miss Baxter is good as the wife of Roger
Dana, member of the Quebec Parliament."

New York Times, 3.23.53: "As the matronly lady of the old
romance, Anne Baxter gives an eloquent show of feeling sorry
for herself and breathing heavily, but the ease with which she
abandons both and resumes a dutiful attitude toward her husband
(Roger Dana) is a bit disheartening."

NOTES: Hitchcock used the actual streets and buildings of
          Quebec for the film. Clift's heavy drinking and
          erratic behavior caused considerable stress on the
          set. His performance mirrored the troubled person
          Clift was in reality.

See: B11, B31, B47, B57, B90, B125, B146, B172, B187, B207,
      B243, B265, B289, B291, B293, B300, B312, B324, B342, B365,
      B380, B415, B435, B452, B462-464, B478, B500, B524

F33   A CARNIVAL STORY (RKO, released 4.16.54)
      Color   95 Minutes

Producers: Maurice and Frank King. Directors: Kurt Newmann
and Hans Jacoby. Screenplay: Kurt Newmann. Photography: Ernest
Haller. Editors: Willy White and Rudolph Griesbach. Music:
Willy Schmitt-Gentner, Tony Sherrell, and Philip Moody. From
the story by Marcel Klauber and C. B. Williams. Available on
video cassette.

CAST: Anne Baxter (Willi), Steve Cochran (Joe), Lyle Bettger
          (Frank), George Nader (Vines), Jay C. Flippen
          (Charley), Helene Stanley (Peggy), and Adi Berber
          (Groppo).

SYNOPSIS: Anne Baxter is a hungry German lass who joins an American carnival on tour in post-war Munich. She is accosted by her ex-lover (Cochran), who insinuates himself into her life again. She is rescued by the star high diver (Bettger), who tutors her into his act, falls in love with her, and marries her. Instead, she falls for a clean-cut Life magazine photographer (Nader). Flippen is the carnival proprietor. Adi Berber is a circus freak who secretly loves her, too, with tragic consequences.

REVIEWS: America, 5.15.54, p. 203
             BFI Monthly Film Bulletin, 6.54, p. 86
             Commonweal, 5.7.54, p. 118
             Film Daily, 3.24.54, p. 6
             Hollywood Reporter, 3.24.54, p. 3
             London Times, 5.17.54, p. 4
             MPHPD, 3.17.54, p. 2237
             National Parent-Teacher, 5.54, p. 38
             New York Times, 4.17.54, p. 8
             New Yorker, 4.24.54, p. 81
             Newsweek, 4.5.54, p. 81
             Saturday Review, 5.8.54, p. 26
             Spectator, 5.14.54, p. 598
             Tatler, 5.26.54, p. 462
             Time, 4.19.54, p. 100
             Variety, 3.24.54, p. 6

Variety, 3.24.54: "The role of the life-buffeted German girl who joins an American carnival in Munich and becomes its high diving star is the best film part Anne Baxter has had in some time. The manner in which she handles it should awaken new interest in her talents because she makes it come over with considerable sexy sing."

New York Times, 4.17.54: "There is nothing about Miss Baxter or that strange iciness in her eyes that makes such a show of hot devotion arresting or sensible. Miss Baxter deserves much more than Mr. Cochran and this sort of corn, dyed blue."

NOTES: Anne loved filming on location in Munich, Germany, where everyone got along famously.

See: B38, B92, B128, B204, B244, B263, B281, B381, B431, B501

F34   BEDEVILLED (M-G-M, released 4.22.55)
      Color   86 Minutes

Producer: Henry Berman.   Director: Mitchell Leisen.   Screenplay:
Jo Eisinger.   Photography: Frederick A. Young.   Editor: Frank
Clarke.   Music: William Alwyn and Muir Mathieson.   Costumes:
Helen Rose and Jean Desses.

CAST: Anne Baxter (Monica Johnson), Steve Forrest (Gregory
           Fitzgerald), Victor Francen (Father Du Rocher), Simone
           Renant (Francesca), Maurice Teynac (Trevelle), Robert
           Christopher (Tony Lugacetti), Ina de la Hye (Mama
           Lugacetti), Joseph Tomelty (Father Cunningham), Olivier
           Hussenot (Remy Hotel Manager), Jean Ozenne (Priest
           in Seminary), Jacques Gilling (Taxi Driver), and
           Raymond Bussieres (Concierge).

SYNOPSIS: Forrest is a young American priest living in Paris,
who encounters a nervous nightclub singer (Anne Baxter).   She
is fleeing gangsters and local gendarmes.   After confessing
to him of her shady past, she dies in his arms.

REVIEWS: America, 5.14.55, p. 194
           Catholic World, 6.55, p. 220
           Commonweal, 5.13.55, p. 150
           National Parent-Teacher, 6.55, p.38
           New York Times, 4.23.55, p. 23
           Saturday Review, 4.23.55, p. 26
           Time, 5.2.55, p. 98
           Variety, 4.13.55, p. 8

Variety, 4.13.55: "Miss Baxter does her character excellently."

New York Times, 4.23.55: In the final, predictable quarter
of the film, Anne Baxter and Steve Forrest "are hard put to
sustain their performances on a respectable level."

NOTES: The entire movie was filmed in the City of Lights
           (Paris).   The wide-screen color camera pulls back
           to reveal a beautiful, panoramic view of back streets,
           hotels, and skylines.   They also scoured the rotunda
           at Napoleon's Tomb and provided an altitude shot of
           traffic around the Arc de Triomphe.

See: B93, B245, B292, B434, B477, B502

F35   ONE DESIRE (Universal, released 9.2.55)
      Color   94 Minutes

Producer: Ross Hunter. Director: Jerry Hopper. Assistant Directors: Tom Shaw and George Dollier. Screenplay: Lawrence Roman and Robert Blees. Photography: Maury Gertsman. Editor: Milton Carruth. Music: Frank Skinner and Joseph Gershenson. Based on the novel Tacey Cromwell by Conrad Richter.

CAST: Anne Baxter (Tacey Cromwell), Rock Hudson (Clint Saunders), Julie Adams (Judith Watrous), Carl Benton Reid (Senator Watrous), Natalie Wood (Seely), William Hopper (Mac Bain), Betty Garde (Mrs. O'Dell), Barry Curtis (Nugget Saunders), Adrienne Marden (Marjorie Huggins), Fay Morley (Flo), Vici Raaf (Kate), Lynne Millan (Bea), Smoki Whitfield (Sam), Robert Hoy and John Daheim (Firemen), Betty Jane Howarth (May), William Forrest (Mr. Wellington), Edward Earlie (Mr. Hathway), and Dennis Moore (Miner).

SYNOPSIS: Anne Baxter and Rock Hudson are one-time gambling house partners who move to a new town and try to gain respectability. Adams is the daughter of the town's richest banker, who falls in love with Hudson. She convinces Hudson to pressure Baxter to leave town after Anne adopts his brother and orphaned Natalie Wood. She is declared an unfit mother and leaves town with the children. Years later they return and Baxter finds Hudson's marriage is very unhappy. A three-alarm fire destroys his home and wife. He is then free to find happiness with his true love -- Baxter.

REVIEWS: America, 9.3.55, p. 548
           Library Journal, 8.55, p. 1674
           New York Times, 9.3.55, p. 9
           Variety, 7.13.55

Variety, 7.13.55: "Miss Baxter delivers commendably as the gambling hall babe in love with gambler Hudson. How she goes off with him and his kid brother, Barry Curtis, to look after the lad while Hudson turns to more respectable ways of earning a living is played believably."

New York Times, 9.3.55: "Rock Hudson, Julie Adams, and Anne Baxter rate credit for pluck and perseverance."

NOTES: This film marked the graduation to "grown-up roles" for child actress Natalie Wood.

See: B38, B178, B188, B395, B450, B503

F36   THE SPOILERS (Universal, released 12.23.55)
      Color   82 Minutes

Producer: Ross Hunter. Director: Jesse Hibbs. Assistant
Directors: Frank Shaw and George Dollier. Screenplay: Oscar
Brodney and Charles Hoffman. Photography: Maury Gertsman.
Editor: Paul Weatherwax. Music: Joseph Gershenson. Costumes:
Bill Thomas. Based on the novel by Rex Beach.

CAST: Anne Baxter (Cherry Malotte), Jeff Chandler (Roy
           Glennister), Rory Calhoun (Alexander McNamara), Ray
           Danton (Bronco), Barbara Britton (Helen Chester),
           John McIntire (Dextry), Carl Benton Reid (Judge
           Stillman), Wallace Ford (Flapjack), Raymond Walburn
           (Mr. Skinner), Dayton Lummis (Wheaton), Willis Bouchey
           (Struve), Roy Barcroft (Marshal), Ruth Donnelly
           (Duchess), Forrest Lewis (Banty), Byron Foulger
           (Montrose), Arthur Space (Bank Manager), Harry Seymour
           (Piano Player), Bob Steele (Mince), Edwin Parker
           (Berry), Lee Roberts (Deputy), John Close (Deputy),
           with John Harmon, Frank Sully, Paul McGuire, Lane
           Bradford, and Terry Frost.

SYNOPSIS: Jeff Chandler is co-owner of the richest mine in
the Alaskan Territory. Baxter is the sole owner of the richest
saloon. Calhoun poses as a gold commissioner who is really
after the gold and the saloonkeeper. Carl Benton Reid is a
phony judge who, with the help of his niece (Britton), almost
pulls off the swindle before being discovered by Chandler.

REVIEWS: Library Journal, 1.15.56, p. 175
           National Parent-Teacher, 1.56, p. 40
           New York Times, 12.24.55, p. 10
           Variety, 12.6.55, p. 6

Variety, 12.6.55: The trio of Anne Baxter, Jeff Chandler, and
Rory Calhoun "brings off the show in suitable fashion for those
who like the action spelled out in a-b-c terms."

New York Times, 12.24.55: "This familiar story has Anne Baxter
as the sole owner of the richest saloon in the territory. (It
should be, she charges $3 for a hard-boiled egg.)"

NOTES: This story was initially filmed in a 1914 silent,
           starring William Farnum and Tom Santschi. In 1930,
           it was remade with Gary Cooper, William Boyd, and
           Kay Johnson. Randolph Scott, John Wayne, and Marlene
           Dietrich reprised the roles in the 1942 version.

See: B54, B159, B189, B419, B430

F37   THE COME ON (Allied Artists, released 4.16.56)
      BW   82 Minutes

Producer: Lindsley Parsons. Associate Producer: John H. Burrows
Director: Russell Birdwell. Screenplay: Warren Douglas and
Whitman Chambers. Photography: Ernest Haller. Editor: Maurice
Wright. Music: Paul Dunlap. Costumes: Edith Head. From the
novel by Whitman Chambers.

CAST: Anne Baxter (Rita Kendrick), Sterling Hayden (Dave
           Arnold), John Hoyt (Harley Kendrick), Jesse White
           (J. J. McGonigle), Walter Cassell (Tony Margoli),
           Alex Gerry (Chalmers), Theodore Newton (Captain Getz),
           Paul Picerni (Jerry Jannings), Lee Turnbull (Joe
           Tinney), Tyler McVey (Hogan), and Karolee Kelly (Tony
           Girl).

SYNOPSIS: Anne Baxter and John Hoyt are blackmailers who join
forces with Hayden, who decides Hoyt should be eliminated.
When their evil deeds backfire, they are all killed.

REVIEWS: New York Times, 4.7.56, p. 13
           Variety, 2.9.56, p. 4

Variety, 2.9.56: "The two stars, other than the physical
appearance put forth by Miss Baxter in her Edith Head costumes,
fail to be very impressive."

New York Times, 4.7.56: "You see Miss Baxter in a two-piece
bathing suit, which is quite interesting."

NOTES: Director Birdwell returned to that rusty job after
           devoting his time and efforts to publicity activities.

See: B160, B162, B452

F38   THE TEN COMMANDMENTS (Paramount, released 11.8.56)
      Color   219 Minutes

Producer: Cecil B. DeMille. Assistant Producer: Henry Wilcoxon.
Director: Cecil B. DeMille. Assistant Directors: Francisco
Day, Michael Moore, Edward Salven, Daniel McCauley, and Fouad
Aref. Screenplay: Aeneas MacKenzie, Jesse L. Lasky, Jr.,

Jack Gariss, and Frederic M. Frank.   Photography: J. Peverell
Marley, John Warren, and Wallace Kelley.   Music: Elmer Bernstein.
Cinematographer: Loyal Griggs.   Editor: Anna Bauchens.   Costumes:
Edith Head, Ralph Jester, John Jenson, Dorothy Jenkins, and
Arnold Friberg.   Based on "The Bible," "Prince of Egypt," by
Dorothy Clarke Wilson, "Pillar of Fire," by Rev. J. H. Ingraham,
and On Eagle's Wings, by Rev. A. E. Southon.

CAST: Charlton Heston (Moses), Anne Baxter (Princess
            Nefretiri), Yvonne De Carlo (Sephora), John Derek
            (Joshua), Nina Foch (Bithiah), Judith Anderson
            (Memnet), John Carradine (Aaron), Douglass Dumbrille
            (Jannes), Henry Wilcoxon (Pentaur), Donald Curtis
            (Mered), B. Warner (Amminadab), Yul Brynner
            (Rameses II), Edward G. Robinson (Dathan), Debra Paget
            (Lilia), Cedric Hardwicke (Sethi), Martha Scott
            (Yochabel), Vincent Price (Baka), Olive Deering
            (Miriam), Frank De Kova (Abiram), Eduard Franz
            (Jethro), Lawrence Dobkin (Hur Ben Caleb), Julia Faye
            (Elisheba), Lisa Mitchell, Joanna Merlin, Joyce
            Vanderveen, Noelle Williams, Pat Richards, Diane Hall
            (Jethro's Daughters), Abbas El Boughdadly (Rameses's
            Charioteer), Fraser Heston (Baby Moses), Tommy Duran
            (Gershom), Eugene Mazzola (Rameses's Son), Ramsay
            Hill (Korah), Esther Brown (Princess Tharbia), John
            Miljan (Blind One), Francis J. McDonald (Simon), Ian
            Keith (Rameses I), Paul De Rolf (Eleazar), Joan
            Woodbury (Korah's Wife), and Woodrow Strode (King
            of Ethiopia).

SYNOPSIS: DeMille's epic film denotes the life of Moses, who,
born a slave child, is rescued as an infant by the Egyptian
royal family. He later returns as the spiritual leader of his
people. He is to lead them to freedom after receiving the Ten
Commandments from God on Mt. Sinai. Yul Brynner is his nemesis,
Rameses II. Anne Baxter is Princess Nefretiri, whose love for
Moses is unreciprocated when he marries De Carlo, a Midianite
shepherdess. John Derek is Moses's reckless follower, Joshua,
who continues the quest when Moses dies.

REVIEWS: America, 12.1.56, p. 284
          American Cinematographer, 4.83, p. 46
          Commonweal, 11.30.56, p. 232
          Film Daily, 10.5.56, p. 7
          Film Quarterly, Fall, 1966, p. 59
          Films and Filming, 10.56, p. 8
          Films and Filming, 1.58, p. 23
          Films in Review, 11.56, p. 461
          Hollywood Reporter, 10.5.56, p. 3

Nation, 12.8.56, p. 506
New Republic, 10.10.56, p. 20
New York Times, 11.9.56, p. 35
New York Times, 11.11.56, p. 1
New York Times, 3.25.84, p. 19
New Yorker, 11.17.56, p. 101
Newsweek, 11.5.56, p. 112
Saturday Review, 11.10.56, p. 28
Sight and Sound, Winter 1957-1958, p. 148
Time, 11.12.56, p. 120
Time, 11.19.56, p. 82
Variety, 10.10.56, p. 6

Newsweek, 11.5.56: "Anne Baxter, as the loving Princess Nefretiri, tries very hard to rise above her material but does not make it."

New York Times, 11.9.56: "Anne Baxter, as the sensual princess and Yul Brynner, as the rival, Rameses, are unquestionably apt and complimentary to a lusty and melodramatic romance."

Variety, 10.10.56: "Performances meet requirements all the way but exception must be made anent Anne Baxter as the Egyptia Princess Nefretiri. In expressing her intense love for Moses, even after discovering his background, Miss Baxter leans close to old-school siren histrionics and in instances this is out of sync with the spiritual nature of 'Commandments.'"

NOTES: The film was re-released in 1990. It is a 3½-hour movie that was the largest and most expensive film made when originally released in 1956. Its remarkabl settings and decor included a facade of the Egyptian city from which the Exocus begins.

See: B (see Index for detailed listings), M1

F39 THREE VIOLENT PEOPLE (Paramount, released 12.15.56)
     Color   100 Minutes

Producer: Hugh Brown. Director: Rudolph Mate. Assistant Director: Richard Caffey. Screenplay: James Edward Grant. Photography: Loyal Griggs. Editor: Alma Macrorie. Music: Walt Scharf. Costumes: Edith Head. Song: Mack Gordon and Martita. From a story by Leonard Praskins and Barbara Slater.

CAST: Charlton Heston (Colt Saunders), Anne Baxter (Lorna Hunter Saunders), Gilbert Roland (Innocencio), Tom

Tryon (Cinch), Forrest Tucker (Cable), Bruce Bennett
(Harrison), Elaine Stritch (Ruby La Salle), Barton
MacLane (Yates), Peter Hansen (Lt. Marr), John Harman
(Massey), Ross Bagdassarian (Asuncion), Raymond
Greenleaf (Carleton), Argentina Brunetti (Maria),
Robert Arthur (One-legged Confederate Soldier), Bobby
Blake (Rafael), Jameel Farr (Pedro), Leo Castillo
(Luis), Don Devlin (Juan), Roy Engel and Don Dunning
(Carpetbaggers), Ernestine Wade (Maid), and Paul Levitt
(Bartender).

SYNOPSIS: Anne Baxter is an ex-saloon hostess who comes between
her rancher husband (Heston) and his brother (Tryon). Heston
is a Confederate veteran, who returns from the Civil War to
his Texas ranch. Tryon covets his sister-in-law as they fight
to outwit carpetbaggers, who try to seize their homestead for
tax arrears.

REVIEWS: National Parent-Teacher, 1.57, p. 37
          New York Times, 2.11.57, p. 34
          Newsweek, 1.28.57, p. 94
          Senior Scholastic, 2.15.57, p. 19
          Time, 2.25.57, p. 96
          Variety, 12.21.56, p. 6

Variety, 12.21.56: "Miss Baxter, trim stuff in a series of
period costumes and matching millinery, has the requisite
sauciness combined with essential sincerity to make the woman's
part stand up. Her inter-relatedness to and with Charlton
Heston, a rugged and believable characterization, gives the
production its underpinning."

Time, 2.25.57: "At one point, Tom Tryon manages to steal a
scene from heroine Anne Baxter, who is probably the most
relentless camera-hugger in the business."

NOTES: Song "Un Momento" by Mack David and Martita.

See: B94, B162, B346, B419, B439, B441

F40 CHASE A CROOKED SHADOW (Warner Bros., released 3.24.58)
     BW   87 Minutes

Producers: Douglas Fairbanks, Jr., and Thomas Clyde. Director:
Michael Anderson. Assistant Director: Robert Lynn. Screenplay:
David Osborn and Charles Sinclair. Editor: Gordon Pilkington.

Music: Matyas Seiber. Costumes: Anthony Mendelson. Plot
borrowed from the British TV series The Whistler.

CAST: Richard Todd (Ward), Anne Baxter (Kimberly), Herbert
            Lom (Vargas), Alexander Knox (Chandler Bridson), Fait
            Brook (Mrs. Whitman), Alan Tilvern (Carlos), and Thel
            d'Aguiar (Maria).

SYNOPSIS: Anne Baxter is a reclusive, beautiful diamond heires
who is recuperating from the suicide death of her father. A
bold young man comes to the villa on the coast of Spain, brazen
claiming to be her long-dead brother. He has the memories and
papers to substantiate his claim. It is revealed, however,
that the young man is really after a cache of hidden diamonds,
of which only Baxter and her elderly uncle know the whereabouts

REVIEWS: America, 4.5.58, p. 28
           Commonweal, 3.28.58, p. 661
           New York Times, 3.25.58, p. 28
           Time, 4.28.58, p. 101
           Variety, 1.29.58, p. 8

Variety, 1.29.58: "Miss Baxter gives a convincing display as
a young woman nearly off her rocker with fear."

New York Times, 3.25.58: "Anne Baxter, as the heiress, and
Richard Todd, as the fellow who moves in, do sufficiently well
in the top roles to keep you casually looking at them, although
there is some handsome seacoast scenery (in black and white)
to catch the eye."

NOTES: This marked actor Douglas Fairbanks, Jr.'s first
           producing effort.

See: B95, B130, B247, B265, B505

F41 CIMARRON (M-G-M, released 2.16.61)
     Color   140 Minutes

Producer: Edmund Grainger. Director: Anthony Mann. Screenplay
Arnold Shulman. Photography: Robert L. Surtees. Special
Effects: A. Arnold Gillespie, Lee Le Blanc, and Robert H. Hoag.
Editor: John Dunning. Art Direction: George W. Davis and Addisc
Behr. Music: Franz Waxman. Song: Paul Francis Webster. Sound:
Franklin Hilton. Costumes: Walter Plunkett. Based on the novel
by Edna Ferber.

CAST: Glenn Ford (Yancey Cravet), Maria Schell (Sabra
           Cravet), Anne Baxter (Dixie), Arthur O'Connell (Tom
           Wyatt), Mercedes McCambridge (Sarah Wyatt), Russ
           Tamblyn (The Kid), Vic Morrow (West), Robert Keith
           (Sam Pegler), Aline MacMahon (Mrs. Pegler), David
           Opatoshu (Sol Levy), Henry Morgan (Jesse Rickey),
           Charles McGraw (Bob Yountis), Lili Darvas (Felicia
           Venable), Edgar Buchanan (Neal Heflin), Royal Dano
           (Ike Howes), George Brenlin (Hoss), L. Q. Jones
           (Willis), Vladimir Sokoloff (Jacob Krubeckoff), Ivan
           Tissault (Lewis Venable), Buzz Martin (Cim Cravet),
           John Cason (Suggs), Dawn Little Sky (Arita Red
           Feather), Eddie Little Sky (Ben Red Feather), with
           Helen Westcott.

SYNOPSIS: Ford and Schell are a young couple who are part of
the hundreds of covered wagon patrons who dash forth in a wild
race to stake out claims on a vast track of land the government
released in the Oklahoma Territory in 1889. He is a loyal,
courageous man whose wife is rather unstable. He fights for
the end of prejudice against Indians and Jewish settlers. Anne
Baxter is the owner of a dance hall, with a heart of gold.
Mercedes McCambridge is the wife of newly-rich oilman O'Connell.
Opatoshu is a Jewish merchant. Robert Keith is the town
newspaperman.

REVIEWS: America, 3.11.61, p. 768
           Commonweal, 3.3.61, p. 587
           Life, 2.10.61, p. 81
           McCall's, 3.61, p. 181
           New York Times, 1.10.60, p. 7
           New York Times, 2.17.61, p. 21
           New York Times, 2.26.61,p. 1
           New Yorker, 2.25.61, p. 126
           Newsweek, 1.16.61, p. 79
           Redbook, 1.16.61,p. 79
           Saturday Review, 2.18.61, p. 31
           Senior Scholastic, 3.22.61, p. 22
           Time, 2.24.61, p. 38
           Variety, 12.7.60, p. 6

Variety, 12.7.60: "Miss Baxter's role is surprisingly short.
However, she makes a vibrant conribution as the Red Light Belle,
Dixie Lee, particularly in her pathetic play to share Yancey
at least with his wife and, this time, with sardonic flippancy,
when she is confronted by Sabra for news about the husband she
hasn't heard from in a couple of years."

New York Times, 2.17.61: Anne Baxter, as a fancy woman, joins other supporting cast members as "gaudy but hollow figures."

NOTES: This novel was previously filmed in 1931, starring Richard Dix, Irene Dunne, Estelle Taylor, Nance O'Neill, William Collier, Jr., and Roscoe Ates.

See: B131, B248, B297, B343, B401, B419, B506, R36

F42 SEASON OF PASSION (United Artists, released 2.4.62)
     BW   94 Minutes

Producer: Leslie Norman. Director: Leslie Norman. Screenplay: John Dighton. Photography: Paul Beeson. Music: Benjamin Frankel. From the play Summer of the Seventeenth Doll by Ray Lawler.

CAST: Ernest Borgnine (Roo), Anne Baxter (Olive), John Mills (Barney), Angela Lansbury (Pearl), Vincent Ball (Dowd) Ethel Gabriel (Emma), Janette Craig (Bubba), Deryck Barnes (Sprulker), Tom Lurica ("Atomic Bomber"), Al Thomas (Cane Cutter), Dana Wilson (Little Girl), Frank Wilson (Cane Cutter), Jessica Noad (Nancy), and Al Garcia (Cane Cutter).

SYNOPSIS: Each year, after months of hard work in the sugar cane fields of Sydney, Australia, Roo and Barney return to their girlfriends. Each year they bring a gift in the form of a doll, to make up for their long separation. Barney's girlfriend, however, has married someone else and is now replaced by Pearl. Roo's girl, Olive, usually is happy-go-lucky; but now their lives are different. They realize they are aging and must change with the times.

REVIEWS: Commonweal, 2.2.62, p. 495
          New York Times, 2.5.62, p. 19
          Newsweek, 1.8.62, p. 64
          Variety, 3.30.62, p. 6

Variety, 3.30.62: "Anne Baxter, stridently taking on an Australian accent, plays Borgnine's love-partner and there's something quite pathetic in the way she, too, refuses to believe that the annual summer layoff can be anything but as sweet at the year before."

New York Times, 2.5.62: "The performances are generally first-rate. Anne Baxter is a bit strident, but Ernest Borgnine, as

her hot-headed escort, and John Mills, as his bantam buddy,
are winning indeed."

NOTES: This movie was filmed on location in Sydney, Australia.
           It was also titled <u>Summer of the Seventeenth Doll</u>.

See: B43, B249, B459, B484

F43   A WALK ON THE WILD SIDE (Columbia/Famous Artists, released
      2.21.62)   BW   114 Minutes

Producer: Charles K. Feldman.   Director: Edward Dmytryk.
Screenplay: John Fante and Edmund Morris. Photography: Joe
MacDonald. Editor: Harry Gerstad. Music: Elmer Bernstein
(credits Saul Bass). From the novel by Nelson Algren. Available
on video cassette.

CAST: Laurence Harvey (Dove Linkhorn), Capucine (Hallie),
           Jane Fonda (Kitty Twist), Anne Baxter (Teresina
           Vidaverri), Barbara Stanwyck (Jo Courtney), Joanna
           Moore (Miss Precious), Richard Rust (Oliver), Karl
           Swensen (Schmidt), Donald Barry (Dockery), Juanita
           Moore (Mama), John Anderson (Preacher), Ken Lynch
           (Frank Bonito), Todd Armstrong (Lt. Omar Stroud),
           Lillian Bronson (Amy Gerard), Adrienne Marden (Eva
           Gerard), Sherry O'Neil (Reba), John Bryant (Spence),
           and Kathryn Card (Landlady).

SYNOPSIS: Harvey is a Texas vagabond, who travels to New Orleans
in search of his long-lost love, Capucine. She now lives in
a French Quarter establishment run by Stanwyck. Jane Fonda
is a fellow traveler, who tries to distract him from his goal.
Anne Baxter is a diner owner, who gives him advice when he seeks
refuge at her place.

REVIEWS: <u>America</u>, 6.2.62, p. 360
           <u>Commonweal</u>, 3.2.62, p. 599
           <u>Film</u>, Summer, 1962, p. 32
           <u>Film Daily</u>, 1.29.62, p. 4
           <u>Filmfacts</u>, 4.6.62, p. 57
           <u>Films and Filming</u>, 4.62, p. 32
           <u>Films in Review</u>, 3.62, p. 171
           <u>Hollywood Reporter</u>, 2.19.62, p. 3
           <u>MPHPD</u>, 2.7.62, p. 436
           <u>New Republic</u>, 7.30.62, p. 30
           <u>New York Times</u>, 5.7.61, p. 9
           <u>New York Times</u>, 2.22.62, p. 20

New Yorker, 2.24.62, p. 111
Newsweek, 3.5.62, p. 84
Redbook, 3.62, p. 32
Saturday Review, 7.28.62, p. 31
Time, 2.23.62, p. 102
Variety, 1.13.62, p. 6
Village Voice, 2.1.62, p. 11

Variety, 1.31.62: "Anne Baxter plays well as a cafe operator with normal affections toward Harvey."

New York Times, 2.22.62: "Anne Baxter is wasted in a weak role

NOTES: This film was noted for portraying lesbianism in an overt manner.

See: B57, B132, B142, B144, B196, B212, B214, B250, B396, B461, B507, B509, M2

F44 MIX ME A PERSON (Wessex-British Lion, released 8.19.62)
     BW   116 Minutes

Producer: Sergei Nolbandov. Director: Leslie Norman. Screenplay; Ian Dalrymple. Editor: Ernie Hosler. Music: Johnny Worth. From the novel by Jack Trevor.

CAST: Anne Baxter (Dr. Anne Dyson), Donald Sinden (Philip Bellamy, Q.C.), Adam Faith (Harry Jukes), David Kernan (Socko), Frank Jarvis (Nobby), Peter Kriss (Dirty Neck), Carole Ann Ford (Jenny), Anthony Booth (Gravy), Topsy Jane (Mona), Jack MacGowan (Terence), Walter Brown (Max Taplow), Glyn Houston (Sam), Dilya Hamlett (Doris), Meredith Edwards (Johnson), Alfred Burke (Lumley), Russell Napier (P. C. Jarrold), Barbara Barnet (Receptionist), Julie Milton (Lorna), Tim Pearce (Tough), Ed Devereaux (Supt. Malley), Ray Barrett (Inspector Wagstaffe), Donald Morley (Prison Governor) Lawrence James (Patrol Officer), Gilbert Wynne (First Prison Officer), and Norman Johns (Second Prison Officer).

SYNOPSIS: Anne Baxter is the psychiatrist wife of an English barrister. She accepts a young client (Adam Faith), who was wrongfully convicted of murder and condemned to death. Thanks to her efforts, the real killer is revealed and caught.

REVIEWS: Variety, 8.14.62, p. 6

<u>Variety</u>, 8.14.62: "Miss Baxter, attractive as ever, does not convince as the East End girl who has become a celebrated doctor of psychiatry, but she has to cope with some very desperate moments."

NOTES: British rock star Adam Faith sings the credit song, which made the British music charts.

F45   THE FAMILY JEWELS (Paramount, released 8.11.65)
      Color   100 Minutes

Producer: Jerry Lewis. Director: Jerry Lewis. Screenplay: Jerry Lewis and Bill Richmond. Photography: W. Wallace Kelly. Editor: Arthur P. Schmidt and John Woodcock. Music: Pete King.

CAST: Jerry Lewis (the Peyton Brothers: Everett, James, Captain Eddie, Julius, Bugsy, Skylock; and Willard Woodward, the Chauffeur), Sebastian Cabot (Dr. Matson), Gene Gaylos (Clown), Donna Butterworth (Donna Peyton), Milton Frome (Pilot), Herbie Faye (Joe), Robert Strauss (Pool Hall Owner), Jay Adler and Neil Hamilton (Lawyers), Marjorie Bennett, Frances Lax, Ellen Corby, Renie Riano, and Jesslyn Fax (Plane Passengers), Anne Baxter (Cameo), with John Lawrence, Francine York, John Hubbard, Michael Ross, John Macchia, Douglas Deane, and Maurice Kelly.

SYNOPSIS: This farce stars Lewis as six brothers. A nine-year-old orphan heiress (Butterworth) must choose one of them as her legal guardian. The brothers are: Captain Eddie, an airline pilot; Julius, a commercial photographer; James, the ferryboat captain; Skylock, the mousy detective; Everett, the clown who hates kids; and Bugsy, the snaggle-toothed, cross-eyed gangster. She ends up choosing Willard, the family chauffeur (also played by Jerry Lewis).

REVIEWS: <u>BFI Monthly Film Bulletin</u>, 1.66, p. 2
           <u>Film Daily</u>, 6.21.65, p. 6
           <u>Films and Filming</u>, 2.66, p. 12
           <u>Hollywood Reporter</u>, 6.21.65, p. 3
           <u>London Times</u>, 11.18.65, p. 8
           <u>MPHPD</u>, 7.7.65, p. 327
           <u>New Statesman and Nation</u>, 11.26.65, p. 853
           <u>New York Times</u>, 8.12.65, p. 30
           <u>New York Times</u>, 8.15.65, p. 1
           <u>Variety</u>, 6.23.65, p. 7

Variety, 6.18.65: "Very good satire on in-flight pix involves Anne Baxter appearing in film clip from Sustenance, a gag scene in which banquet guests, silverware, and food slide about with aircraft motion."

See: B98, B133

F46   THE TALL WOMEN (Allied Artists, released 1967)
      Color   95 Minutes

Producers: Danny L. and L. M. Danubia. Director: Cechet Grooper Screenplay: Mino Rolli.

CAST: Anne Baxter (Mary Ann), Maria Perschy, Gustavo Rojo,
           Rossella Como, Adriana Ambesi, Mara Cruz, Christa
           Linder, and John Clarke.

SYNOPSIS: This European-made western was about seven women who survive an Indian massacre and are forced to fight for their lives while crossing the desert.

REVIEWS: Filmfacts, 1967

NOTES: This movie was filmed in Spain and had limited
           distribution. It suffered from poor dubbing and
           mediocre acting. It quickly disappeared.

See: B12, B419

F47   THE BUSY BODY (Paramount, released 6.7.67)
      Color   102 Minutes

Producer: William Castle. Director: William Castle. Screenplay: Ben Starr. Photography: Hal Stine. Editor: Edwin H. Bryant. Music: Vic Mizzy. Song: Edward Heyman and John Green. From the novel by Donald E. Westlake.

CAST: Sid Caesar (George Norton), Robert Ryan (Charles
           Barker), Anne Baxter (Margo Foster), Kay Medford (Ma
           Norton), Dom DeLuise (Brock), Jan Murray (Murray
           Foster), Richard Pryor (Whittaker), Arlene Golonka
           (Bobbi Brody), Charles McGraw (Fred Harwell), Ben
           Blue (Felix Rose), Bill Dana (Archie Brody), Godfrey
           Cambridge (Mike), Marty Ingels (Willie), George Jessel
           (Mr. Fessel), Mickey Deems (Copy #1), Paul Wexler

(Mr. Merriwether), Marina Koshely (Marcia Woshikowski), Choo Choo Collins (Woman #1), Norman Bartold, Mike Wagner, Larry Gelman, and Don Brodie (Board Members).

SYNOPSIS: Caesar is a wimp suspected of fleecing money from gangster boss Ryan and his cronies. The money was actually collected by Dana, who is murdered for being disloyal. Caesar's wife selects the wrong suit for his funeral -- it contains the money wanted by the mob. The case soon evolves into missing corpses, missing suits, and the $1 million cache. Dom DeLuise is a hairdresser who turns mortician's aide. Baxter and Murray are a conniving married couple. Jessel has a self-satiric bit as a professional eulogist. Medford is Caesar's doting Jewish mother.

REVIEWS: New York Times, 6.8.67, p. 52
          Variety, 1.24.67, p. 6

Variety, 1.24.67: "Miss Baxter scores a standout performance."

NOTES: This marked the film debut of young comedian Richard Pryor. Edward Heyman and John Green wrote the featured song "Out of Nowhere."

See: B485

F48   THE LATE LIZ (Dick Ross and Associates, released 9.22.71)
      Color   119 Minutes

Producer: Dick Ross. Directors: Dick Ross and Arthur Levinson. Screenplay: Bill Rega. Photography: Harry Stradling, Jr. Editor: Mike Pozan. Music: Ralph Carmichael. Art Direction: Bill Malley. Set Decoration: James W. Payne. From the autobiographical novel by Elizabeth Burns. Available on video cassette.

CAST: Anne Baxter (Elizabeth Burns/Liz Addams Hatch), Steve Forrest (Jim Hatch), James Gregory (Sam Burns), Coleen Grey (Sue Webb), Joan Hotckkis (Sally), Jack Albertson (Rev. Rogers), Eloise Hardt (Laura), Steve Dunne (Si Adams), Reid Smith (Alan), Bill Katt (Peter), Ivor Francis (Dr. Murray), Gail Bonney (Maid), and Jackson Bostwick (Randall Trowbridge).

SYNOPSIS: Anne Baxter has the title role of Elizabeth Burns (real name Gert Behanna), the daughter of a dominating millionaire (Gregory), who tries to mold her into his image.

Instead, she drifts into three unhappy marriages that produce
two sons (Smith and Katt) and a battle with the bottle. After
an unsuccessful suicide attempt, she is saved by her newfound
Christian faith at the age of 53, in 1947. Forrest is her third
husband, a cold, unsympathetic plastic surgeon, who only marries
her to meet her rich drinking friends. Jack Albertson is the
minister who comes to her rescue. Joan Hotckis is a lovable,
tragi-comic drunk.

REVIEWS: Christianity Today, 10.22.71, p. 25
          Variety, 9.15.71, p. 6

Variety, 9.15.71: "Miss Baxter, plus a large cast, makes it
very credible. The tedious overlength (119 minutes, perhaps
a half-hour too much) results in dampening the effect of Miss
Baxter's versatile performance."

Christianity Today, 10.22.71: "Anne Baxter, in the title role,
contributes to the success of the movie, imitating mannerisms
that make her a believable Gert Behanna, though at times she
becomes too melodramatic."

NOTES: Anne was not able to attend the premiere on
          September 22 in San Antonio, because she was starring
          on Broadway in Applause. The producer and cast member
          Coleen Gray and Bill Katt attended. Mrs. Behanna
          began an extensive public speaking career following
          her conversion. Her son was Reverend Bardwell Smith,
          Dean of Carleton College, in Northfield, Minnesota.
          Proceeds from the premiere were donated to the
          San Antonio chapter of the Salvation Army.

See: B359, B407

F49 FOOL'S PARADE (Columbia, Stanmore Productions and Penbar
     Productions, released 8.18.71)
     Color   98 Minutes

Producer: Andrew V. McLaglen and Harry Bernsen. Directors:
Andrew V. McLaglen and Howard W. Koch, Jr. Screenplay: James
Lee Barrett. Photography: Harry Stradling, Jr. Editors: David
Bretherton and Robert Simpson. Music: Henry Vars. Costumes:
Guy C. Verhille. From the novel by David Grubb.

CAST: James Stewart (Mattie Appleyard), George Kennedy (Doc
         Council), Anne Baxter (Cleo), Strother Martin (Lee
         Cottrill), Kurt Russell (Johnny Jessus), William Windo

(Roy K. Sizemore), Mike Kellin (Steve Mystic), Kathy
Cannon (Chanty), Morgan Paull (Junior Kilfong), Robert
Donner (Willis Hubbard), David Huddleston (Homer
Grindstaff), Dort Clark (Enoch Purdy), James Lee
Barrett (Sonny Boy), Kitty Jefferson Doepken (Clara),
Dwight McConnell (Stationmaster), Richard Carl (Police
Chief), Arthur Cain (Prosecuting Attorney), Paul
Merriman (Fireman), Walter Dove (Engineer), Peter
Miller (Trusty), George Metro (Train Dispatcher),
Suzann Stoehr (Bank Teller), and John Edwards (Bank
Clerk).

SYNOPSIS: James Stewart is one of a trio of ex-convicts released
from a West Virginia prison in 1935, who try to leave town on
the train. Stewart is owed $25,452.32 by the state, which the
local dishonest bank has no intention of remitting. Kennedy
is a religiously zealous prison guard assigned to see that nobody
collects. Anne Baxter is an operator of a river houseboat.

REVIEWS: America, 10.2.71, p. 235
           Life, 6.11.71, p. 20
           New York Times, 8.19.71, p. 42
           Variety, 6.23.71, p. 7

Variety, 6.23.71: "Stewart tries to evoke sympathy, and Kennedy
is menacing as a brutal killer, even though his role has been
over-written character-wise. Anne has little more than a bit
part."

NOTES: Long-time TV western director Andrew V. McLaglen filmed
           this "Faulkneresque" story.

See: B205, B508, B515

F50 JANE AUSTEN IN MANHATTAN (Putnam Square Productions,
     released 11.17.81)   Color   108 Minutes

Producer: Ismail Merchant. Director: James Ivory. Screenplay:
Ruth Prawer Jhabvala. Photography: Ernst Vincze. Music: Richard
Robbins. Sets: Michael Yeargan. Costumes: Jenny Beavan.
From "The Libretto of Sir Charles Grandison," by Jane Austen
and Samuel Richardson. Available on video cassette.

CAST: Anne Baxter (Lilianna), Robert Powell (Pierre), Sean
           Young (Ariadne), Kurt Johnson (Victor), Katrina Hodiak
           (Katya), Tim Choate (Jamie), Nancy New (Jenny), Chuck

McCaughan (Billie), John Guerrasio (Gregory), and Michael Wager (George Midash).

SYNOPSIS: This is a fictitious account of the discovery of a real play written by 12-year-old Jane Austen, based on an 18th-century novel by Samuel Richardson. Two quite different acting teachers hope to produce the play. Robert Powell is a very charismatic instructor who causes a rift between two young married students when he takes the wife (Young) into his commune of actors. Anne Baxter is a selfless teacher-producer who wants to stage the work as an operetta.

REVIEWS: Film Comment, November-December, 1980, p. 4
          New York Times, 11.18.81, p. 15
          Variety, 7.22.81, p. 6

Variety, 7.22.81: "Anne Baxter, as a contrastingly altruistic teacher-producer -- is hardly less preposterous, or more sympathetic."

New York Times, 11.18.81: "Mr. Powell's icy magnetism and Miss Baxter's flair for the sweeping gesture are perfectly contrasted here, and they are indeed powerful opposites. While Mr. Powell projects an eerie, unnerving calm, Miss Baxter makes the most of the screenplay's distracted brand of comedy."

NOTES: Anne's daughter, Katrina Hodiak, co-starred with her mother for the first time. The film was co-financed by Polytel and London Weekend TV, and was first shown on television in Britain.

See: B2, B252, B332, B402, B437, B455

Television Productions

This chapter compiles Anne Baxter's appearances on television. They are listed in chronological order and include episodic guest-starring roles, as well as series work. TV movies are catalogued in a format similar to that used in the filmography.

T1   "Bitter Choice," <u>G.E. Theater</u>, CBS, 4.21.57

Anne Baxter and Vince Edwards co-star in this tense drama about an Army nurse and the young soldier in her care who awakens her deep feelings of compassion.

See: B347

T2   "The Right Hand Man," <u>Playhouse 90</u>, CBS, 3.20.58

Dana Andrews is a successful talent agency director who starts to rely increasingly on a young aide (Leslie Nielsen), both in his personal life and professional career, to the consternation of his young wife (Anne Baxter).

T3   "Stopover," <u>G.E. Theater</u>, CBS, 4.27.58

Anne Baxter and Beverly Washburn co-star in this drama about a southern girl who brings cheerfulness into the lives of a drab western family.

T4   "The Four," Lux Video Theater, NBC, 10.17.58

Anne Baxter stars as a school teacher who is being forced
to resign by vicious students.

T5   "The Kitty Angel Story," Wagon Train, ABC, 1.7.59

Kitty Angel is an ex-saloon girl traveling out west on
the wagon train. She adopts a sickly, orphaned Indian
baby and incurs the wrath of the members of the caravan,
who want her and the baby to be thrown off the train.
CAST: Ward Bond (Major Seth Adams), Robert Horton (Flint
McCullough), Terry Wilson (Bill Hawks), with Anne Baxter
(Kitty Angel), Henry Hull, and Kathleen Freeman.

T6   "Race to Cincinnati," Riverboat, NBC, 10.4.59

A desperate woman (Anne Baxter) hires the captain of the
Enterprise, a 100-ft.-long stern-wheeler, to quickly take
her to Cincinnati. CAST: Darren McGavin (Capt. Grey
Holden), Burt Reynolds (Ben Frazer), William D. Gordon
(Travis), Richard Wessell (Carney), Jack Lambert (Joshua),
Mike McGreevey (Chip), Jack Mitchum (Pickalong), Bart Patton
(Terry Blake), with Anne Baxter, Monica Lewis, and Robert
Lowery.

T7   "Hand on the Latch," Zane Grey Theater, CBS, 10.29.59

This western anthonology's episode featured Anne Baxter
as a young woman who takes care of hearth and home while
her husband fights the enemy in the Civil War.

NOTE: This series was also known as Dick Powell's Zane
       Grey Theater.

T8   "Death Runs Wild," Checkmate, NBC, 9.17.60

This episode premiered the series based on Eric Ambler's
tale of private eyes and their criminologist, who are hired
to solve their clients' cases. CAST: Anthony George (Don
Corey), Doug McClure (Jed Sills), Sebastian Cabot
(Dr. Carl Hyatt), with Anne Baxter and Frankie Darro.

T9   "The Dance Man," The DuPont Show with June Allyson, CBS, 10.6.60

Host June Allyson introduces the story of a lonely woman (Anne Baxter) who receives the attention she needs and desires from a young man (Dean Stockwell) she meets at a dance, although she doesn't realize he is not as innocent as he seems.

NOTE: This series was also known as The June Allyson Show.

T10   "Goodbye, My Love," G.E. Theater, CBS, 10.16.60

This romantic story featured host of the series Ronald Reagan, with Anne Baxter, Nestor Pevis, and Chet Stratton.

T11   "The Shame of Paula Marsten," The U.S. Steel Hour, CBS, 4.19.61

A young woman (Anne Baxter) suffers a traumatic breakup of her romance with a young man (Mark Richman) that leads her to attempt suicide. Gene Raymond is the psychiatrist who treats her depression.

T12   "A Nice Touch," Alfred Hitchcock Presents, CBS, 10.4.63

A theatrical agent leaves her husband for an ambitious young actor, who already has a girlfriend. CAST: Anne Baxter (Janice Brandt), George Segal (Larry Duke), with Harry Townes and Charlene Holt.

T13   "A Day to Remember," Dr. Kildare, NBC, 4.2.64

Nora Willis is deeply disturbed by the death of her husband. She poses as a volunteer worker to help a fatally stricken, abandoned little boy. Screenplay by Calvin Clements. CAST: Richard Chamberlain (Dr. James Kildare), Raymond Massey (Dr. Gillespie), with Anne Baxter (Nora Willis), Michel Petit (Jerome Sebrell), Yvonne Craig (Carol Devon), and Edith Atwater (Miss Thorton).

T14   "Inescapable Doom Trap," Batman, ABC, 2.9.66

Magician Zelda the Great wreaks havoc on Gotham City in
this two-part episode. CAST: Adam West (Bruce Wayne -
Batman), Burt Ward (Dick Grayson - Robin), Alan Napier
(Alfred Pennyworth), Madge Blake (Aunt Harriet Cooper),
Neil Hamilton (Police Commissioner Gordon), Stafford Repp
(Chief O'Hara), with Anne Baxter (Zelda), Jack Kruschen,
and Barbara Helere.

See: B218, B440

T15   "Zelda Takes the Rap," Batman, ABC, 2.10.66

An evil female magician (Anne Baxter) kidnaps Aunt Harriet.
Second of a two-part episode.

See: T14, B385, B440

T16   "Enter Batgirl, Exit Penguin," Batman, ABC, 9.14.67

Batgirl (Yvonne Craig) joins the Caped Crusaders. She
is kidnapped by the Penguin, who intends to make her his
bride. CAST: Regulars, with Burgess Meredith (the
Penguin), Vincent Price (the Ogg), and Anne Baxter (Zelda).

See: T14, B440

T17   "Search for Survival," Cowboy in Africa, ABC, 10.9.67

Erica Holloway is a pitiless owner of a ranch oasis, who
refuses to offer the natives relief from a draught. CAST:
Chuck Connors (Jim Sinclair), Tom Nardini (John Henry),
Ronald Howard (Wing Cdr. Howard Hayes), Gerald Edwards
(Samson), with Anne Baxter (Erica Holloway) and Izack Field
(Kanya).

NOTE: The series was based on producer Ivan Tors's film
       Africa - Texas Style, shot in Africa (backgrounds)
       and at Africa, U.S.A. Park in southern California.

T18   STRANGER ON THE RUN (Universal Television), NBC, 10.31.67,
       110 Minutes

Producer: Richard E. Lyons. Director: Don Siegel. Writer:
Dean E. Riesner. Photography: Bud Thackery. Editor:
Richard G. Wray. Art Direction: William D. De Cinces. Music:
Leonard Rosenman. Song: Kay Scott (performed by Bill Anderson).
From a story by Reginald Rose.

CAST: Henry Fonda (Ben Chamberlain), Anne Baxter (Valverda
         Johnson), Michael Parks (Vince McKay), Dan Duryea (O.
         E. Hotchkiss), Sal Mineo (George Blaylock), Lloyd
         Bochner (Mr. Gorman), Michael Burns (Matt Johnson),
         Tom Reese (Leo Weed), Bernie Hamilton (Dickory), Madlyn
         Rhue (Alma Britten), Zalman King (Larkin), Walter Burke
         (Berk), Rodolfo Acosta (Mercurio), George Dunn (Pilney,
         and Pepe Hern (Monolo).

SYNOPSIS: Henry Fonda is a drifter who finds himself wrongly
accused of murder by a hostile sheriff (Parks). The sheriff's
posse chases Fonda, first giving him a horse, supplies, and
a one-hour head start in the desert.

NOTE: Ford and Baxter made their television movie debuts
         in this above-average western.

See: B63, B416

T19 "The Ogg and I," Batman, ABC, 11.2.67

     Gothamites are agog when Egghead and Olga kidnap
     Commissioner Gordon and demand an "eggsorbitant" ransom:
     10¢ on every egg eaten in Gotham City. CAST: Regulars,
     with Vincent Price (Egghead) and Anne Baxter (Olga).

     NOTE: This was another first of a two-part episode.

     See: T14, B440

T20 "Designing Woman," My Three Sons, ABC, 11.4.67

     Steve is taken in by an attractive woman. CAST: Fred
     MacMurray (Steve Douglas), Don Grady (Robbie Douglas),
     Stanley Livingston (Chip Douglas), William Demarest (Uncle
     Charley O'Casey), Barry Livingston (Ernie Thompson Douglas),
     Tina Cole (Katie Miller), John Howard (Dave Welch), and
     Anne Baxter.

T21   "How to Hatch a Dinosaur," <u>Batman</u>, ABC, 11.9.67

Egghead schemes to become a crime czar by hatching a
dinosaur egg and feeding the Caped Crusaders to the reptil
CAST: Regulars, with Vincent Price (Egghead), Anne Baxter
(Olga), and Jon Lormer (Professor Dactyl).

See: T14

T22   "The Ogg Couple," <u>Batman</u>, ABC, 12.21.67

Egghead and Olga join forces with the Joker and Catwoman
to continue their evil deeds. CAST: Regulars, with Vince
Price (Egghead), Anne Baxter (Olga), Cesar Romero (the
Joker), and Eartha Kitt (Catwoman).

See: T14

T23   "Measure of a Man," <u>The Danny Thomas Show</u>, CBS, 1.22.68

An illiterate backwoodsman becomes a tool for big city
numbers game players. CAST: Anne Baxter, Bradford Dillma
and Richard Kiley.

T24   "Regions of Peril," <u>The F.B.I.</u>, ABC, 2.25.68

A search is launched for a homicidal robber, who has
kidnapped Katherine Daly and is forcing her to guide him
through the grueling heat of the Arizona desert. CAST:
Efrem Zimbalist, Jr. (Inspector Lewis Erskine), Philip
Abbott (Arthur Ward), William Reynolds (Special Agent Tom
Colby), with Anne Baxter (Katherine Daly), Steve Ihnat
(Frank Padgett), Mark Roberts (Will Channahon), and Arthur
Franz (Joseph Daly).

NOTE: The program, based on real cases, always portrayed
       the agency in a favorable light. Many telecasts
       closed with a short "most wanted" segment. In Apri
       1968, the audience was asked for information on
       the whereabouts of fugitive James Earl Ray, suspect
       assassin of Martin Luther King, Jr.

T25   "Live Among the Meat Eaters," <u>Run for Your Life</u>, NBC,
       3.13.68

On the island of Sardinia, Paul receives mysterious threats
agains his life after joining a group of jetsetters
gathering for a millionairess's seventh wedding. CAST:
Ben Gazzara (Paul Bryan), Anne Baxter (Mona Morrison),
Jacques Bergerac (Alejandro Orsini), Peter Donat (Burton
Wells), and Philip Chapin (Willem).

NOTE: Based on an episode of Kraft Suspense Theater
         telecast in April, 1965, Run for Your Life ran three
         years despite the fact that Paul Ryan had only two
         years to live!

T26   "The Reluctant Redhead," Get Smart, NBC, 4.6.68

Maxwell Smart (Agent 86) trains a rank amateur to pose
as the estranged wife of Kinsey Krispin, who has a list
of all the enemy agents. Krispin will exchange the list
for his wife's return. CAST: Don Adams (Maxwell Smart),
Barbara Feldon (Agent 99), Edward Platt (Chief Thaddeus),
Bernie Kopell (Conrad Siegfried), King Moody (Starker),
Dick Gautier (Hymie the CONTROL Robot), Victor French (Agent
44), Robert Karvelas (Larrabee), Jane Dulo (99's Mother),
with Cesar Romero (Krispin), Julie Sommars (Mimsey), and
Anne Baxter (Mrs. Krispin).

NOTE: The catch-phrase, "Would you believe?" was made
         very popular by Agent 86. During the latter part
         of the series's run, Agents 86 and 99 married and
         became parents of twins (boy and girl).

See: B314

T27   "An Obvious Case of Guilt," Ironside, NBC, 11.14.68

Carolyn White is an old friend of Robert Ironside. She
is suspected of killing her unfaithful husband. Ironside
doggedly refuses to book her and looks beyond the
circumstantial evidence and lack of hard facts to clear
her. CAST: Raymond Burr (Chief Robert Ironside), Don
Galloway (Detective Sgt. Ed Brown), Barbara Anderson (Eve
Whitfield), Don Mitchell (Mark Sanger), Gene Lyons
(Commissioner Dennis Randall), with Anne Baxter (Carolyn
White) and Warren Stevens (District Attorney Chapman).

T28 "The Protector," <u>The Name of the Game</u>, NBC, 11.15.68

The death of an inquisitive reporter forces publisher Glen
Howard to encounter veteran Herman Allison, a political
fanatic, who has organized his own army. The investigatio
reveals a crew that includes an influence-peddling senator
a fading movie star (who likes younger men), a gruff
restaurateur, and another murder victim. CAST: Gene Barr
(Glenn Howard), Cliff Potter (Andy Hill), Susan St. James
(Peggy Maxwell), with Robert Young (Herman Ellison), Anne
Baxter (Magda Blain), Ralph Meeker (Senator Goddard),
Stephen McNally (Albert Lang), and Jeff Morrow
(Dr. Wallace).

NOTE: This series was actually three-in-one, with the
        stars Gene Barry, Anthony Franciosa (as Jeff Dillon
        and Robert Stack featured in their own,
        self-contained episodes. The connection between
        them was Howard Publications, a Los Angeles-based
        publishing empire started by Howard, who confronts
        business and political adversaries. Jeff Dillon
        is an investigative correspondent. Farrell (Robert
        Stack) is a former F.B.I. agent, now editor, who
        fights organized crime. Peggy Maxwell is their
        trusty but kooky secretary, who later became an
        editorial assistant to all three men.

T29 COMPANIONS IN NIGHTMARE (Universal Television), NBC
     11.23.68,   120 Minutes

Producer: Norman Lloyd and John Wallace Hyde. Director: Norman
Lloyd. Writer: Robert L. Joseph. Photography: William
Margulies. Editor: Douglas Stewart. Art direction: Alexander
A. Mayer. Costumes: Burton Miller. Music: Bernard Herrmann.

CAST: Gig Young (Eric Nicholson), Anne Baxter (Carlotta
        Mauridge), Patrick O'Neal (Jeremy Siddack), Dana Wynte
        (Julia Klanton), Leslie Nielsen (Dr. Neesden), Melvyn
        Douglas (Dr. Lawrence Strelson), William Redfield
        (Richard Lyle), Bettye Ackerman (Sara Nicholson), Lou
        Gossett (Lt. Adam McKay), Stacy Harris (Phillip Rootes
        Thomas Bellin (Detective Cort), Greg Mullavey (Man
        in Funeral Parlor), David Fresco (David), Connie Hunte
        (Waitress), and Syl Lamont (Cab Driver).

SYNOPSIS: Melvyn Douglas is a psychiatrist who brings together
handpicked professionals to group therapy, where it is discover
that one of them is a murderer.

NOTE: This television movie was originally titled <u>The Midnight Patient</u>. Melvyn Douglas made his TV movie debut in this film.

See: B416

T30   "Nora," <u>The Virginian</u>, NBC, 12.11.68

A conniving Army wife visits Shiloh ranch with her officer husband, who has been frequently passed over for promotion. Word of an Indian uprising threatens to cut short their visit, but it kindles a scheme by Nora to advance her husband's Army career. CAST: James Drury (The Virginian), John McIntire (Clay Grainger), Jeanette Nolan (Holly Grainger), Ross Elliott (Sheriff Abbott), with Anne Baxter (Nora Carlton), Hugh Beaumont (Major James Carlton), Tim McIntire (Lt. Tim O'Hara), Harry Lauter (Captain Sam Harris), and Ken Renard (Gray Feather).

NOTE: This was the first 90-minute television western series. It was based on the 1902 novel by Owen Wister (<u>The Virginian</u> was also filmed twice as movies). Tim McIntire is the son of John McIntire and Jeanette Nolan.

T31   "The 25 Graves of Midas, <u>The Big Valley</u>, ABC, 2.3.69

The graves belong to 25 men killed in a mine cave-in. The Barkleys own the mine with the town boss, Webb Dutton. The grieving inhabitants vow to take revenge for their tragic loss. CAST: Barbara Stanwyck (Victoria Barkley), Richard Long (Jarrod Barkley), Peter Breck (Nick Barkley), Lee Majors (Heath Barkley), Linda Evans (Audra Barkley), and Napoleon Whiting (Silas), with Anne Baxter (Hannah), Linda Marsh (Nora), Arch Johnson (Webb Dutton), and Kevin Hagen (Jack Case).

See: B142

T32   "The Bobby Currier Story," <u>The Name of the Game</u>, NBC, 2.21.69

This episode featured a story of an indepth examination of raw, untempered violence in the Midwest. Crime reporter Dan Farrell gets to the heart of the story of a young loner, who kidnaps a sheriff's daughter and embarks on a cross country killing spree. CAST: Robert Stack (Dan Farrell), Susan St. James (Peggy Maxwell), with Anne Baxter (Betty Jean Currier), Brandon De Wilde (Bobby Currier), Steve Forrest (Sheriff A. G. Ward), Tisha Sterling (Alice Ward), Julie Harris (Verna Ward), Lonny Chapman (Ralph Currier), and Parley Baer (Doctor).

NOTE: Anne Baxter received an Emmy nomination for her role as the distraught mother of the murdering young man.

See: B287, B288

T33   MARCUS WELBY, M.D. (Universal Television), ABC, 3.26.69, 110 Minutes

Producers: David Victor and David J. O'Connell. Director: David Lowell Rich. Writer: Don M. Mankiewicz. Photography: Russell Metty. Editor: Gene Palmer. Art Direction: George Patrick. Music: Leonard Rosenman.

CAST: Robert Young (Marcus Welby), James Brolin (Steven Kiley), Penny Stanton, later Elena Verdugo (Consuelo Lopez), Anne Baxter (Myra Sherwood), Susan Strasberg (Tina Sawyer), Lew Ayres (Dr. Andrew Swanson), Tom Bosley (Tiny Baker), Peter Deuel (Lew Sawyer), Sheila Larkin (Sandy Welby), Richard Loo (Kenji), Mercer Harri (Ray Wells), with Larry Linville, Ben Wright, Ron Stokes, Allison McKay, Craig Littler, Sheila Rogers, and Fran Ryan.

SYNOPSIS: In this pilot TV movie for a proposed television series (1969-1976), Anne Baxter is the romantic interest of Dr. Welby, who suffers a heart attack and must acquire a younger assistant (Kiley) to ease his workload.

See: B329, B416

T34   "Programmed for Danger," Ironside, NBC, 11.20.69

Undercover cop Eve Whitfield acts as bait to snare an attacker who preys on young blonde women who live alone. He gets his victims through a computer dating service. CAST: Raymond Burr (Ironside), Barbara Anderson (Eve Whitfield), Don Galloway (Ed Brown), with Anne Baxter (Alic Flynn), Roger Perry (Roy Flynn), Herbert Anderson (Jim Saunders), and Dick Walessa (Harry Kane).

T35 "A Time for Lying," Paris 7000, ABC, 1.22.70

U.S. Consulate troubleshooter Jack Brennan investigates
when a distinguished American jurist is accused of fathering
an illegitimate child during World War II. CAST: George
Hamilton (Jack Brennan), Jacques Aubuchon (Jules Maurois),
with Anne Baxter (Estelle), E. G. Marshall (Judge
Banderman), Robert Ellenstein (Pierre), and Pamela McMyler
(Danielle).

NOTE: This episode was the series premiere.

T36 "The Takeover," The Name of the Game, NBC, 1.23.70

Special envoy Glenn Howard gets help from two ladies when
he visits a crisis-torn Asian nation, whose chief of state
allegedly robbed the treasury and disappeared. The ladies
reinforce Howard's suspicions of a frame-up and spark a
probe that sends him into enemy territory. CAST: Gene
Barry (Glenn Howard), with Anne Baxter (Magda), Gloria
Grahame (Madame Noh), David Sheiner (Col. Bander), Michael
Ansara (Ben Kallman), Warren Stevens (Lawrence), David
Opatoshu (Anartha), H. M. Wynant (Col. Mara), Anna Navarro
(Madame Bandar), and Robert Carricart (Kraston).

T37 THE CHALLENGERS (Universal Television), CBS, 2.20.70,
     120 Minutes

Producers: Roy Huggins and Frederick Shorr. Director: Leslie
H. Martinson. Writer: Dick Nelson. Photography: Jack Marta.
Editors: Edward A. Biery and Nick Archer. Art Direction:
John T. McCormack. Costumes: Burton Miller. Music: Pete Rugolo.
From the story by Robert Hammer and John Thomas James.

CAST: Darren McGavin (Jim McCabe), Sean Garrison (Cody
         Scanlon), Nico Minardos (Paco), Anne Baxter (Stephanie
         York), Richard Conte (Ritchie), Farley Granger (Nealy),
         Juliet Mills (Mary McCabe), Sal Mineo (Angel de Angelo),
         Susan Clark (Catherine Burroughs), Michael Evans
         (Jules), John Holland (Ambrose), William Sylvester
         (Brad York), and Alan Caillou (Byron Toomey).

SYNOPSIS: This TV movie focused on racing drivers competing
in the Grand Prix.

NOTE: The film, which was filmed in March, 1968, was to be
         originally broadcast on March 28, 1968. It was

pre-empted because of the death of former President
Dwight D. Eisenhower.

See: B416

T38   RITUAL OF EVIL (Universal Television), NBC, 2.23.70,
      120 Minutes

Producer: David Levinson. Director: Robert Day. Writer: Robert
Presnell, Jr. Photography: Lionel Lindon. Editor: Douglas
Stewart. Art Direction: William D. De Cinces. Music: Billy
Goldenberg. From characters created by Richard Alan Simmons.

CAST: Louis Jourdan (David Sorell), Anne Baxter (Jolene
           Wiley), Diana Hyland (Leila Barton), John McMartin
           (Edward Bolander), Wilfrid Hyde-White (Harry Snowden),
           Belinda J. Montgomery (Loey Wiley), Carla Borelli (Alin
           Wiley), Georg Stanford Brown (Larry Richmond),
           Regis J. Cordic (Sheriff), Dehl Berti (Mora), Richard
           Alan Knox (Hippie), Johnny Williams (Newscaster), Jimmy
           Joyce, and James La Shane (Reporters).

SYNOPSIS: A noted psychiatrist delves into the death of a young
heiress patient (Montgomery).

NOTE: Jourdan and Hyde-White reprise their roles in this
           occult-chiller sequel to Fear No Evil (1969). The
           original title was Next Time, My Love.

See: B416, B441

T39   "Diffusion," Bracken's World, NBC, 3.13.70

      A veteran movie star's vanity causes serious problems for
      her young director. She wants to believe she is still
      young -- even to the detriment of her role. CAST: Eleanor
      Parker (Sylvia Caldwell), Peter Haskell (Kevin Grant),
      Dennis Cole (Davey Evans), Elizabeth Allen (Laura Deane),
      Laraine Stephens (Diane Waring), Linda Harrison (Paulette
      Douglas), Karen Jensen (Rachel Holt), Stephen Oliver (Tom
      Hudson), Jeanne Cooper (Grace Douglas), Gary Dubin (Mark
      Grant), Leslie Nielsen (John Bracken), Bettye Ackerman
      (Ann Frazier), with Anne Baxter (Marian Harper), Don Knight
      (Monty Brooks), Zooey Hal (George Patakis), Fred Sadoll
      (Wally), Olive McGowan (Cari Manning), Barry Coe (Assistant
      Director), Harry Hickox (Electrician), Robert Shayne (Sound
      Mixer), and Alida Ihle (Marian's Secretary).

NOTE: The series was actually filmed at 20th Century-Fox
        Studios.

See: B441

T40 "All the Old Familiar Faces," The Name of the Game, NBC,
     11.13.70

     After receiving death threats, Glenn Howard launches an
     investigation to find out who wants to see him dead (their
     motives are established via flashbacks). CAST: Gene Barry
     (Glenn Howard), Mark Miller (Ross Craig), Susan St. James
     (Peggy Maxwell), with Anne Baxter (Louise Harris), Burgess
     Meredith (Garver), Michael Constantine (Johnson), Lois
     Nettleton (Laura Garver), Stephen McNally (James Andry),
     Frank Maxwell (Lieutenant), and Jonathan Lippe and Lucille
     Meredith.

T41 IF TOMORROW COMES (Aaron Spelling Production), ABC, 12.7.71,
     120 Minutes

Producers: Aaron Spelling and Richard Newton. Director: George
McCowan. Writer: Lew Hunter. Photography: Arch R. Dalzell.
Editor: Art Seid. Art Direction: Paul Sylos. Music: Gil Melle.

CAST: Patty Duke (Eileen Phillips), Frank Michael Liu (David
         Tayaneka), Anne Baxter (Miss Cramer), James Whitmore
         (Frank Phillips), Pat Hingle (Sheriff), Mako (Tadashi),
         John McLiam (Father Miller), Beulah Quo (Midori),
         Richard McGreevy (Harlan Phillips), Kay Stewart (Helen
         Phillips), Bennett Ohta (Hachito), Bert Remsen (Coslow),
         Michael Fox (Judge), Frank Hotchkiss (Lieutenant),
         and Ron Stokes (Corporal).

SYNOPSIS: Just minutes before the announcement that Pearl Harbor
has been bombed on December 7, 1941, a California girl (Duke)
and a Japanese-American boy (Liu) ignore local prejudices and
secretly marry, to the consternation of their parents. Their
only support comes the local school teacher, Miss Cramer
(Baxter).

NOTE: This TV movie was originally titled The Glass Hammer.

See: B149

T42   THE CATCHER, CBS, 6.2.72, 120 Minutes

Producers: Stanley Neufield and Herbert B. Leonard. Director:
Allen H. Miner. Writer: David Freeman. Music: Bill Walker.
Song: Jackie De Shannon.

CAST: Michael Witney (Noah Hendrix), Jan Michael Vincent
         (Sam), Anthony Franciosa (Joe Cade), Catherine Burns
         (Sara), David Wayne (Armand Faber), Mike Kellin (Capt.
         Mike Keller), Anne Baxter (Kate), Kiel Martin (Wes
         Watkins), Jackie De Shannon (Amy Lee), Andrew Robinson
         (Andy), Marshall Efron (Shooting Gallery Attendant),
         Piano Red (Himself), Naomi Thornton (Woman), Jacqueline
         Bertrand (Jewelry Saleslady), David Williams (Young
         Clerk), Eugene Ray Katz (Arcade Manager), Louis
         Criscuolo (Fruit Vendor), Reuben Figueroa (Billy
         Figueroa), Reggie Baff (Car Rental Girl), Rehn Scofield
         (Record Producer), and Kay Mason (Memphis Tourist).

SYNOPSIS: This unsold pilot crime drama featured Witney as
a cop-turned-missing persons investigator, who works for his
friend's newspaper. He searches for a missing co-ed and becomes
involved in a murder.

T43   "Requiem for a Falling Star," Columbo, NBC, 1.21.73

      A fading movie star kills her secretary while trying to
      slay a gossip columnist. She tries to incriminate the
      columnist, but her scheme backfires. CAST: Peter Falk
      (Lt. Columbo), Anne Baxter (Nora Chandler), Mel Ferrer
      (Jerry Parks), Kevin McCarthy (Officer Frank Simmons),
      Frank Converse (Fallon), Pippa Scott (Jean Davis), Sid
      Miller (Director), and William Bryant (Jeffries).

      NOTE: This series was one of the rotating elements on
              the NBC Sunday Mystery Movie. The others were
              McMillan and Wife and McCloud.

T44   "He Who Digs a Grave," Cannon, CBS, 9.12.73

      An old war buddy of heavy-weight private eye Frank Cannon
      is stuck in a small town jail on a double-murder charge.
      CAST: William Conrad (Frank Cannon), with Anne Baxter
      (Helen Blye), David Janssen (Ian Kirk), Barry Sullivan
      (Sheriff Luke), Tim O'Connor (Martin Ross), Martine Bartlet
      (Hannah Friel), Lee Purcell (Marian), Royal Dano

(Dr. Binns), Murray Hamilton (Arthur Gibson), R. G.
Armstrong (Banner), and Dennis Rucker.

NOTE: This episode was filmed on location in Grass Valley,
California.

T45 "All My Tomorrows," Love Story, NBC, 10.10.73

Lee McKinley, a wealthy art patroness, loves Richard Donner,
a struggling pianist, who sees her money as a barrier to
their love. CAST: Susan Anspach (Lee McKinley), Robert
Foxworth (Richard Donner), Anne Baxter (Elaine McKinley),
Barnard Hughes (Andrew Corby), and Bill Quinn (Dr. Wellman),
with John Sebastian.

T46 "If Max is so smart, why doesn't he tell us who he is?"
Banacek, NBC, 11.7.73

Leslie Lyle is the wealthy owner of Max, an electronic
computer with a highly prized medical brain. When Max
disappears from the lab fortified by sensitive alarms and
electric fences, Banacek is called to investigate. CAST:
George Peppard (Thomas Banacek), Ralph Manza (Jay Drury),
Murray Matheson (Felix Mulholland), Christine Belford
(Carlie Kirkland), with Anne Baxter (Leslie Lyle), Paul
Richards (Kenton), Alan Fudge (Howard), Richard Jordan
(Bailey), and Jim Davis (McCKay), plus John Zaremba and
Sabrina Scharf.

NOTE: Originally, this series was aired as one of the
rotating elements of NBC's Wednesday Mystery Movie.

T47 LISA, BRIGHT AND DARK (Universal Television), NBC, 11.28.73,
90 Minutes

Producers: Bob Banner and Tom Egan. Director: Jeannot Szwarc.
Writer: Lionel E. Siegel. Photography: Richard C. Glovner.
Editor: Keith Olson. Music: Rod McKuen. Based on novel based
on fact by John Neufield.

CAST: Kay Lenz (Lisa Schilling), Anne Baxter (Margaret
Schilling), John Forsythe (William Schilling), Debralee
Scott (Mary Nell), Jamie Smith Jackson (Betsy), Anne
Lockhart (Elizabeth), Anson Williams (Brian), with
Erin Moran, Stuart Kistner, Richard Stahl, Jessica
Myerson, and Lawrence Casey.

SYNOPSIS: Friends of a teenager with a "split personality"
try to help her overcome her problems by conducting their own
group therapy sessions.

NOTE: This TV movie was broadcast as a segment of the Hallmark
         Hall of Fame.

T48 "Deadly Madonna," Mannix, CBS, 12.2.73

    After being released from a mental hospital, an actress
    has her sanity questioned once again. She claims a
    grotesque masked man tried to kill her, but there's no
    evidence to show he even exists. CAST: Mike Connors (Joe
    Mannix), Gail Fisher (Peggy Fair), Robert Reed (Lt. Adam
    Tobias), with Anne Baxter (Victoria), Barbara Babcock
    (Janet), Walter Brooke (Baxter), Ned Glass (Nemo), Leonard
    Stone (Seagrave), and Jock Gaynor (Allen).

    NOTE: This series was one of the most violent detective
             shows of its time.

T49 ARTHUR HAILEY'S "THE MONEYCHANGERS," (Paramount Pictures
     Television), NBC Mini-series, 6½ hours, 12.4.76, 12.5.76,
     12.12.76, and 12.19,76

Producers: Ross Hunter, Marvin Miller, and Jacque Mapes.
Director: Boris Sagal. Writers: Dean E. Reisner and Stanford
Whitmore. Photography; Joseph Biroc. Editor: Richard Bracken.
Art Direction: Jack De Shields. Music: Henry Mancini.

CAST: Kirk Douglas (Alex Vandervoort), Christopher Plummer
         (Roscoe Heyward), Anne Baxter (Edwina Dorsey), Ralph
         Bellamy (Jerome Devereaux), Tim Bottoms (Miles Eastin),
         Joan Collins (Avril Devereaxu), Susan Flannery (Margot
         Bracken), Robert Loggia (Tony Bear), Marisa Pavan (Celia
         Vandervoort), Jean Peters (Beatrice Heyward), Percy
         Rodriguez (Nolan Wainwright), Hayden Rorke (Lewis
         Dorsey), James Shigeta (Wizard Wong), Amy Twill (Juanita
         Nunez), Patrick O'Neal (Harold Austin), Lorne Greene
         (George Quartermain), Helen Hayes (Dr. McCartney),
         Roger Bowen (Fergus Gatwick), Douglas Fowley (Danny
         Kerrigan), Basil Hoffman (Stanley Inchbeck), Lincoln
         Kilpatrick (Deacon Euphrates), Leonard Cimino (Ben
         Rosselli), Woodrow Parfrey (Mr. Tottenhoe), Stan Shaw
         (John Dinkerwell), Joseph R. Sincari (Jules La Rocca),
         Nancy Hseuh (Moonbeam), Bing Russell (Timberwell),
         Lynnette Metty (Teller), Virginia Gregg (Miss Callahan)

Jon Lormer (Depositor), Burt Mustin (Jack Henderson), Marla Gibbs (Mrs. Ephrates), Redmond Gleason (Vernon Jax), Miiko Taka (Mom), and Barry Coe (TV Newsman).

SYNOPSIS: This televised bestselling novel is a tale of power and greed in the banking business. Two ambitious vice presidents become rivals when an imminent board room vacancy arises.

NOTE: This mini-series was retitled <u>The Moneychangers</u> when shown in repeat broadcasts.

See: B68, B329

T50 LITTLE MO (Mark VII Ltd., Worldvision Enterprises), NBC, 9.5.78, 120 Minutes

Producers: David Hallet, Jack Webb, and George Sherman. Director: Jack Webb. Writer: John McGreevey. Photography: Harry L. Wolf. Editors: Michael Berman, Bill E. Gant, Doug Hines, Robert L. Swanson. Art Direction: Carl Anderson. Music: Billy May and Carl Brandt.

CAST: Glynnis O'Connor (Maureen Connolly), Michael Learned (Eleanor "Teach" Tennant), Anne Baxter (Jess Connolly), Claude Akins (Gus Berste), Martin Milner (Wilbur Folsom), Anne Francis (Sophie Fisher), Mark Harmon (Norman Brinker), Tony Trabert (Himself), Fred Holliday (Dr. Bruce Kimball), Len Wayland (Johnson), Justin Lord (Maxwell), Maggie Wellman (Susan), Jean Kard (Nancy Shaffee), Susan Partridge (Cindy Brinker), K. C. Keller (Laura Lou Jahn), Tony Gretz (Doris Hart), Stacy Keach, Sr. (Chamber of Commerce President), Beatrice Manley (Duchess of Kent), Tracey Gold (Cindy Brinker), Missy Gold (Missy Brinker).

SYNOPSIS: This is the story of Maureen Connolly, the first woman to win the Grand Slam of tennis twice. Anne Baxter is her mother, and Michael Learned is Mo's beloved instructor. Together they witness Mo's rise to fame and her personal tragedy: she died of cancer at age 34.

NOTE: Anne was very effective in her role as Mo's mother. Anne replaced Lana Turner, who was originally slated for the part.

See: B446, B455

T51 NERO WOLFE (Paramount Pictures TV), ABC, 12.19.79,
     120 Minutes

Producers: Emmett Lavery, Jr., and Everett Chambers. Director:
Frank D. Gilroy. Writer: Frank D. Gilroy. Photography: Ric
Waite. Editor: Harry Keller. Art Direction: John Beckman.
Music: Leonard Rosenman. Based on the novel The Doorbell Rang
by Rex Stout.

CAST: Thayer David (Nero Wolfe), Tom Mason (Archie Goodwin)
          Anne Baxter (Rachel Bruner), Brooke Adams (Sarah
          Dacos), Bill McGuire (Inspector Cramer), Sarah
          Cunningham (Mrs. Athaus), John Randolph (Lou Cohen),
          David Hurst (Fritz), Allen Case (Agent Fredericks),
          with John Hoyt, John O'Leary, Frank Campanella, Jim
          Gerstead, Robert Phalen, Davis Lewis, Sam Weisman,
          and Katherine Charles.

SYNOPSIS: Gourmet, orchid-tending, private investigator Nero
Wolfe is enmeshed in a puzzling murder mystery after escaping
the case of a woman tycoon (Anne Baxter), who wants to know
why she's being investigated by the F.B.I.

See: B329

T52 JOHN STEINBECK'S EAST OF EDEN, ABC, 8-hour Mini-series,
     2.8.81, 2.9.81, and 2.11.81

Producers: Mace Neufeld, Barney Rosenzweig, and Ken Wales.
Director: Harvey Hart. Writer: Richard A. Shapiro. Photography
Frank Stanley. Editors: Michael Brown and Bill Brame. Art
Direction: Kim Swados and Ray Storey. Music: Lee Holdridge.
From the novel by John Steinbeck.

CAST: Timothy Bottoms (Adam Trask), Jane Seymour (Cathy/Kate
          Adams), Bruce Boxleitner (Charles Trask), Soon-Teck
          Oh (Lee), Karen Allen (Abra), Hart Bochner (Aaron
          Trask), Sam Bottoms (Cal Trask), Warren Oates (Cyrus
          Trask), Howard Duff (Jules Edwards), Anne Baxter
          (Faye), Richard Masur (Will Hamilton), Nicholas Pryor
          (James Grew), Lloyd Bridges (Samuel Hamilton), Nellie
          Bellflower (Mrs. Trask), M. Emmett Walsh (Sheriff
          Horace Quinn), Vernon Weddle (Bill Ames), Grace
          Zabriskie (Mrs. Ames), Stymie Beard (Cotton Eye),
          Wendell Burton (Tom Hamilton), Timothy Agoglia Carey
          (Preacher), with Walter Brooke, Fredric Cook, John
          Michael Johnson, Harry Lewis, Bret Williams, Brian

Ann Zoccola, Buck Taylor, Peter Maloney, and Paul
Harper.

SYNOPSIS: This is the indepth television mini-series exploration
of John Steinbeck's classic story of the Trask family and the
women who haunted their lives for two generations. Anne Baxter
is Faye, an aging bordello proprietress. Evil-minded Cathy
deserts her twin sons and husband, leaves town, and gains
ownership of Faye's establishment by forcing her to drink gin
until she dies. Years later, when her sons learn of her
whereabouts and try to regain their family ties, she rejects
them.

NOTE: Emmy nominations were conferred for Outstanding Limited
         Series, Photography, Art Direction (Award), and Set
         Decoration (Award). This mini-series was later titled
         East of Eden when shown in repeat broadcasts.

T53 The Dean Martin Celebrity Roast, NBC, 2.23.84

     This honorary "roast" of actress Joan Collins was hosted
     by Dean Martin. Executive Producer: Greg Garrison.
     Producer: Lee Hale. Director: Greg Garrison. Writers:
     Bill Box, Sol Weinstein, Howard Albrecht, Greg Garrison,
     Jay Burton, and Tom Waldron.

CAST: Dean Martin, Joan Collins, Milton Berle, Beatrice
         Arthur, Anne Baxter, Red Buttons, Dom DeLuise, Angie
         Dickinson, Phyllis Diller, John Forsythe, Zsa Zsa
         Gabor, Rich Little, Gavin MacLeod, and Don Rickles.

T54 Hotel, ABC, First Telecast: 9.21.83. Second Season:
     9.26.84. Third Season: 9.25.85.

     The St. Gregory Hotel in San Fancisco is the elegant
     setting for romance, drama, and occasional comedic episodes
     of this television series that featured different guest
     stars each week in stories that ended happily. Victoria
     Cabot (Anne Baxter) is a wealthy aristocrat, who takes
     over the operation of the hotel on behalf of her ill sister-
     in-law, Laura Trent. Peter McDermott (James Brolin), is
     the bearded, suave general manager. Christine Francis
     (Connie Selleca) is McDermott's assistant and love interest.
     Mark Danning (Shea Farrell) is the public relations
     director. Billy Griffin (Nathan Cook) is a black ex-convict
     hired to be the hotel's new security director. Julie
     Gillette (Shari Belafonte-Harper) is in charge of the
     information center. Newlyweds Dave Kendall (Michael Spound)

and Megan Kendall (Heidi Bohay) are the bellhop and desk clerk, respectively.

NOTE: The series was loosely based on Arthur Hailey's bestselling novel. The model for the series hotel was the real San Francisco Fairmont Hotel on Nob Hill. Its imposing facade was seen in exterior shots. The giant lobby was re-created on a Hollywood sound stage.

Anne Baxter replaced Bette Davis, who was original. to appear as the proprietress of the hotel. When Anne died in 1985, during the 1985-1986 season, her character died also. It was then revealed that Victoria's half-interest in the hotel was given to Peter McDermott.

Real-life co-stars Spound and Bohay married and left the series. Their story line had them exit the show by having them finally find success together to make it on their own after he graduated from law school.

See: B26, B139, B273-274, B279, B327-329, B458, B489, B492-493

T55   Hollywood Stars' Screen Tests, NBC, 10.5.84

This variety special spotlighted the never-before-seen screen tests of famous movie stars. CAST: George Peppard (Host), Anne Baxter, Morgan Brittany, Jane Russell, Pia Lindstrom, Imogene Coca, and Byron Allen.

T56   Night of 100 Stars II, NBC, 3.10.85

This special featured 100 movie and television entertainers and was presented on Sunday evening, February 17, 1985; however, it was televised on Sunday, March 10, 1985. It was written and produced by Hildy Parks and presented by Alexander H. Cohen and Bentwood Television Productions. The show was a benefit for the Actors' Fund of America. It included film segments and musical tributes to stars of the past and present. The participants marched on stage one-by-one, escorted by dancers.

Radio Productions

Movie stars were very popular as guest on the many radio shows that greeted the airwaves before the advent of television. Performances of new plays, scenes from currently released films, skills that focused on down-home comedy, and interviews brought these entertainers into the nation's homes on a regular basis. Anne Baxter appeared as a guest on the following radio shows, listed in chronological order.

R1 "Dead End," <u>Theaetre Guild on the Air</u>, CBS, a play, starring Anne Baxter and Richard Conte, 1943

    See: B418

R2 "Five Graves to Cairo," <u>Lux Radio Theatre of the Air</u>, CBS, starring Anne Baxter and Franchot Tone, who recreated their film roles, 12.13.43

    See: B107, B418

R3 "The Ghost Goes West," <u>The Ronald Colman Show</u>, sponsored by Electric Auto Lite, a radio play, 3.14.44

R4 Guest on <u>Chase and Sanborn's The Edgar Bergen Show</u>, sponsored by Standard Brands, 9.24.44

R5 "Nothing But the Truth," <u>Comedy Theatre</u>, a radio play by P. Lorillard, 1.14.14

R6   Guest on <u>Chase and Sanborn's The Edgar Bergen Show</u>,
     sponsored by Standard Brands, originating from
     Victorville Army Air Base in Victorville, California,
     3.4.45

R7   "My Wayward Parents," <u>Cavalcade of America</u>, a radio play,
     starring Anne Baxter and Brian Donlevy, 4.2.45

R8   Guest on <u>Bill Stern Sports</u>, sponsored by Colgate Palmolive
     Peet, 6.1.45

R9   Guest on <u>Adelaide Hawley</u>, making war bond plea, 6.4.45

R10 Guest on <u>Chase and Sanborn's The Charlie McCarthy Show</u>,
     sponsored by Standard Brands, starring Edgar Bergen,
     Ray Noble, Anne Baxter, and Keenan Wynn, 9.23.45

R11 "Angel Street," <u>Theater of Romance</u>, CBS, a radio play,
     starring Anne Baxter, Vincent Price, Sir Cedric
     Hardwicke, 10.9.45

R12 Guest on <u>Chase and Sanborn's The Charlie McCarthy Show</u>,
     sponsored by Standard Brands, 9.8.46

R13 Guest on <u>The Drene Show</u>, sponsored by Procter and Gamble,
     11.3.46

R14 Guest on <u>Kraft Music Hall</u>, sponsored by Kraft Food
     Company, 1.23.47

R15 "A Tree Grows in Brooklyn," <u>Screen Guild Theatre</u>, a radio
     adaptation of the film, starring Anne Baxter, 3.10.47

R16 Guest on <u>Chase and Sanborn's The Charlie McCarthy Show</u>,
     sponsored by Standard Brands, 3.23.47

R17   "Frontier Widow," Cavalcade of America, sponsored by
          DuPont, starring Anne Baxter, as Anne Robertson
          Johnston, a radio play, 4.28.47

R18   "Apartment for Peggy," Truth or Consequences, sponsored
          by Procter and Gamble, where Anne Baxter appeared
          in front of a Los Angeles apartment house for the
          premiere of the film Apartment of Peggy, 10.2.48

R19   Guest on Dewey-Warren Bandwagon, sponsored by Dewey-
          Warren Clubs of America, 11.1.48

R20   "You're My Everything," Camel Screen Guild Theatre,
          sponsored by R. J. Reynolds, starring Anne Baxter
          and Dan Dailey, in scenes from their film You're My
          Everything, 1.5.50 and 6.29.50

      See: B40, B85, B119, B237, B256, B264, B318, B336, B375,
          B464, B465, B489, B509, F24

R21   "Yellow Sky" and "A Letter to Three Wives," Screen
          Writer's Guild Annual Award Show, sponsored by Screen
          Writers, starring Anne Baxter in scenes from her movie
          Yellow Sky and recent release A Letter to Three Wives,
          2.5.50

      See: B80, B84, B118, B151, B179, B183, B208, B255, B286,
          B317, B337, B419, B464, B497, B518, F23

R22   Guest of honor on The Anacin Hollywood Star Theatre,
          sponsored by American Home Products, 2.18.50

R23   "House of Strangers," Lux Radio Theatre of the Air, CBS,
          starring Richard Conte and Anne Baxter, 10.16.50

R24   "Seventh Veil," Screen Guild Theatre, starring Anne
          Baxter and Van Heflin, 12.14.50

R25   "Morning Glory," The Theatre Guild on the Air,
          sponsored by U.S. Steel Corporation, starring Anne
          Baxter, as Eva Lovelace, in a radio play, 1.28.51

R26   "The Walls of Jericho," <u>Hedda Hopper</u>, starring Anne
           Baxter in a scene from her recently released film
           <u>The Walls of Jericho</u>, 2.18.51

       See: B82, B374, B408, B409, B448, B488, F21

R27   "All About Eve," <u>Screen Guild Theatre</u>, starring Anne
           Baxter, Bette Davis, and George Sanders, reprising
           their roles from their new film <u>All About Eve</u>, 3.8.51

       See: F26 and Index for detailed listing

R28   "The Thirteenth Sound," <u>Suspense</u>, a radio play, 4.26.51

R29   "The Death of Barbara Allen," <u>Suspense</u>, a radio play,
           10.20.52

R30   "Trial by Forgery," <u>Theater Guild on the Air</u>, sponsored
           by U.S. Steel Corporation, starring Anne Baxter, as
           Hannah, a radio play, 1.18.53

R31   Guest on <u>The Oscar Awards</u>, RCA and SUS, where Anne Baxter
           presented the honorary award for Scientific and
           Technical Achievement, from Hollywood, 3.19.53

R32   Guest on <u>The Bob Hope Show</u>, sponsored by General Foods,
           4.1.53

R33   Guest on <u>The Martin and Lewis Show</u>, sponsored by Liggett
           and Myers, 5.5.53

R34   "Friend to Friend," <u>American Red Cross</u>, taped from
           Hollywood, dealing with Greek islands stricken by
           a devastating earthquake and appeals for disaster
           relief funds. Anne Baxter appeared in a skit as
           Helene, sister of Bishop George Maudakas, 9.14.53

R35   Guest on <u>The Bob Hope Show</u>, sponsored by the American
           Dairy Association, 10.16.53

R36   "Swamp Water," Playhouse 25, for American Forces Radio
        Television Services only, starring Anne Baxter and
        Dana Andrews in a scene from the film Swamp Water,
        1974

      See: B221, B471, F4

R37   "The Plow and the Candle," Playhouse 25, for American
        Forces Radio and Television Services only, starring
        Anne Baxter, 1975

Musical Recordings/Soundtracks

M1   THE TEN COMMANDMENTS

Composer: Elmer Bernstein

DOT (M) DLP-3054-D, 1956
DOT (S) DLP-25054-D*
United Artists (S) UAS-6495, 1956
United Artists (S), UA-LA304-G

> *The stereo LP differs from the original mono in that
> it was completely re-recorded especially for this
> album.

See: F38

M2   A WALK ON THE WILD SIDE

Composer-Conductor: Elmer Bernstein

Choreo (M) A-4ST, 1962
Choreo (S) AS-4-ST
Ava (M) AS-4-ST, 1962
AVA (S), AS-4-ST
Mainstream (M) 56083, 1962
Mainstream (S) 56083

There were some issues in a Choreo jacket that had the
Ava label.

See: F43

M3   APPLAUSE

Composer: Charles Strousse and Lee Adams
Conductor: Donald Pippin
Cast: Lauren Bacall, Len Cariou, and Robert Mandan

Original Cast ABC(S)OCA-11, 1970
Original Cast Reissue MCA(S)-OC-11, 1970

See: S12

Stage Plays

   Anne Baxter made her stage debut at the tender age of 13,
appearing on Broadway. Throughout her long acting career, she
returned to the stage in a variety of roles. This chapter
presents those plays in which she appeared.

S1   SEEN BUT NOT HEARD

   Debuted at the Henry Miller Theater, New York, 9.17.36
   Run: 60 performances

   Playwrights: Marie Baumer and Martin Berkeley.

   CAST: Frankie Thomas, Paul McGrath, Kent Smith, Eleanor
           Phelps, and Anne Baxter (as Elizabeth Winthrop).

   SYNOPSIS: This play was a murder mystery.

   REVIEWS:
   New York Times, 9.18.36: This melodrama features the cast
   stars "and a good many others, adult and younger than
   adult."

   Variety, 9.18.36: Anne Baxter is a "cute kidlet."

   See: B47, B54, B294, B319

S2   THERE'S ALWAYS A BREEZE

   Debuted at the Windsor Theatre, New York City, 3.2.38

Producers: Joseph M. Hyman and Irving Cooper. Director:
Harry Wagstaff Gribble. Playwright: Edward Caulfield.
Setting: Frederick B. Fox.

CAST: Leslie Barrett (Tommy Hammond), Anne Baxter (Lita
         Hammond), Cecilia Loftus (Mrs. Weatherby), Blanche
         Sweet (Carrie Hammon), Leona Powers (Julia
         Weatherby), Curtis Cooksey (Oscar Jarvis), William
         Lynn (Ernest Hammond), Sara Floyd (Miss Walsh),
         George Volk (First Detective), Boris de Vadetzky
         (Second Detective), Otto Hulett (Harold O'Brien),
         Hume Cronyn (Abe Sherman), Herbert Duffy (Inspector
         Martin), Gordon Nelson (Assistant District Attorney
         Roberts), Jeanne Hart (Lilly Jerome), Alexander
         Campbell (Mr. Buckman), and Rena Mitchell (Maria).

SYNOPSIS: This three-act play tells of Mr. Hammond, a
"Caspar Milquetoast" bank teller, who gets a reprieve from
his cage by confessing to a murder. Even though he gets
entangled with a glamorous actress and is jailed, he cannot
convince anyone, including the authorities, that he is
the guilty party. His family write stories of their lives
and testimonials pour in on his behalf. For a time,
Mr. Milquetoast is a big-shot hero.

REVIEW:
New York Times, 3.3.38: "To play it, the Messrs.
Joseph M. Hyman and Irving Cooper have assembled a cast
considerably better than the script. On the left: William
Lynn, the best Caspar in the business. Next to Mr. Lynn:
Cecilia Loftus, the best scattered, grandmotherly alcoholic
in the business. On the right: Blanche Sweet, Curtis
Cooksey, Otto Hulett and the rest, all fighting for a cause
lost in the shuffling of paper. A poor play."

See: B54, B163, B389

S3   MADAME CAPET

Debuted at the Cort Theatre, New York City, 10.25.38

Producer: Eddie Dowling. Director: Jose Ruben. Playwright:
Marcelle Maurette. Adaptation: George Middleton. Sets:
Watson Barratt. Costumes: Helene Pons. Music: Lehman
Engel.

CAST: Eva Le Gallienne (Marie Antoinette), Staats
         Cotsworth (Count de Vaudreuil), George Coulouris

(Mirabeau), Marian Eversen (Madame Elizabeth),
Anne Baxter (Rosalie), Alice John (Madame de
Misery), and Merle Maddern (Madame Brunier).

SYNOPSIS: The Reign of Terror in France is the setting
of this biographical drama, staging the last days of Marie
Antoinette. At the onset, she is reckless and happy, living
in ornate style at Versailles in 1777. She refuses her
loyal brother's anxious counsel and indulges in the luxury
of the court. However, Marie is taken as a political
prisoner and sentenced to die by the fanatical president
of the tribunal, who wishes to overthrow the royal ruler.
As she is led to the guillotine, her strength and resolute
character emerge. Anne Baxter is one of Marie Antoinette's
handmaidens.

REVIEW:
New York Times, 10.26.38: "Some good actors help to trace
the changing colors of this biography. Miss Le Gallienne
plays the 'serene Queen with a clear, submissive voice.'
It is a pity that the play as a whole does not make a more
searching use of a daughter of political doom."

NOTE: Miss Le Gallienne returned to the stage following
         a two-year absence. She coveted the role after
         seeing the play in Paris. She wore elaborate
         costumes beautifully. The play, termed "a court
         calendar drama," consisted of panels of scenes.

See: B28, B54, B163, B445

S4   SUSAN AND GOD

Summer, 1938, Cape Playhouse, Dennis, Massachusetts

S5   SPRING MEETING

Summer, 1939, Cape Playhouse, Dennis, Massachusetts

S6   JOHN BROWN'S BODY

Debuted at the Santa Barbara Lobero Theatre, Santa Barbara,
California, 11.1.52

Producer: Charles Laughton. Director: Charles Laughton.
Based on the epic poem by Stephen Vincent Benet.

CAST: Raymond Massey, Tyrone Power, Judith Anderson,
          Anne Baxter (second tour), and John Hodiak.

SYNOPSIS: This national road tour was informally staged
to adapt to any milieu. Benet's epic poem deals with eve
of the Civil War and includes narrations of the "Harper
Ferry Raid," the trial of John Brown and his group of
rebels, "John Brown's Soliloquy," the "Lincoln Sequence,"
and two passages on Robert E. Lee.

NOTE: The first tour ended after 80 performances. The
          second tour, in which Anne Baxter replaced Judith
          Anderson, began in the fall of 1953, and ran for
          another 80 performances.

See: B303, B319, B333

S7   THE SQUARE ROOT OF WONDERFUL

Debuted at the National Theatre, New York City, 10.30.57,
Closed 12.7.57, after 45 performances

Producer: Saint Subber and Figaro, Inc. Director: George
Keathley. Playwright: Carson McCullers. Scenery and
Lighting: Jo Mielziner. Costumes: Noel Taylor. General
Manager: C. Edwin Knill. Company Manager: George Oshrin.
Press: Dorothy Ross. Stage Managers: John Maxtone-Graham
and John Connolly.

CAST: Kevin Coughlin (Paris Lovejoy), Anne Baxter (Moll.
          Lovejoy), Philip Abbott (John Tucker), Martine
          Bartlett (Loreena Lovejoy), Jean Dixon (Mother
          Lovejoy), William Smithers (Philip Lovejoy), Kipp;
          Campbell (Joey Barnes), with understudies Carol
          Grace (Mollie and Loreena) and Kippy Campbell
          (Paris).

SYNOPSIS: This is a love story in three acts, taking plac
on an apple farm in Rockland County, New York, in early
spring. Mollie is a naive young woman, twice divorced
from an irascible, half-mad writer. His mother is
tyrannically obsessive of her son and has illusions of
grandeur about his writing abilities. She also has very
odd ideas about what is proper in "good society." The
problem is that Mollie has fallen in love with an architec
(Abbott).

REVIEW:
New York Times, 10.31.57: "Anne Baxter, as sweet-looking
as ice cream and peach pie, plays the part of the naive
woman with charm and good humor." However, "the characters
are hardly indistinguishable from inhabitants of the
conventional comedy of manners. Very little of
Mrs. McCullers's odd genius has gotten into the fabric
of this frail, delicate, though listless, play."

NOTE: This was Carson McCullers's second play, set in
          a plausible territory. She was a stylist, who
          evoked strange images from ordinary situations,
          making the familiar "other-worldly."

See: B54, B163

S8   THE JOSHUA TREE

Debuted at the Duke of York Theatre, London, 7.9.58
Run: 5 months

Producer: Alec Coppel.

Anne Baxter appears as Louise Shaeffer.

S9   APPLAUSE

Debuted at the Palace Theatre, New York City, 3.30.70
Closed 7.27.72, after 900 performances

Producers: Joseph Kipness and Lawrence Kasha, in association
with Nederlander Productions and George M. Steinbrenner
III. Director-Choreographer: Ron Field. Scenery: Robert
Randolph. Costumes: Ray Aghanyan. Lighting: Tharon Musser.
Musical Direction-Vocal Arrangements: Donald Pippin.
Orchestrations: Philip J. Lang. Dance and Incidental Music
Arrangements: Mel Marvin. Music: Charles Strouse. Lyrics:
Lee Adams. Based on the book by Betty Comden and Adolph
Green. Based on the film All About Eve and original short
story by Mary Orr.

CAST: John Anania (Tony Announcer and Peter), Alan King
          (Tony Host), Anne Baxter (Margo Channing), Janice
          Lynde (Eve Harrington), Lawrence Weber (Howard
          Benedict), Tom Urich (Bert), Brandon Maggart (Buzz
          Richards), Keith Charles (Bill Sampson), Tom Rolla
          (Duane Fox), Peggy Hagan (Karen Richards), Jerry

Wyatt (Bartender), Gene Aguirre (Dancer in Bar),
John Herbert (Bob), Joseph Neal (Piano Player),
Ray Becker (Stan Harding), Bonnie Franklin (Bonnie)
Kathleen Robey (Carol), John Medeiros (Joey), with
Gene Kelton, Nat Horne, and David Anderson
(Musicians).

SYNOPSIS: This two-act (16 scenes) play, set in New York
City, is based on the 1950 classic film All About Eve.
Margo Channing is an aging actress, who is the victim of
a usurping ingenue, Eve Harrington. Margo accepts young
Eve into her entourage and witnesses Eve's rise to stardom
at her expense.

REVIEW:
New York Times, 3.31.70: "The cast as a whole was superior
the look of the show proved sweet and glossy."

NOTE: Anne Baxter replaced Lauren Bacall in the role
         of Margo Channing on July 19, 1971.

See: B467, B487, M3

S10   NOEL COWARD IN TWO KEYS

Debuted at the Ethel Barrymore Theatre, New York City,
2.17.74
Closed 6.29.74 after 140 performances and 4 previews.
Reopened at the Playhouse in Wilmington, Delaware,
2.17.75
Closed 8.2.75

Producers: Richard Barr and Charles Woodward. Director:
Vivian Matalon. Setting and Lighting: William Ritman.
Costumes: Ray Diffen. Hairstylist: Ray Iagnocco. Wardrobe
Sophie Fields. From plays by Noel Coward.

"Come into the Garden, Maude"

CAST: Jessica Tandy (Anna-Mary Conklin), Hume Cronyn
         (Verner Conklin), Anne Baxter (Maude Caragnani),
         Thom Christopher (Felix, the Waiter).

SYNOPSIS: Cronyn is an American millionaire who takes
his temperamental, social-climbing wife to Europe, where
she becomes even more unbearable. While in Switzerland,
she unceremoniously orders him to leave after a disastrous
dinner party. He leaves and meets friendly, recently

divorced Princess Maude, who has no qualms about conducting a tryst with the downtrodden husband.

"A Song at Twilight"

CAST: Jessica Tandy (Hilde Latymer), Hume Cronyn (Hugo
         Latymer), Anne Baxter (Carlotta Gray), and Thom
         Christopher (Felix, the Waiter).

SYNOPSIS: This longer play is about a recently knighted,
aging author whose celebrity doesn't save him from now
revealing his homosexuality. Anne is a not-so-famous
actress who would like to use him in her memoirs.

STANDBY CAST MEMBERS: For both plays, Shepperd Strudwick,
         for Hume Cronyn; Jan Farrand, for Miss Tandy and
         Miss Baxter; and Joel Parks, for Thom Christopher.

REVIEWS:
Los Angeles Times, 6.29.75: "Anne Baxter tried to soften
her accent as the princess, so as not to let the audience
think, 'Isn't Anne Baxter putting on the dog?'"

Los Angeles Times, 7.2.75: "Miss Baxter suggests an aging
actress who has done her best to preserve her beauty but
is about to say the hell with it. Her vocal patterns also
evoke, ever so delicately, the fine lunge of a Tallulah
Bankhead."

NOTE: The novelist in the play "A Song at Twilight" is
         loosely based on friend and fellow author W.
         Somerset Maugham, with whom Coward had a falling
         out later in life. The play was inspired by the
         meeting of Max Beerbohm with his one-time lady
         friend and love, Constance Collier, when they were
         both in their seventies.

See: B140, B313, B475

S11 CAUSE CELEBRE

Debuted at the Ahmanson Theatre, Los Angeles, California,
10.12.79
Closed 5.31.80.

Producer: Terence Rattigan. Director: George Keathley.
Setting: David Emmons. Costumes: Noel Taylor. Lighting:

Martin Aronstein. Music: Robert Prince. Technical
Supervisor: Robert Rourolo. Sound: William Young.

CAST: Anne Baxter (Alma), Dorothy McGuire (Edith), Willi
         Roerick (O'Connor), Jack Gwillim (Judge), Jeanette
         Landis (Joan), Tom Covert-Nolan (George), John
         Eames (Francis), Ian Abercrombie (Coronore), Val
         Bettin (Croom-Johnson), Chad Christian Cowgill
         (Christopher), Joshua Daniel (Randolph), Kate
         Fitzmaurice (Irene), Patricia Fraser (Stella),
         James Charles-Garrett (Court Clerk), Daniel Grace
         (Sgt. Bagwell), Wiley Harker (Caswell), Charles
         Nicklin (Montagu), and Eric Williams (Tony).

SYNOPSIS: This courtroom drama centers around the guilt
or innocence of a middle-aged woman and her teenaged lover
who assisted in the demise of her impotent husband. Dorot
McGuire is the jury forewoman, who also has troubles with
her teenaged son, whose father takes him to nightclubs.
Gwillim is the judge, Bettin is the chief proesecutor,
Fitzmaurice is Baxter's best friend, and Fraser is McGuire
snobby sister.

REVIEW:
Los Angeles Times, 10.13.79: Although Anne Baxter is
"posey," she is quite watchable in a warm way. "She's
a love."

See: B474

S12 HAMLET

Debuted at the American Shakespeare Theatre in Stratford,
Connecticut, 8.3.82

Executive Director: Roger Sherman. Director: Peter Coe.
Playwright: William Shakespeare. Sets/Costumes: David
Chapman. Lighting: Marc B. Weiss. Music: Joe Griffiths.

CAST: Michael Allinson (Ghost/Player King), Anne Baxter
         (Queen Gertrude), Roy Dotrice (Polonius), Fred
         Gwynne (King Claudius), Chris Sarandon (Laertes),
         Christopher Walken (Hamlet), Norman Allen
         (Lucianus), Lisabeth Bartlett (Ophelia), Chet Carl
         (Osric), Patrick Clear (Fortinbras), Sophie
         Gilmartin (Harpist), Michael Guido (Guildenstern),
         Stephen Lang (Horatio), Joel Leffert (First

Soldier), Matt Mulhern (Second Soldier), Scott
Rhyne (Third Soldier), Gary Roberts (Fourth
Soldier), Brian Rose (King Mime/Bernardo), David
Sabin (Marcellus), Sylvia Short (Understudy), Fritz
Sperberg (Rosencrantz), Karen Trott (Player Queen),
and John Wojda (Fifth Soldier).

SYNOPSIS: Anne Baxter is Queen Gertrude, completely
dependent and not very bright, who has strong maternal
longings for children since she lost a baby girl at age
six months. She later does have a son (Walken), who becomes
king after his father's death. The melancholy Hamlet
discovers from his ghostly father that his Uncle Claudius
murdered his father and married his mother. The ghost
demands that Hamlet seek revenge, which causes Hamlet a
distressing dilemma. He knows killing is against God's
will, but he also knows he must obey his father. Hamlet
laments in the soliloquy "To be or not to be." His
indecision causes him to take his angry feelings out on
Ophelia, the woman he loves. He also betrays his friends
and they are slain. In the end, he challenges his uncle
to a sword fight. As he kills his uncle, his uncle's
poison-tipped epee pierces his chest and he dies, too.

REVIEW:
New York Times, 8.4.82: On Anne's portrayal of Gertrude,
the critic wrote, "Her queen is completely independent."

NOTE: Just a couple of days before she was to make her
         Shakespearean theater debut, Anne fell and broke
         her ankle. She appeared in a walking cast
         throughout the play's run.

See: B103, B370

Bibliography

The following annotated bibliography consists of summarized citations from books, newspapers, and periodicals (using the prefix B). Additionally, unannotated articles from books, newspapers, and periodicals are listed separately (using the prefix UB).

B1   Aaronson, Charles. <u>The International Television Almanac</u>. Quigley Publications. New York. 1960.

Featured is a short biography on actress Anne Baxter.

B2   Adair, Gilbert. "Moving Picture Review." <u>Film Comment</u>. November-December, 1980.

Anne Baxter is featured in the review of <u>Jane Austen in Manhattan</u>.

See: F50

B3   Affron, Charles. <u>Star Acting: Gish, Garbo, Davis</u>. Dutton Books. New York. 1977.

The author provides an indepth critique of the film <u>All About Eve</u>.

See: F26

B4   Agee, James. <u>Agee on Film</u>. Grosset and Dunlap. New York.
         1969.

Anne Baxter is mentioned in the recap of the film <u>North
Star</u>.

See: F9

B5   _____. "Films." <u>The Nation</u>. 6.3.44.

In <u>The Eve of St. Mark</u>, the suffering of wartime love is
conveyed in gentle glimmers by the sweetheart (Anne Baxter)
and her drafted hero (William Eythe).

See: F10

B6   _____. "Films." <u>The Nation</u>. 1.27.45.

Anne Baxter hated, feared, and understood the girl she
portrayed in <u>Guest in the House</u>. The writing gave her
a chance to get to know the character and communicate her
to the audience.

See: F13

B7   _____. "Films." <u>The Nation</u>. 2.3.45.

Most of the performers in <u>Sunday Dinner for a Soldier</u> seem
to have loved appearing in the film, believed in it, and
had great hopes for its originality and worthiness. One
of the ads for the film says of star John Hodiak's romance
with co-star Anne Baxter, "Their eyes met! Their lips
questioned!   Their arms answered."

See: F12

B8   Agin, Patrick. <u>The Decline and Fall of the Love Goddesses</u>
         Pinnacle Books. Los Angeles, California. 1979.

Betty Grable was considered for the heavy, dramatic role
in <u>The Razor's Edge</u>. She knew what the public wanted of
her ("People would have expected me to come on like a
chorus."). She starred in <u>Mother Wore Tights</u>, for which
Anne Baxter did the narration. Anne co-starred with

beautiful Linda Darnell in <u>The Walls of Jericho</u>. Marilyn
Monroe held her own against Anne Baxter and Bette Davis
in <u>All About Eve</u>. Also mentioned were the films <u>A Ticket
to Tomahawk</u>, which featured Marilyn Monroe in a small role,
and <u>O. Henry's Full House</u>.

See: F17, F19, F21, F25, F26, F30

B9   "All About Anne Baxter." <u>Photoplay</u>. September, 1943.

Rising dramatic actress Anne Baxter is featured in this
article.

B10   Alpert, Hollis. "The Case of Joseph L. Mankiewicz."
        <u>Saturday Review</u>. 10.21.50.

In <u>All About Eve</u>, Anne Baxter has the hardest acting job
in order to convince the audience she is as conniving as
she comes across, since her character is so transparent.

See: F26

B11   _____. "The Star Behind the Camera." <u>Saturday Review</u>.
        2.21.53.

Anne Baxter lends excellent support in her role of the
priest's young sweetheart and later suspect in a murder
mystery in <u>I Confess</u>.

See: F32

B12   Alvarez, Max Joseph. <u>Index to Motion Pictures Reviewed
        by Variety, 1907-1980</u>. The Scarecrow Press, Inc.
        Metuchen, New Jersey, and London. 1982.

All of Anne Baxter's films are reviewed by <u>Variety</u> magazine,
except <u>The Tall Women</u> and <u>Lapin 300</u>. <u>The Tall Women</u> had
a short-lived release in the United States. <u>Lapin 300</u>
was not released.

See: F46

B13   Anger, Kenneth. <u>Hollywood Babylon II</u>. E. P. Dutton,
       Inc. New York. 1984.

       Barbara Bates (as Phoebe) appeared in the last important
       scene in <u>All About Eve</u>, as the ambitious girl who
       ingratiates herself with Eve (Anne Baxter). Bates killed
       herself on March 18, 1986.

       See: F26

B14   "Anne Baxter Condition Is Reported as Critical."
       <u>New York Times</u>. 12.6.85.

       Spokesperson Joyce Wagner reported today that actress
       Anne Baxter is in critical condition at Lenox Hill
       Hospital in New York City after collapsing on Madison
       Avenue.

B15   "Anne Baxter Dies." <u>London Times</u>. 12.13.85.

       Oscar-winning American actress Anne Baxter succumbs eight
       days after collapsing on a New York street at age 62
       from a stroke.

B16   "Anne Baxter Divorces John Hodiak." <u>New York Times</u>.
       1.28.53.

       The two actors' final divorce decree was granted.

B17   "Anne Baxter Divorces Randolph Galt." <u>New York Times</u>.
       1.30.70.

       Anne Baxter was issued a final decree of divorce from
       second husband, Randolph Galt. They separated in 1967.

B18   "Anne Baxter Expects a Divorce." <u>New York Times</u>.
       2.9.67.

       Anne Baxter will live in Los Angeles with her three
       daughters following her separation from second husband,
       Randolph Galt. He has leased a home in Newport Beach,
       California.

B19   "Anne Baxter, Hodiak to Wed." New York Times. 4.25.46.

Actors Anne Baxter and John Hodiak announced their
engagement to be married in June at the home of her
parents. It will be the first marriage for both.

B20   "Anne Baxter in Hospital." New York Times. 9.17.46.

Actress Anne Baxter was rushed to the hospital after
suffering an attack of appendicitis.

B21   "Anne Baxter Near Death." Los Angeles Times. 12.5.85.

The actress was unconscious and near death after suffering
a stroke. At her side were her three daughters.

B22   "Anne Baxter to Divorce Hodiak." New York Times.
         12.23.52.

Citing the "cruel and inhuman manner that she has suffered
great humiliation, mental anguish and embarrassment,"
Anne Baxter filed for divorce from actor John Hodiak.
She received custody of their 17-month-old daughter,
Katrina. He agreed to contribute toward Katrina's
support, as well as Anne's.

B23   "Anne Baxter to Narrate Film About her Grandfather's
         Life." London Times. 11.13.83.

Anne Baxter, granddaughter of architect Frank Lloyd
Wright, is scheduled to narrate a documentary on the
life of her grandfather.

B24   Arce, Hector. The Secret Life of Tyrone Power.
         William Morrow and Company, Inc. New York. 1979.

Anne was a teenager when she co-starred with Tyrone Power
in Crash Dive. She won the part of Sophie by default
in The Razor's Edge. She later co-starred with Power
in The Luck of the Irish, a nonmusical version of Finian's
Rainbow.

See: F7, F17, F22

B25   Armour, Robert A. _Fritz Lang_. Twayne Books.
        New York. 1978.

        One of Lang's best movies was _The Blue Gardenia_, a murder
        mystery with a wonderful soundtrack.

        See: F31

B26   Armstrong, Lois. "Anne Baxter Has a New Career in Hotel
        Management -- And One More Debt to Bette Davis."
        People Weekly. 6.11.84.

        Anne Baxter's role in the TV series _Hotel_ was won after
        Davis suffered a mastectomy and disabling stroke and
        had to bow out.

        See: T54

B27   "At the Roxy." _New York Times_. 6.27.46.

        The new film _Smoky_ is as pretty as a picture card,
        although not as satisfactory a horse romance as the
        earlier filmed versions about a wild stallion and an
        understanding cowhand, starring Fred MacMurray and Anne
        Baxter.

        See: F15

B28   Atkinson, Brooks. "Theatre Reviews." _New York Times_.
        10.26.38.

        Anne Baxter is a handmaiden to Catherine the Great (Eva
        Le Gallienne) in _Madame Capet_.

        See: S3

B29   Barnes, Howard. _New York Herald Tribune_. 5.27.43.

        Five Graves to Cairo is a pleasantly unpretentious film
        fable that's been executed with enough finesse to make
        it an "exciting pipedream."

        See: F8

B30   _____. "Yellow Sky." New York Herald Tribune. 2.1.49.

Anne Baxter gives a touch of sincerity and compunction
to conventional material in Yellow Sky.

See: F23

B31   Barsocchini, Peter. From Where I Sit: Merv Griffin's
            Book of People. Pinnacle Books. New York. 1982.

On the set of I Confess, Alfred Hitchcock made his famous
statement that actors are like cattle. He restated his
quote, "All actors should be treated like cattle."

See: F32

B32   Bartelt, Chuck, and Bergeron, Barbara. Variety
        Obituaries. Garland Publishing, Inc. New York and
            London. 1988.

Anne Baxter's extensive obituary gives major highlights
of her life and career.

B33   Basten, Fred E. Glorious Technicolor, The Movies' Magic
            Rainbow. A. S. Barnes and Company. New York. 1980.

Anne Baxter is mentioned in the chapter on Betty Grable.
Darryl F. Zanuck offered Grable the role of Sophie
MacDonald in the 1946 film The Razor's Edge. Because
she would be playing against type, Grable declined the
offer. The role went to Anne Baxter, who gained prestige
by winning an Academy Award for the role. Also featured
is a full-page advertisement from Crash Dive, which co-
starred Tyrone Power.

See: F7, F17

B34   Bawden, J.E.A. "Anne Baxter." Films in Review. October,
            1977.

Bawden perfectly relates the biography of Hollywood
stalwart Anne Baxter. Anne's interest in becoming an
actress at an early age and carrying through on her
aspirations show a person of great conviction and
perseverance. The article is liberally sprinkled with

quotes from Anne's interview with Bawden. Anne is
portrayed as strong as many of her movie characters.
Her films to date are chronicled, as well.

B35   Baxter, Anne. Intermission: A True Story. G. P. Putnam'
        Sons. New York. 1976.

Anne's autobiography spans the four-year period during
which she married her second husband, gave birth to two
daughters, and lived a pioneer's life in the outback
of Australia.

See: B44, B60, B152, B156, B177, B195, B442

B36   Bayer, William. The Great Movies. Grosset and Dunlop,
        Inc. New York. 1973.

All About Eve is compared to Sunset Boulevard and The
Barefoot Contessa. The difference between Anne's Eve
and Ava Gardner's role in The Barefoot Contessa is that
Eve really wanted to be a star and was willing to pay
the price.

See: F26

B37   "Beauty with a Broken Nose." American Magazine. 11.42.

Anne Baxter is the feature of this article. She is an
up-and-coming actress, who may not be conventionally
beautiful, but her acting is sure to make an impression
in the future.

B38   Bego, Mark. Rock Hudson: Public and Private. New
        American Library. New York. 1986.

In 1954, Rock Hudson appeared opposite Anne Baxter in
One Desire. Also mentioned is Rock's good personal
friend, George Nader, who co-starred with Anne in A
Carnival Story.

See: F33, F35

B39   Behlmer, Rudy. America's Favorite Movies: Behind the
          Scenes. F. Ungar Publishing Group. New York. 1982.

       Among the author's favorite films is All About Eve.

       See: F26

B40   _____, and Thomas, Tony. Hollywood's Holywood.
          The Citadel Press. Secaucus, New Jersey. 1975.

       In You're My Everything, Anne Baxter's character is a
       composite "It Girl," "Dancing Daughter," "Modern Maiden,"
       and "Baby Vamp." She does a charleston on a tabletop
       reminiscent of Joan Crawford in Our Dancing Daughters.

       See: F24, R20

B41   _____. Memo From: David O. Selznick. Avon Books.
          New York. 1972.

       Anne gave the most touching test for Gone with the Wind.

B42   Berg, Z. Scott. Goldwyn: A Biography. Ballantine Books.
          New York. 1989.

       Samuel Goldwyn borrowed Darryl F. Zanuck's new discovery,
       Anne Baxter, to replace a pregnant Teresa Wright for
       the ingenue role in North Star. Screenwriter Lillian
       Hellmann expressed pleasure at the choices for the cast.
       The film was photographed by Margaret Bourke-White in
       1943. Goldwyn joked later that "Whenever Stalin got
       depressed, he ran that picture."

       See: F9

B43   Bergan, Ronald. The United Artists Story. Crown
          Publishers. New York. 1986.

       Anne's starring roles were described in A Guest in the
       House, Angel on My Shoulder, and Summer of the Seventeenth
       Doll (or Season of Passion).

       See: F13, F16, R42

B44   Berkinow, Louise. "Intermission." <u>New York Times Book
          Review</u>. 9.10.76.

       Berkinow compares Anne Baxter's writing style in her
       autobiography <u>Intermission: A True Story</u> to that of Doris
       Lessing. She feels this is a serious book that
       beautifully balances the internal and external plots
       of Baxter's life in Australia.

B45   "The Best of the Weekend." "Films: A Movie Exocus."
          <u>Los Angeles Times</u>. 5.5.90.

       Charlton Heston and Anne Baxter are seen in a photograph
       from the re-release of <u>The Ten Commandments</u>.

       See: F38

B46   Blake, Groverman. "Aisle Say." <u>Chicago Sun Times</u>
          3.28.53.

       Anne Baxter is more than capable at her chores in <u>The
       Blue Gardenia</u>. She keeps a reasonably literate script
       going at a good clip. She is never one to let herself
       get typecast.

       See: F31

B47   Bosworth, Patricia. <u>Montgomery Clift</u>. Harcourt Brace
          Jovanovich, Inc. New York. 1978.

       Anne Baxter appeared in <u>Seen But Not Heard</u> on Broadway
       at age 15. She met Montgomery Clift while auditioning.
       Neither won the roles they were vying for, so he asked
       her to a concert at Carnegie Hall to commiserate.
       According to Anne, the 18-year-old Monty was
       hyper-energetic and hypersensitive. He didn't date often
       but when he did, it was usually with Anne or Louisa
       Horton. Later, when they co-starred in <u>I Confess</u>, it
       was rumored that he had been unhappy with the casting
       of Anne as his love interest. He had wanted Swedish
       actress Anita Bjork.

       See: F32, S1

B48   "Brat to Match." Newsweek. 1.1.45.

In A Guest in the House, Anne Baxter is the waifish yet
mentally unstable guest of an unsuspecting family who
take her in.

See: F13

B49   Brian, Denis. Tallulah, Darling. Macmillan Publishing
          Co., Inc. New York. 1972, 1980.

Ernst Lubitsch was angry with the daily rushes on A Royal
Scandal. One scene called for Tallulah to keep her eyes
closed while talking with the young Anne Baxter. Instead,
she kept them open the entire time.

See: F14

B50   Briggs, Colin. "Ann Sothern's Career." Hollywood Studio
          Magazine. 12.82.

Ann Sothern's movie comeback after a long illness was
in The Blue Gardenia, co-starring Anne Baxter and Jeff
Donnell.

See: F31

B51   _____. "Remembering: Capucine." Hollywood Studio
          Magazine. 9.90.

Capucine's second film for Columbia Pictures was A Walk
on the Wild Side, which featured a bizarre plot. "Anne
Baxter and Joanna Moore, who had relatively normal parts,
got the best reviews."

See: F43

B52   Brode, Douglas. Fifty from the Fifties: Sunset Boulevard
          to On the Beach. The Citadel Press. Secaucus,
          New Jersey. 1976.

Among Brode's compilations were All About Eve and The
Ten Commandments.

See: F26, F38

B53   No entry.

B54   Bronner, Edwin. The Encyclopedia of the American Theatr
       1900-1975. A. S. Barnes and Company, Inc. San Dieg
       New York, and London. 1976.

       Included are Anne Baxter's appearances on stage or in
       a film based on a stage play: There's Always a Breeze,
       The Square Root of Wonderful, The Spoilers, Seen But
       Not Heard, Madame Capet, A Guest in the House, The Eve
       of St. Mark, and The Czarina (A Royal Scandal).

       See: F10, F13, F14, F36, S1-3, S7

B55   Brooks, Tim, and Marsh, Earle. The Complete Directory
       to Prime Time Network TV Shows, 1946-Present,
       Ballantine Books. New York. 1979, 1981, 1985, 1988

       Anne appeared on The G.E. Theater, which was first
       telecast on February 1, 1953; last broadcast on
       September 16, 1962, on CBS, Sunday nights, from 9:00-
       9:30. Ronald Reagan was host/star from 1954-1962. In
       1960, she was a woman of ill repute in an episode of
       Wagon Train ("The Kitty Angel Story"). She also
       co-starred in the pilot TV movie Marcus Welby, M.D.,
       as Myra Sherwood. Later, Anne appeared as Victoria Cabo
       in Hotel, 1983-1986, Wednesdays, 10:00-11:00, on ABC.

       See: T1, T5, T33, T54

B56   _____. The Complete Directory to Prime Time TV Stars,
       1946-Present. Ballantine Books. New York. 1987.

       Brooks gives a brief biography and filmography for Anne
       Baxter.

B57   Brown, Jay A. Rating the Movies for Home Video, TV,
       and Cable. Publications International, Ltd. Skokie,
       Illinois. 1982-1987.

       Anne received "Star" ratings for each of her films.
       All About Eve and The Magnificent Ambersons received
       four stars. The Ten Commandments received
       three-and-a-half stars. The Razor's Edge, Angel on
       My Shoulder, Charley's Aunt, Five Graves to Cairo, and

I Confess received three stars. _The Luck of the Irish_
and _A Walk on the Wild Side_ received two stars.

See: F3, F5, F8, F16, F17, F22, F26, F32, F38, F43

B58   Bumgardner, C. W. _Movie Trivia Quiz Book_. Ventura
        Associates, Inc. New York. 1981.

Gary Merrill played the object of Anne Baxter's scheming
in _All About Eve_. Anne Baxter and Fred MacMurray co-
starred with a horse in _Smoky_.

See: F15, F26

B59   Burgess, Patricia. _The Annual Obituary, 1985_. St. James
        Press. Chicago, Illinois, and London. 1988.

A lengthy tribute is paid to actress Anne Baxter.

B60   Burns, Ernest D. _Cinemabilia_. Cinemabilia, Inc.
        New York. 1980.

The Academy Award-winning actress writes about her years
in the Australian outback in _Intermission: A True Story_.

B61   Callow, Simon. _Charles Laughton: A Difficult Actor_.
        Grove Press. New York. 1988.

Callow provides a review of _O. Henry's Full House_, which
included the story "The Last Leaf," in which Anne Baxter
starred.

See: F30

B62   Campbell, Richard H, and Pitts, Michael R. _The Bible
        on Film: A Checklist, 1897-1980_. The Scarecrow Press.
        Metuchen, New Jersey, and London. 1981.

The Ten Commandments was cast with stars, former stars,
and character actors who had previously worked with
Cecil B. DeMille. This was just as important to him
as were the production aspects of the film.

See: F38

B63   Campbell, Robert. <u>The Golden Years of Broadcasting</u>.
       Charles Scribner's Sons. New York. 1976.

The television movie <u>Stranger on the Run</u> was detailed
in the chapter titled "Two on the Aisle, World Premieres,"
as an acclaimed feature broadcast in 1967. The film
was a western set in the bleak railroad town of Banner,
New Mexico, circa 1885, and co-starred Henry Fonda.

See: T18

B64   Carey, Gary. <u>Judy Holliday: An Intimate Life Story</u>.
       Seaview Books. New York. 1982.

Judy felt that she had an edge over Anne Baxter (for
<u>All About Eve</u> or Eleanor Parker (<u>Caged</u>) the year she
was nominated for an Academy Award. She felt Gloria
Swanson (<u>Sunset Boulevard</u>) had an edge on Bette Davis,
who was also nominated for her role in <u>All About Eve</u>.
Judy Holliday won the Oscar for her role in <u>Born
Yesterday</u>.

See: F26

B65   _____. <u>More About "All About Eve</u>." Random House.
       New York. 1951, 1972.

Carey gives more tidbits about the cast, crew, and filming
of <u>All About Eve</u>.

See: F26

B66   Carlson, Timothy. "Dream on: The Sitcom Where Old TV
       Shows Get a Weird New Life." <u>TV Guide</u>. 7.29.90.

In the pilot for the HBO series <u>Dream On</u>, old clips from
television shows shown in the 1950s are part of Martin
Tupper's (Brian Benben) thoughts. In one episode, his
ex-wife, Judith (Wendie Malick), comes to his apartment
for an unscheduled talk. Martin smiles dreamily and
says, "I think I know what you are going to say." The
scene cuts to a vintage tele-clip of Anne Baxter emoting,
"I'm in love with you. I want what you want. I want

to come back. I want to be your wife." This clip from
"Bitter Choice" cuts back to Judith saying to Martin,
"I want you to sign those divorce papers." Another clip
from the same archived show was broadcast on August 25,
1990, in which Anne says, "You don't have the guts!"

B67   Cassini, Oleg. <u>Oleg Cassini: In My Own Fashion</u>. Simon
           and Schuster. New York. 1987.

       Cassini designed the clothes for Anne Baxter, as well
       as his then-wife, Gene Tierney,in the film <u>The Razor's
       Edge</u>.

       See: F17

B68   Castleman, Harry, and Podrazik, Walter J. <u>Harry and
           Wally's Favorite TV Shows</u>. Prentice-Hall. Englewood
           Cliffs, New Jersey. 1989.

       Anne's performances are mentioned in the TV mini-series
       <u>The Moneychangers</u> and the series <u>Hotel</u>.

       See: T49, T54

B69   "Catherine Baxter." <u>New York Times</u>. 1.3.79.

       The 85-year-old mother of actress Anne Baxter died in
       a Laguna Hills, California, convalescent hospital.

B70   Champlin, Charles. "Heston Revisits 'Ten Commandments.'"
           <u>Los Angeles Times</u>. 5.16.90.

       Cecil B. DeMille had an icy rebuke for those who were
       late on the set during filming of <u>The Ten Commandments</u>.
       For instance, when Anne Baxter was late one day, he said
       to the makeup artists, "Do you realize that you've delayed
       Miss Baxter for 20 minutes? Don't you realize how
       important this scene is to her, and to the picture?"

       See: F38

B71   Chaneles, Sol, and Wolsky, Albert. <u>The Movie Makers</u>.
           Derbibooks, Inc. Secaucus, New Jersey. 1974.

The brief biography on Anne Baxter describes her roles
from wholesome, girl-next-door types to nightclub singer,
saloonkeeper, dance hall girl, and Princess Nefretiri.
In The Razor's Edge, she was a victim of drugs and drink.

See: F17

B72   "Cinema." Time. 8.10.42.

Anne Baxter affects a fine French accent as the girl
who helps children and an old man to safety from Nazi
henchmen in The Pied Piper.

See: F6

B73   _____. Time. 5.10.43.

Anne Baxter stars as the love interest in Crash Dive,
a submarine story to appear to every boy who would like
to be an officer and a gentleman.

See: F7

B74   _____. Time. 5.24.43.

Anne Baxter co-stars in the unusual World War II drama
Five Graves to Cairo. In a united effort, the wits of
Franchot Tone and Anne Baxter turn the entire tide of
a battle in Rommel's campaign in North Africa.

See: F8

B75   _____. Time. 1.29.45.

Anne Baxter is the whey-faced invalid Evelyn Heath in
the heavily melodramatic A Guest in the House. Her
psychotic behavior is ended when the aunt strikes the
key nerve to end her evil harassment -- Evelyn's fear
of birds.

See: F13

B76   _____.   Time.   2.5.45.

Sunday Dinner for a Soldier is sincere but misguided
in its attempt to present an unusual, simple film.   Anne
Baxter is the marriageable daughter of a very poor family
who invite home a lonely soldier for a meal before leaving
for Europe.

See: F12

B77   _____.   Time.   4.9.45.

In A Royal Scandal, the jealous fiancee (Anne Baxter)
of a young rider (William Eythe) for the Russian Czarina
Catherine (Tallulah Bankhead), some further conspiracies,
and the rider's own self-esteem bring him to his senses
and send Catherine the Great on to other victims.

See: F14

B78   _____.   Time.   7.8.46.

The beautifully photographed film Smoky co-starred Anne
Baxter and Fred MacMurray, although their love interest
was only faintly evident.

See: F15

B79   _____.   Time.   12.9.46.

In The Razor's Edge, Anne Baxter gives a fine, effective
characterization of the horribly unhappy Sophie.

See: F17

B80   _____.   Time.   3.24.47.

As the romance builds in Blaze of Noon, Anne Baxter plays
a waiting game, and the story falls apart.   She is married
to one of four aviator brothers, while another cherishes
her.   At its weakest point, however, it never quite
becomes an unlikable movie.

See: F18

B81   _____. <u>Time</u>. 5.10.48.

Clark Gable is a doctor married to a nice wife, Anne
Baxter, in <u>Homecoming</u>. But he falls for nurse Lana
Turner, whose death makes him realize he's able to be
a more caring, good person.

See: F20

B82   _____. <u>Time</u>. 8.30.48

In <u>The Walls of Jericho</u>, Anne Baxter's sincerity in the
love scenes helps to bring a glimmer of reality and
interest to the film.

See: F21

B83   _____. <u>Time</u>. 10.4.48.

<u>The Luck of the Irish</u> is a pleasant comedy with fine
performances by Anne Baxter, Tyrone Power, and Cecil
Kellaway.

See: F22

B84   _____. <u>Time</u>. 12.13.48.

Anne Baxter is the trigger-happy heroine in <u>Yellow Sky</u>.
She coyly takes pot-shots at her hero's (Gregory Peck)
head.

See: F23

B85   _____. <u>Time</u>. 8.8.49.

<u>You're My Everything</u> is the perfect family movie about
a movie family, with Anne Baxter as the singing and
dancing actress, Dan Dailey as her devoted entertainer
husband, and Shari Robinson as their sprightly moppet
daughter.

See: F24

B86   _____. Time. 5.15.50.

Anne Baxter once again co-stars with Dan Dailey in A
Ticket to Tomahawk. They are excellent in their roles,
she as a lady sharpshooting, peace officer, and he as
a traveling salesman.

See: F25

B87   _____. Time. 10.16.50.

In All About Eve, the sensitively modulated playing of
Anne Baxter counts heavily in the film's effectiveness.
Baxter is one of Hollywood's most versatile performers.

See: F26

B88   _____. "Made in Hollywood." Time. 5.5.52.

After filming My Wife's Best Friend, Anne Baxter would
like to be known as a glamour girl, especially after
wearing a topaz in her navel!

See: F29

B89   _____. Time. 5.26.52.

Anne Baxter's role in The Outcasts of Poker Flat has
been transformed into a good girl for the purpose of
a movie romance.

See: F28

B90   _____. Time. 3.2.53.

Anne Baxter co-stars in I Confess, a good, workmanlike
thriller, although only fair-to-middling Hitchcock.

See: F32

B91   _____. Time. 3.23.53.

Anne Baxter makes a thoroughly attractive murder suspect
in The Blue Gardenia.

Anne Baxter

    See: F31

B92   _____. Time. 4.19.54.

In Carnival Story, Anne Baxter gives a horribly
fascinating portrayal as she writhes and yowls. "Sure
to assure her succession to the Bette Davis roles."

    See: F33

B93   _____. Time. 5.2.55.

In the ecclesiastical striptease that comes repulsively
close to "priestitution" in Bedevilled, Anne Baxter is
a blues singer who becomes involved in murder.

    See: F34

B94   _____. Time. 2.25.57.

Three Violent People starred Anne Baxter and Charlton
Heston, with whom she previously worked in The Ten
Commandments. Anne is probably the most relentless
camera-hugger in the business.

    See: F38, F39

B95   _____. Time. 4.28.58.

Anne Baxter is the powder-pale beauty, who writhes in
her "poor-little-rich-girl loneliness" in Chase a Crooked
Shadow.

    See: F40

B96   _____. Time. 2.23.62.

Anne Baxter and Jane Fonda positively seethe with vitality
in their roles in A Walk on the Wild Side.

    See: F43

B97   Coburn, Marcia Froelke. "Ten Tough Broads: A Collection
        of Role Models for Those Who Detest Cheap Sentiment."
        <u>American Film</u>. July-August, 1983.

        In <u>All About Eve</u>, Bette Davis provides the broadest of
        all the female toughies -- earnest, opportunistic, and
        smart-alecky in her role of Margo Channing. Anne Baxter
        plays a younger, more ruthless version of Margo.

        See: F26

B98   Coleman, John. "Lady Loren." <u>New Statesman</u>. 11.26.65.

        Jerry Lewis directed and acted in <u>The Family Jewels</u>,
        a silly comedy where he plays six roles. The film had
        bad press, unusual in its unanimity. "There are four
        or five amusing sight-gags drowning in a sea of moronic
        bad taste." Anne Baxter had a cameo role.

        See: F45

B99   Colombo, John Robert. <u>Popcorn in Paradise</u>. Holt,
        Rhinehart, and Winston. New York. 1979.

        Quotes from Anne Baxter: "I am an actress first and
        last." "I don't want any of this whole schmeer about
        being a movie star." "See into life, don't just look
        at it." "Best to have failure happen early. It wakes
        up the phoenix bird in you."

B100   Considine, Shaun. <u>Bette and Joan: The Divine Feud</u>.
        E. P. Dutton. New York. 1989.

        Anne attended a party at Joan Crawford's house. Anne
        had to work the entire ten weeks of filming on <u>All About</u>
        <u>Eve</u>, because she had the most dialogue.

        See: F26

B101   "Conte Unravels Paramount Puzzle, 'The Blue Gardenia.'"
        <u>San Francisco Chronicle</u>. 5.10.53.

        "Anne Baxter emotes once she realizes it was probably
        she who did in the wolfish calendar artist (Raymond Burr),
        although she can't remember a thing because of all the

rum drinks she's had." It is later discovered that Anne
was not the killer.

See: F31

B102   Conway, Michael, and Ricci, Mark. The Films of Marilyn
        Monroe. Cadillac Publishing Co., Inc. New York.
        1964.

Anne Baxter gives a tip-top performance in O. Henry's
Full House. Anne, Jean Peters, and Gregory Ratoff were
directed by Jean Negulesco in their chapter, "The Last
Leaf."

See: F30

B103   Cooper, Roberta Krensky. The American Shakespeare
        Theatre, Stratford, 1955-1985. Folger Shakespeare
        Library Press and Associate University Press.
        Washington, London, and Toronto. 1986.

Anne Baxter played Gertrude in Hamlet, on August 4, 1982
A Variety review was mentioned which said that this play
was a "catastrophic staging in perversity." Anne used
too many gestures and facial expressions too reminiscent
of the 19th-century school of acting.

See: S12

B104   Crane, Ralph. "The Story of a Single Scene Shows How
        Magazine's Novel Is Translated into a $3,000,000
        Movie." Life. 8.12.46.

The Razor's Edge has raw material in its script and cast
Included is a photograph of the principal actors and
their stand-ins. Anne Baxter won the role of Sophie
MacDonald over Bonita Granville, Susan Hayward, and
Annabelle Shaw.

See: F17

B105   Crowther, Bosley. New York Times. 10.18.40.

The Great Profile stars "The Great Profile" John Barrymor
in a pathetic film, where he sell his talent at cut-rate.

See: F2

B106   _____.   New York Times.   4.29.43.

Crash Dive is Hollywood at its wildest, in Technicolor.
"This movie has no more sense of reality than a popular
song."

See: F7

B107   _____.   New York Times.   5.27.43.

Erich Von Stroheim gave the only key performance in Five
Graves to Cairo, an incredible comedy-melodrama.   "It
had a little something for all tastes, provided you don't
give a darn."

See: F8, R2

B108   _____.   New York Times.   11.5.43.

North Star is a lyric and savage movie that suggests
in passionate terms the outrage committed upon peaceful
Russian people by the invading armies of Nazi Germany.
"It offers a clamorous tribute to the courage and tenacity
of those who have sacrificed their homes, themselves,
and their families in resisting the Fascist hordes in
this war."

See: F9

B109   _____.   New York Times.   5.31.44.

John M. Stahl directed The Eve of St. Mark in a variety
of cinematic styles, "ranging from farce to grimmest
tragedy, which only adds to the discredit of the whole
thing."

See: F10

B110   _____.   New York Times.   1.25.45.

Sunday Dinner for a Soldier is a warm, sentimental tale
about an impoverished, parentless brood who have their

hearts set on entertaining a young soldier in the best
way they know how.

See: F12

B111   _____. New York Times. 4.12.45.

A Royal Scandal, for all of Tallulah Bankhead's presence
is "an oddly dull and generally witless show."

See: F14

B112   _____. New York Times. 2.16.46.

A Guest in the House is a cracked, incredible tale about
a mischief-making female. "The story is cheaply syntheti
and about as logical as a crooner's song. No help is
rendered by Anne Baxter, who plays her role with much
coyness."

See: F13

B113   _____. New York Times. 10.21.46.

The story of Angel on My Shoulder is pretty good, althou
hokey. "The story is so imitative -- and is repeated
so dutifully -- that it's hard to feel any more towards
it than a mildly nostalgic regard."

See: F16

B114   _____. New York Times. 11.20.46.

The Razor's Edge is a long and elaborate film in which
"the grasp for some shining revelation of spiritual
quality exceeds its reach."

See: F17

B115   _____. New York Times. 3.5.47.

Blaze of Noon cannot be called a good picture in concept
or cinematic style. "But the younger generation will
probably like it."

See: F18

B116   _____.   New York Times.   4.30.48.

Homecoming pretends to be a serious film about the war
and medicine, but it is really "nothing more than a cheap,
synthetic chunk of romance designed to exploit two gaudy
stars -- Clark Gable and Lana Turner."

See: F20

B117   _____.   New York Times.   9.16.48.

The Luck of the Irish is a "whimsey-wishful film that
is somewhat like a Chauncey Olcott-type of Irish comedy."

See: F22

B118   _____.   New York Times.   2.2.49.

Yellow Sky is a "tough, taught, and good, scorching
western."

See: F23

B119   _____.   New York Times.   7.23.49.

You're My Everything is a spoof of Hollywood careerdom,
with Anne Baxter as "fair flower of Boston."

See: F24

B120   _____.   New York Times.   5.20.50.

"Anne Baxter is fair and more than middling" as the
marshal's daughter in the pleasant western A Ticket to
Tomahawk, which is reminiscent of Annie Get Your Gun.

See: F25

B121   _____. New York Times. 10.14.50.

All About Eve is a witty, mature, worldly-wise, witherin
satire of theater life that includes excellent music
and an air of ultra-class. "The legitimate theater had
better look to its laurels."

See: F26

B122   _____. New York Times. 5.16.52.

The personalities in The Outcasts of Poker Flat are
involved in unrelievably grim situations and settings.
The film improvises fancifully and enlarges Bret Harte's
blueprint "but only fitfully succeeds in adding movement
or tension to the tale."

See: F28

B123   _____. New York Times. 10.11.52.

My Wife's Best Friend features a very pleasant woman
(Anne Baxter) at the center of the story.

See: F29

B124   _____. New York Times. 10.17.52.

"The Last Leaf" is a rampantly sentimental climax to
the tales of O. Henry's Full House, which audiences will
easily foresee and find a trifle manufactured. Even
so, "the story is so appealingly dramatized and played
that the smack of their terminal surprises will not be
too greatly missed."

See: F30

B125   _____. New York Times. 3.23.53.

Although I Confess has moments of tension and power,
and the whole thing is scrupulously acted by a tightly
professional cast, "the consequence is an entertainment
that tends to drag, sag, and generally grow dull."

See: F32

B126   _____ . <u>New York Times</u>. 4.28.53.

The Blue Gardenia is a routine melodrama rendered
hackneyed and tedious from beginning to end by the script.
"The happiest cast member is Nat King Cole. He sits
at a piano and sings one run-through of the title song
of the picture then goes home."

See: F31

B127   _____ . <u>New York Times</u>. 4.17.54.

Carnival Story is too arbitrary and contrived then
dwindles into monotonous and dull. There is nothing
about Steve Cochran that makes his role credible. "And
there is nothing about Miss Baxter or the strange iciness
in her eyes that makes such a show of hot devotion
arresting or sensible."

See: F33

B128   _____ . <u>New York Times</u>. 11.9.56.

The Ten Commandments is a three-hour and thirty-nine
minutes film that tells the arresting story of Moses,
the Israelite slave who struggled to set his people free
in Egypt. "It is a moving story of the spirit of freedom
that is thrilling and spiritually profound."

See: F38

B129   _____ . <u>New York Times</u>. 3.25.58.

Chase a Crooked Shadow is a moderately well-done program,
"with Anne Baxter as an heiress harassed by a young man
passing as her long-dead brother."

See: F40

B130   _____ . <u>New York Times</u>. 2.17.61.

Edna Ferber's Cimarron is sprawlingly filmed. After
the land rush, however, "the movie becomes another
frontier pastiche from Hollywood."

See: F41

B131   _____. New York Times. 2.22.62.

Anne Baxter is wasted in A Walk on the Wild Side, a
sluggish film that "smacks of sentimentality and social
naivete. It's as naughty as a cornsilk cigarette."

See: F43

B132   _____. New York Times. 8.12.65.

Anne Baxter has a cameo appearance in the Jerry Lewis
farce The Family Jewels, "an unfunny vehicle for dyed-
in-the-wool fans of his."

See: F45

B133   _____. Vintage Films. G. P. Putnam's Sons. New York.
        1977.

In All About Eve, Anne Baxter played her role of Eve
Harrington with balanced measures of unction and stealth.

See: F26

B134   "Current Cinema: A Bad Girl." The New Yorker. 2.24.45.

Anne Baxter underplays her role as the diabolical Evelyn
in Guest in the House so well and intelligently that
she really could have deceived a group of more or less
rational people.

See: F13

B135   "Current Cinema: Katie's in Pain," The New Yorker.
        4.21.45.

"Anne Baxter and the rest of the supporting cast of A
Royal Scandal are kept in discreet focus."

See: F14

B136   Da, Lottie, and Alexander, Jan. Bad Girls of the Silver
          Screen. Carroll and Graf Publishers, Inc.
          New York. 1989.

        In a captioned photograph from The Razor's Edge, Anne
        Baxter goes from nice girl to Parisian slut. She is
        quoted, "It never occurred to me that they'd even consider
        me for the part."

        See: F17

B137   Datillo, Peggy. National Enquirer. 3.18.86.

        At the season-end party for the television series Hotel,
        the producers paid Anne Baxter a tribute by showing scenes
        from her films.

        See: T54

B138   Davis, Bette. Bette Davis: The Lonely Life, an
          Autobiography. Putnam Books. New York. 1962.

        Davis talks about her film All About Eve and mentions
        her co-star, Anne Baxter.

        See: F26

B139   Davis, Bette, with Herskowitz, Michael. This 'n That.
          G. P. Putnam's Sons. New York. 1987.

        After illness caused Davis to be replaced on the
        television series Hotel, Anne Baxter took the role of
        the manager-proprietress of the posh San Francisco hotel.
        When Davis was recovered enough to consider returning
        to work, producer Aaron Spelling sent her scripts that
        Davis considered unsuitable. One called for her to cure
        Baxter of drug addiction.

        See: T54

B140   De Vine, Lawrence. "Three Stars in 'Two Keys.'"
          Los Angeles Times. 6.29.75.

        Anne Baxter returns to California to co-star in Noel
        Coward's final stage play, Noel Coward's In Two Keys.

It opened on Broadway on February 17, 1974, running for
18 weeks, then resumed with a national tour that closed
on August 2, at the Hartford in Chicago.

See: S10

B141   "Debbie's Do!" _Movie Land and TV Time Annual_. Fall,
       1968.

Popular actress Debbie Reynolds hosted a party to welcom
French actor Maurice Ronet, her co-star in _How Sweet_
_It Is_. Among the celebrities attending was Anne Baxter,
who was the first to be introduced to him.

B142   Di Orio, Al. _Barbara Stanwyck_. Coward-McCann, Inc.
       New York. 1984.

Anne reported that the atmosphere on the set of _A Walk_
on the Wild Side was extremely ghastly because of the
royally spoiled male star (Laurence Harvey), who fought
with the director and was continually late. Both Anne
and Stanwyck were furious with his unprofessionalism
to the point that Stanwyck gave him a "good chewing out."
Anne claimed she baldly lied about being pregnant so
she wouldn't have to personally confront him. He never
did it again. Anne was one of the many guest stars who
appeared in one of the 112 episodes of _The Big Valley_,
starring Stanwyck. On April 13, 1981, Anne was one of
the stars who lauded Stanwyck's contribution to film
at the Film Society of Lincoln Center.

See: F43, T31

B143   Dick, Bernard F. _Joseph L. Mankiewicz_. Twayne
       Publishers. New York. 1983.

Anne's "smarmy" role of Eve Harrington is covered in
the chapter that mentions _All About Eve_.

See: F26

B144   Dickens, Homer. _The Films of Barbara Stanwyck_.
       The Citadel Press. Secaucus, New Jersey. 1984.

Anne Baxter has one of the few normal roles in the film
<u>A Walk on the Wild Side</u>, with Barbara Stanwyck as a
lesbian owner of a brothel.

See: F43

B145   Druxman, Michael B. <u>Make It Again, Sam</u>. A. S. Barnes.
           New York. 1975.

The elaborate epic film <u>The Ten Commandments</u> gives credit
to its cast and special effects.

See: F38

B146   _____. <u>Merv</u>. Award Books. New York. 1976.

Astute late-night movie viewers can catch Merv Griffin's
voice on the telephone in the Alfred Hitchcock thriller
<u>I Confess</u>, starring Anne Baxter.

See: F32

B147   _____. <u>Paul Muni: His Life and His Films</u>. A. S. Barnes.
           New York. 1974.

Anne Baxter co-starred with Paul Muni in <u>Angel on My
Shoulder</u>, a popular movie of the time.

See: F16

B148   Dudar, Helen. "Anne Baxter's Road to Shakespeare."
           <u>New York Times</u>. 8.1.82.

The long, varied career of Anne Baxter has prepared her
to competently handle the small but important role of
Queen Gertrude in Shakespeare's <u>Hamlet</u>, to be staged
at the American Shakespeare Theatre in Stratford,
Connecticut. Anne broke her anke in a fall but will
perform her debut on August 3, 1982, in a walking cast.

See: S12

B149   Eberly, Stephen L. <u>Patty Duke: A Bio-Bibliography</u>.
            Greenwood Press. New York, Westport, Connecticut,
            and London. 1988.

Anne Baxter co-starred with Miss Duke in the television
movie <u>If Tomorrow Comes</u>, as a teacher who tries to help
the determined young woman in her quest to marry a
Japanese young man at the time Pearl Harbor was bombed.

See: T41

B150   Edwards, Anne. <u>Vivien Leigh</u>. Simon and Schuster.
            New York: 1977.

Anne Baxter was a major contender for the leading role
in <u>Rebecca</u>. It went to Joan Fontaine.

B151   Edwards, Bill. "Anne Baxter Dies in New York at
            62 -- 'Eve' Beacon is Felled by Stroke." <u>Variety</u>.
            12.18.85.

A quite extensive biography gives a wonderful recap of
actress Anne Baxter's life and career as a dedicated
and reliable survivor of Hollywood. She never quite
achieved superstardom, but she never let anyone down.

B152   Eichelbaum, Stanley. "A Different Hollywood
            Autobiography." <u>San Francisco Chronicle</u>. 9.26.76.

The 53-year-old actress Anne Baxter has a bestseller
in <u>Intermission: A True Story</u>, and she's embarrassed
about the rave reviews and success. The book may be
made into a film.

B153   Einstein, Xavier. <u>Trivia Mania</u>. Kensington Publishing
            Corporation. New York. 1984.

Question: "In the Cecil B. Demille film <u>The Ten
Commandments</u>, the role of Nefretiri was played by what
actress?"

Answer: Anne Baxter.

B154   Eisner, Joel, and Krinsky, David. <u>Television Comedy</u>
        <u>Series: An Episode Guide to 1953 TV Sitcoms in</u>
        <u>Syndication</u>. McFarland and Company, Inc.,
        Publishers. Jefferson, North Carolina, and London.
        1984.

        Listed are Anne Baxter's credits for work on the series
        <u>My Three Sons</u> and <u>Batman</u>.

B155   Eisner, Lotte H. <u>Fritz Lang</u>. Oxford University Press.
        New York. 1977.

        Anne Baxter's role in <u>The Blue Gardenia</u> is critiqued.

        See: F31

B156   Elliott, Deborah. "Book Review." <u>Library Journal</u>.
        6.15.76.

        Elliott feels Anne Baxter's writing style in her
        autobiography <u>Intermission: A True Story</u> was too "flowery,
        pretentious, overdramatic, and loaded down with romantic
        fluff."

B157   Elmo, Don. <u>The Giant Book of Trivia</u>. Modern Promotions.
        New York. 1980.

        Anne Baxter and Rock Hudson make "smoldering love while
        Julie Adams goes up in smoke" in <u>One Desire</u>.

        See: F35

B158   Essoe, Gabe. <u>The Films of Clark Gable</u>. The Citadel
        Press. Secaucus, New Jersey. 1970.

        Anne Baxter co-starred with Clark Gable in <u>Homecoming</u>,
        as the long-suffering young wife, who tries to save her
        marriage while her hard-as-nails hubby finds comfort
        in the arms of beautiful nurse, Lana Turner.

        See: F20

B159   Esterow, Milton. New York Times. 12.24.55.

The Spoilers is the fourth filming of the boomtown
inhabitants' fight for gold, "a very familiar tale, this
time filmed in color, that will probably be filmed again
in another ten years."

See: F36

B160   _____. New York Times. 4.7.56.

The Come On is a mediocre film about "a girl, a man and
fate all tangled up together."

See: F37

B161   Everson, William K. A Pictorial History of the Western
            Film. The Citadel Press. Secaucus, New Jersey.
            1969.

The Outcasts of Poker Flat was "optic symphony" according
to Photoplay magazine. Anne is pictured with Gregory
Peck in a scene from Yellow Sky.

See: F23, F28

B162   _____. The Bad Buys. Cadillac Publishing Co., Inc.
            New York. 1964.

Every so often a performance such as Anne Baxter's in
All About Eve reminds us that there is a volcanic power
that exists in the villain roles that actresses of her
calibre get when they sink their teeth into the
characterizations. She could be the outwardly sweet,
straightforward girl, who can inwardly be a psycho in
Guest in the House, the murderess in The Come On, or,
in her most famous role of all, the schemer Eve Harringto
in All About Eve.

See: F13, F26, F37

B163   Falk, Byron A., Jr. New York Times Theatre Reviews.
            New York Times Company. New York. 1976.

Stage productions that feature Anne Baxter: There's
Always a Breeze, March 3, 1938; Madame Capet,
October 26, 1938; and The Square Root of Wonderful,
October 31, 1967.

See: S2, S3, S7

B164   Farber, Manny. "Andersen's Fairy Tale." The New
              Republic. 6.19.44.

         Anne Baxter and her film parents in The Eve of St. Mark
         go through the farm scenes with a "pleased-as-punch look
         in this cliched war movie."

         See: F10

B165   _____. "Murder, She Says." The New Republic. 3.24.47.

         "Due to the cost of living, Anne Baxter lends herself
         to Blaze of Noon as she makes coffee and awaits the four
         brothers' planes to land."

         See: F18

B166   _____. "Never Sharp." The New Republic. 12.9.46.

         Anne Baxter is very moving and strange as a memory-ridden,
         heartbroken harlot in The Razor's Edge. "The precise,
         slow, rhythmical movements of the film are often very
         interesting."

         See: F17

B167   "Film Review." Christian Century. 5.24.50.

         Anne Baxter is the gun-toting granddaughter of the local
         marshal, who saves the day in A Ticket to Tomahawk.

         See: F25

B168   _____. Christian Century. 11.29.50.

         Anne Baxter co-stars in All About Eve, "an unusually
         discerning view of human nature and the theater."

See: F26

B169   _____. <u>Christian Century</u>, 7.25.51.

Anne Baxter plays the wife of pro golfer Ben Hogan in
<u>Follow the Sun</u>. Her acting, as well as Glenn Ford's,
provided inspiration yet unsentimentality in the simple
truth of their story.

See: F27

B170   _____. <u>Christian Century</u>. 7.23.52.

Anne Baxter co-stars in <u>The Outcasts of Poker Flat</u>, "a
disappointing film vaguely based on a Bret Harte story."

See: F28

B171   _____. <u>Christian Century</u>. 11.26.52.

Anne Baxter starred in "The Last Leaf," one of four
stories in <u>O. Henry's Full House</u>. Each story shared
qualities of sentimentality, irony, and predictability.
The other three stories were "The Cop and the Anthem,"
"The Clarion Call," and "The Ransom of Red Chief."

See: F30

B172   _____. <u>Christian Century</u>. 4.15.53.

<u>I Confess</u> is "a strangely unsuspenseful" Hitchcock film
starring Anne Baxter.

See: F32

B173   "Film Review." <u>National Parent-Teacher</u>. May, 1953.

<u>The Blue Gardenia</u> stars Anne Baxter in a foolish murder
mystery only given suspense and plausibility by skillful
direction and acting. The film received a "poor" rating.

See: F31

B174   "Films in Review." <u>Theatre Arts</u>. January, 1945.

       <u>Guest in the House</u> provides Anne Baxter with a role to
       challenge her fine acting talents.

       See: F13

B175   _____. <u>Theatre Arts</u>. January, 1947.

       The stars of <u>The Razor's Edge</u>, save Clifton Webb, all
       "suffer from the vague unrest that comes from a lack
       of definition at the core."

       See: F17

B176   Fireman, Judy. <u>TV Book</u>. Workman Publishing Company.
       New York. 1977.

       Anne Baxter is a guest on the new <u>Jerry Lewis Show</u>, a
       disastrous two-hour talk show that aired in 1963.

B177   Fisher, Craig. "The Adjustment of Anne Baxter."
       <u>Los Angeles Times</u>. 10.24.76.

       Although her autobiography is well-written in describing
       Anne Baxter's crushing loneliness and adjustment to living
       in Australia's outback while married to Randolph Galt,
       <u>Intermission: A True Story</u> leaves the reader with a sense
       that her book's primary human conflict is incomplete.
       Fisher feels that the book had some of the same appeal
       as those written by Betty MacDonald in the 1930s and
       1940s (<u>The Egg and I</u> and <u>Onions in the Stew</u>). "Finishing
       'Intermission' a reader may feel that he or she has
       happened to meet Anne Baxter at a party and then spent
       an evening with her." The only fault is what she omits.

B178   Fitzgerald, Michael G. <u>Universal Pictures</u>. Arlington
       House Publishers. Westport, Connecticut. 1977.

       Anne Baxter co-starred with Rock Hudson, Julie Adams,
       and teenaged Natalie Wood in <u>One Desire</u>, released in
       July.

       See: F35

B179   Florin, John. "The Great American Horse Opera." <u>Life</u>.
           1.10.49.

       Anne Baxter stars as a gun-toting girl living with her
       prospector grandfather in a small town that is invaded
       by outlaws in the western <u>Yellow Sky</u>. At first, she
       is distrustful of the hero (Gregory Peck), but eventuall
       they fall in love.

       See: F23

B180   "For Her Performance in...Best Supporting Actress
           Winners!" <u>Academy Awards, 54 Years of Oscar
           Winners</u>. Magazine Special Issue. 1983.

       Profiled is Anne Baxter's role as the tragic Sophie in
       <u>The Razor's Edge</u>, for which she won the Oscar. It
       mentions that four years later, she was nominated for
       Best Actress in <u>All About Eve</u>. It also indicates she
       has acted on Broadway and written her autobiography.

       See: F17, F26

B181   Fraser, George MacDonald. <u>The Hollywood History of the
           World</u>. Fawcett Columbine. New York. 1988.

       Anne Baxter was a distinct success as Nefretiri in <u>The
       Ten Commandments</u>. The cast included luminaries, but
       the real stars of the film were the huge sets, special
       effects, and crowds of extras.

       See: F38

B182   Fredrik, Nathalie. <u>Hollywood and the Academy Awards</u>.
           Award Publications. Los Angeles, California. 1968

       The bright, pretty granddaughter of Frank Lloyd Wright
       received an Academy Award for Best Suporting Actress
       for her role of Sophie MacDonald in <u>The Razor's Edge.</u>

       See: F17

B183   Freedland, Michael. <u>Gregory Peck</u>. William Morrow and
           Company, Inc. New York. 1980.

In 1949, Gregory Peck co-starred with Anne Baxter in
Yellow Sky, a post-Civil War western. He was a robber
with a heart, especially for the daughter of the house
(Anne) where the robbers hid after their robbery. Anne
never looked lovelier and Peck considered her a delightful
companion.

See: F23

B184   Freeman, Marilla Waite. "Current Feature Films."
          Library Journal. 4.1.51.

Follow the Sun is an autobiographical drama starring
Glenn Ford and Anne Baxter, in modest and appealing
performances as the Ben Hogans. The film "illustrates
the long struggle for excellence which goes into the
making of champions."

See: F27

B185   _____. "New Films from Books." Library Journal.
          5.15.52.

Mary H. Zipprich, of the New York Public Library,
critiques The Outcasts of Poker Flat, based on a novel
by Bret Harte. Anne Baxter plays Cal (taking the place
of Mother Shipton in the book), who is married to one
of the meanest bad men on film (Cameron Mitchell).

See: F28

B186   _____. "New Films from Books." Library Journal.
          11.15.52.

Ms. Freeman critiques O. Henry's Full House.

See: F30

B187   _____. "New Films from Books." Library Journal.
          3.1.53.

Herbert Cahoon, of the Research Division of the New York
Library, reviews I Confess, based on a play by Louis
Verneuil. Alfred Hitchcock filmed the story in which
Anne Baxter is the ex-love of a priest, who is involved

in a murder cover-up. This film was based on an actual
event.

See: F32

B188   _____. "New Films from Books." Library Journal.
            8.10.55.

Herbert Cahoon reviews One Desire, based on the novel
by Conrad Richter. "Anne Baxter is fine in a meaty role

See: F35

B189   _____. "New Films from Books. Library Journal.
            1.15.56.

Earle F. Walbridge, Reference Assistant at the Washingto
Square Library, New York University, critiques The
Spoilers, based on the novel by Rex Beach. In the film,
Anne Baxter plays her role of Cherry Malote "with her
usual cast-iron seductiveness."

See: F36

B190   Freiberg, Warren. "Star Talk from Beyond the Grave:
            Dead Celebrities Answer Sun Readers' Letters Thru
            Psychic Channelers." Sun. 11.15.88.

Freiberg, a Chicago-area broadcaster and psychic
investigator, publishes a column where readers can reque
interviews, through mediums and channelers, to answer
inquiries. One such letter from Carla B. in Vancouver,
B.C., wanted to get some encouraging words from the
unfortunate victim of a stroke (which the requester
survived), her favorite star, the late Anne Baxter.
Anne's reply was, "No one should go before their time."

B191   Garbicz, Adam. Cinema, the Magic Vehicle: A Guide to
            Its Achievement. The Scarecrow Press. Metuchen,
            New Jersey. 1975.

Featured is Anne Baxter's contribution to the critically
acclaimed film All About Eve.

See: F26

B192   Gareffa, Peter M. Contemporary Newsmakers. Gale Press.
        New York. 1987.

        The author includes a biographical sketch of the 1986
        people in the news, including Anne Baxter.

B193   Geist, Kenneth L. Pictures Will Talk: The Life and Films
        of Joseph Mankiewicz. Scribner. New York. 1978.

        All About Eve and its stars are featured in a 16-page
        spread.

        See: F26

B194   "Gentleman's Leprechaun." Newsweek. 9.13.48.

        In The Luck of the Irish, Anne Baxter, fortified with
        an appealing brogue, seems as much at home in Ballynabun
        as if she had been born there.

        See: F22

B195   George, George L. "The Bookshelf: Busy Headliners."
        American Cinematographer. November, 1977.

        George flowingly describes Anne's autobiography
        Intermission: A True Story as brilliant and moving.
        She displayed remarkable literary ability in relating
        the four years she lived with her husband and children
        in the Australian bush, with occasional movie jobs in
        the United States.

B196   Gill, Brendan. "The Current Cinema." The New Yorker.
        2.24.62.

        Anne Baxter is among the actors and actreses who walk
        through A Walk on the Wild Side looking less surprised
        and dismayed than they should.

        See: F43

B197   _____. Many Masks: The Life of Frank Lloyd Wright.
        G. P. Putnam's Sons. New York. 1987.

Frank Lloyd Wright worked hard to gain celebrity. He
was very pleased that his granddaughter, Anne Baxter,
became famous as an actress. She last saw him at an
Easter celebration just days before his death from an
intestinal blockage on April 4, 1959.

B198   Gottesman, Ronald. <u>Focus on Orson Welles</u>.
        Prentice-Hall. Englewood Cliffs, New Jersey. 1976.

Gottesman mentions Anne Baxter for her role in <u>The
Magnificent Ambersons</u>.

See: F5

B199   Gould, Michael. <u>Surrealism and the Cinema</u>. A. S. Barnes
        New York. 1976.

The special effects of <u>The Ten Commandments</u> were chosen
as one of the contributions to this subject.

See: F38

B200   Graham, Sheila. "As You Were, Annie." <u>Photoplay</u>.
        April, 1953.

Miss Graham features popular actress Anne Baxter in an
article presenting Anne as a woman who knows what she
wants and is willing to work to get it.

B201   Graham, Virginia. "Cinema." <u>The Spectator</u>. 12.8.50.

In <u>All About Eve</u>, Anne Baxter, as the rising young
actress, and the other roles are dissected and magnified
to produce an absorbing, although long, story.

See: F26

B202   _____. "Cinema." <u>The Spectator</u>. 9.26.52.

<u>My Wife's Best Friend</u> is an unassuming comedy. Anne
Baxter "has a whale of a time in a creditable
performance." She is so good indeed that she must "arouse
in every breast a feeling of wildest irritation," as
her character changes attitude very ten minutes. She

means to torture her husband following their survival
of a plane crash. Although they both admit past
indiscretions, she will not let him live his down.

See: F29

B203   _____. "Cinema." The Spectator. 10.3.52.

Anne Baxter is a sick woman, who belives she will die
when the vine opposite her window is bare in "The Last
Leaf," one of four stories in O. Henry's Full House.
"She manages beautifully to make her sweet role
palatable."

See: F30

B204   _____. "Cinema." The Spectator. 5.14.54.

Anne Baxter acts sufficiently as the woman who does not
like the man she loves in the well-directed Carnival
Story. She wears a selection of bathing suits!

See: F33

B205   Greenspun, Roger. New York Times. 8.17.71.

Fool's Parade is a rare film in recent years that
"restores faith in ordinary movie-going as a reasonable
and even privileged way of passing time." It is an action
film concerned with its place and period, as well as
its genre.

See: F49

B206   Griffin, Ann. Films in Review. December, 1950.

For her role in All About Eve, Anne Baxter, as Eve (Little
Miss Evil), responds nimbly to direction but does not
bring much to her role "beyond a satisfactory physique."

See: F26

B207   _____. Films in Review. March, 1953.

Miss Griffin critiques Anne's role in I Confess.

See: F32

B208   Griggs, John. The Films of Gregory Peck. The Citadel
        Press. Secaucus, New Jersey. 1984.

In the 20th Century-Fox film Yellow Sky, Anne Baxter
"plays her role with just the right touch of
self-assurance and the proper amount of femininity."

See: F23

B209   Gross, Martin A. The Nostalgia Quiz Book 2. New American
        Library, Inc. New York. 1974.

"Match the clue with the movie." The "curtain goes up
on the behind-the-scene's movie, with Bette Davis, Anne
Baxter, and Celeste Holm...and Marilyn Monroe" (All About
Eve).

B210   Guernsey, Otis L., Jr. Broadway Song and Story. Dodd,
        Mead and Company. New York. 1985.

The night they announced on Broadway that choreographer
Gower Champion had died, Anne Baxter dropped into her
seat and wept.

B211   _____. New York Herald Tribune. 4.29.43.

The final climactic scene in Crash Dive is tops in the
field of film melodrama.

See: F7

B212   Guiles, Fred Lawrence. Jane Fonda: The Actress in Her
        Time. Pinnacle Books. New York. 1981.

Anne Baxter was annoyed once with the headstrong, willful
Jane Fonda during filming of A Walk on the Wild Side.
Anne was six months pregnant when she journeyed to
Hollywood from Australia to appear in the film. It seems

that Jane had misplaced her bra pads and borrowed Anne's
bra!

See: F43

B213   Gurvitz, Ian. The Great TV and Movie Quiz. Prestige
          Books, Inc. New York. 1980.

Anne Baxter was part of the star-studded cast in All
About Eve; a question was included about the career of
Bette Davis.

See: F26

B214   Haddad-Garcia, George. The Films of Jane Fonda. The
          Citadel Press. Secaucus, New Jersey. 1981.

According to Bosley Crowther, Anne Baxter was wasted
in a weak role in A Walk on the Wild Side.

See: F43

B215   Halliwell, Leslie. The Filmgoer's Companion. Avon
          Books. New York. 1965, 1967, 1970, 1974, 1976,
          1977, 1989.

A short biography stated that Anne was a leading lady,
who usually played shy, innocent characters but could
be equally at home as a schemer. Her films are listed.

B216   _____. Halliwell's Film Guide. Charles Scribner's Sons.
          New York. 1977.

Two of Anne Baxter's films (All About Eve and Angel on
My Shoulder) are included with synopses and running times.

See: F16, F26

B217   _____. Halliwell's Hundred. Charles Scribner's Sons.
          New York. 1982.

This book contained one hundred films that Leslie
Halliwell considered the best of all time. Included

is the classic movie about what goes on behind the scene
of a Broadway coterie in <u>All About Eve</u>.

See: F26

B218   Harris, Jay S. <u>TV Guide: The First 25 Years</u>. Simon
        and Schuster. New York. 1978.

Anne Baxter portrayed Olga the criminal as a "special
guest villain" on the TV series <u>Batman</u>.

See: T14

B219   Harris, Marilyn J. <u>The Zanucks of Hollywood</u>. Crown
        Publishers. New York. 1989.

Anne Baxter gave Darryl F. Zanuck's daughter, Darrylin,
wedding gifts of demitasse teaspoons when Darrylin marrie
Robert Livingston Jacks in 1949.

B220   Hartung, Philip T. "Stage and Screen." <u>Commonweal</u>.
        8.29.41.

Anne Baxter is one of the young people in <u>Charley's Aunt</u>
who benefits from Jack Benny's making a fool of himself
in the corny comedy.

See: F3

B221   _____. "Stage and Screen." <u>Commonweal</u>. 11.28.41.

In <u>Swamp Water</u>, Anne Baxter is included in the cast whose
performances are beautifully in keeping with the spirit
of the harrowing story set in the Okefenokee Swamp (where
filming actually took place).

See: F4

B222   _____. "Stage and Screen." <u>Commonweal</u>. 8.21.42.

Anne Baxter is the fresh young girl in <u>The Magnificent
Ambersons</u>, whose love for George Amberson Minafer does
not blind her to the fact that the once properous family

is decaying -- she is not fooled by the magnificence
of the Ambersons.

See: F5

B223   _____. "Stage and Screen." Commonweal. 8.21.42.

Anne Baxter is Nicole in The Pied Piper. She agrees
to show the group of refugees the escape route through
the French Alps in June, 1940, to reach safety and cross
the English Channel.

See: F6

B224   _____. "Stage and Screen: Two Wrapped in Technicolor."
          Commonweal. 5.14.43.

Crash Dive is a slick love story about two World
War II officers (Dana Andrews and Tyrone Power) who fall
for the same girl (Anne Baxter).

See: F7

B225   _____. "Stage and Screen." Commonweal. 6.11.43.

In Five Graves to Cairo, another World War II film, Anne
Baxter is a French barmaid, who feels no kindliness toward
the British who deserted the French after Dunkirk.

See: F8

B226   _____. "Stage and Screen." Commonweal. 11.19.43.

North Star is a true-to-life, moving war film set in
Russia. Anne Baxter "is fine in her role as a member
of the younger generation who defend their homeland
against invading Nazis."

See: F9

B227   _____. "Stage and Screen." Commonweal. 2.25.44.

Although set in World War II, The Fighting Sullivans,
also titled The Sullivans, is not a war film. It is

"the basically true story of five brothers who each lost
his life and posthumously won Purple Hearts." This movie
is noted for its realism and simplicity, where the parent
are the true heroes for keeping the rest of the family
together.

See: F11

B228   _____. "Stage and Screen." Commonweal. 6.16.44.

The Eve of St. Mark is a faithful retelling of Maxwell
Anderson's play set in the Second World War. Anne is
the love interest of a farm boy, who goes off to war
but doesn't return to her. Anne plays her so honestly
and simply that she "seems like the girl next door."

See: F10

B229   _____. "Stage and Screen." Commonweal. 2.2.45.

Anne Baxter's character victimizes her opponents in the
psychological thriller A Guest in the House. "She is
a sadistic nymphomaniac, played with disarming simplicity
and full understanding of evil implications of her
actions."

See: F13

B230   _____. "Stage and Screen." Commonweal. 3.23.45.

The greatest asset to the film Sunday Dinner for a Soldier
was the romance between the girl (Anne Baxter) and the
soldier (John Hodiak). Their real-life romance enhanced
their performances. The longing and uncertainty of their
relationship at the end of the film provided a refreshing
realistic note.

See: F12

B231   _____. "Stage and Screen: The Girls and Their Affairs."
        Commonweal. 4.13.45.

In A Royal Scandal, Anne Baxter has a small role as the
lieutenant's fiancee. She has her big moment when she
tells off Czarina Catherine the Great (Tallulah Bankhead)

The czarina has eyes for Anne's love, because he saved her life.

See: F14

B232   _____. "Stage and Screen: Cowboy's Best Friend."
          Commonweal. 6.26.46.

Anne Baxter is a ranch owner with a yen for Fred MacMurray, special friend of Smoky, a beautiful horse. Smoky is based on the popular story by Will Jones, filmed sentimentally by director Louis King.

See: F15

B233   _____. "Stage and Screen.' Commonweal. 12.13.46.

Although the cast is handsome in The Razor's Edge, they are given little opportunity to act in this tiresome film about Tyrone Power's search for the meaning of life. Anne Baxter "goes completely to the dogs" after the deaths of her husband and child.

See: F17

B234   _____. "Stage and Screen." Commonweal. 3.21.47.

Blaze of Noon is an American war film that spoils the realistic background material with an effectual plot. William Holden is the oldest of four brothers, who is married to dutiful nurse wife, Anne Baxter. She resents the informal living arrangements in this unsuspenseful movie.

See: F18

B235   _____. "Stage and Screen." Commonweal. 5.28.48.

Clark Gable is a callow surgeon in Homecoming. He learns to consider his patients as human beings from his comely nurse (Lana Turner), while suffering wife (Anne Baxter) agonizes at home, anxious to share his problems when he returns.

See: F20

B236   _____. "Stage and Screen: Gold Is Where You Find It."
        Commonweal. 9.24.48.

Anne Baxter is an Irish lass in the intelligently
delightful film The Luck of the Irish. Anne provided
a brogue that doesn't sound amateurish.

See: F22

B237   _____. "Stage and Screen." Commonweal. 8.5.49.

Dan Dailey is a musical comedy hoofer, who is happily
married to proper Bostonian Anne Baxter in You're My
Everything. She becomes a famous movie star and is named
the "It" girl of silent movies. Anne's impersonation
of a hot-cha girl provides some of the most brilliant
satire ever one film.

See: F24

B238   _____. "Stage and Screen." Commonweal. 5.19.50.

A Ticket to Tomahawk is a thoroughly enjoyable satire
of western films. Dan Dailey is a drummer selling The
Saturday Evening Post. Anne Baxter is a girl who can
outspit, outride, and outshoot any man. Walter Brennan
is the engineer taking his train from Epitaph to Tomahawk
to win a franchise.

See: F25

B239   _____. "Stage and Screen." Commonweal. 10.27.50.

In All About Eve, Anne Baxter "handles her role as the
vicious Eve well and succeeds in making the heartless,
calculating, and mean character into a living person."

See: F26

B240   _____. "Stage and Screen." Commonweal. 5.11.51.

Anne Baxter is excellent as Mrs. Valerie Hogan in Follow
the Sun, especially in the last third of the film when

Ben (a pro golfer) courageously learns to walk and play golf again after a horrible, near-fatal car accident.

See: F27

B241   _____. "Stage and Screen." Commonweal. 6.6.52.

In The Outcasts of Poker Flat, Anne Baxter is excellent as Cal, the shady character who is secretly wed to the robber (Cameron Mitchell), who turns up to collect his loot and wife. She is among a group of people stranded in a snowstorm.

See: F28

B242   _____. "Stage and Screen." Commonweal. 11.7.52.

My Wife's Best Friend is a giddy comedy featuring Anne Baxter in a tour de force performance as the wife who shares confessions with her husband (Macdonald Carey) when they think they are about to be killed in a plane crash. She uses the confession to full advantage when they don't die! Anne "handles her role expertly, adopting a series of attitudes him: noble, forgiving, patient, and vampish."

See: F29

B243   _____. "Stage and Screen: Cucullus non Facit Monachum."
        Commonweal. 3.6.53.

Anne Baxter is hard and brash in her role of the married woman who had been in love with a priest in I Confess.

See: F32

B244   _____. "Stage and Screen." Commonweal. 5.7.54.

A Carnival Story is a shoddy tale of a woman (Baxter) of loose morals in post-war Germany, who cannot resist her ex-lover carnival barker (Steve Cochran), even after she marries the respectable high diver (Lyle Bettger). He is order to leave the circus, but returns following the death of her husband. She falls in love with a writer (fictional) from Life magazine, but Cochran won't leave

her alone.   "This carnival story is more interested in
sex than in the glamour of circus life."

See: F33

B245   _____. "Stage and Screen." Commonweal. 5.13.55.

Although Anne Baxter doesn't play her fallen woman with
the finesse of Deborah Kerr (as in The End of the Affair)
"Bedevilled is still a fascinating movie that has a
definite Catholic slant."

See: F34

B246   _____. "Stage and Screen." Commonweal. 11.30.56.

In The Ten Commandments, Anne Baxter plays the Egyptian
Princess Nefretiri to the hilt as she joins a cast of
Hollywood's who's who. The film should have been titled
"Moses," since "it concentrates on him more than the
Ten Commandments."

See: F38

B247   _____. "Stage and Screen." Commonweal. 3.28.58.

Creepy goings on occur in Chase a Crooked Shadow, but
it is hard to decide whose side the audience should be
on: the recuperating heiress (Anne Baxter) or her return-
from-the-dead brother (Richard Todd). He gives her a
frightening time and she, in turn, puts him through some
harrowing tests.

See: F40

B248   _____. "Stage and Screen." Commonweal. 3.3.61.

Cimmaron stars many good actors, who are saddled with
rather skimpy roles that "leave one longing for more
depth to the characterizations."

See: F41

B249   _____. "Stage and Screen." Commonweal. 2.2.62.

In Summer of the Seventeenth Doll (later titled Season
of Passion), Anne Baxter plays Olive, the girlfriend
of Roo (Ernest Borgnine). He brings her a doll each
year during his annual lay-off season in the cane fields
of Australia. She desperately refuses to let go of the
past and wants what she's been given each year for the
past sixteen years: a kewpie doll.

See: F42

B250   _____. "Stage and Screen." Commonweal. 3.2.62.

"Anne Baxter, as the solicitous diner owner in A Walk
on the Wild Side, provides the only decent female role
in the movie."

See: F43

B251   Haskell, Molly. From Reverence to Rape: The Treatment
        of Women in the Movies. Holt, Rinehart and Winston.
        New York. 1973.

Anne Baxter is the ingenue in The Magnificent Ambersons,
Orson Welles's second film. In the fifties, serious
actresses, such as Anne Baxter, were filmed mostly in
black and white. In All About Eve, Anne's Eve is like
a cat clawing its way up the theater curtain.

See: F5, F26

B252   Hatch, Robert. "Films." The Nation. 11.28.81.

Anne Baxter is Lilianna in Jane Austen in Manhattan.
She is a celebrated actress and drama coach who undertakes
to wrest a manuscript from her former student (Robert
Powell), who has become guru to acolytes.

See: F50

B253   _____. "Movies: Hail to Bette Davis." The New Republic.
        11.6.50.

Eve Harrington (Anne Baxter) is the viper in Margo
Channing's (Bette Davis) bosom in <u>All About Eve</u>. "Anne
plays her with the serene malevolence of one of the
poisoning Borgias." "She does her devil's work capably,
but the personality inflicted on her is both improbably
and unnecessarily revolting."

See: F26

B254   _____. "Movies: Love Under Fire." <u>The New Republic</u>.
          5.17.48.

Anne Baxter is surgeon Clark Gable's long-suffering wife
in <u>Homecoming</u>. She has yet to learn the lesson that
the only really invincible rival is the dead one.

See: F20

B255   _____. "Movies: The Quiet One." <u>The New Republic</u>.
          2.21.49.

Anne Baxter is a wild girl of the hills raised by Navajos
in <u>Yellow Sky</u>. She is the object of desire of a gang
of unemployed veterans, whose lust for gold brought them
to the girl and her old prospector grandfather.

See: F23

B256   ____. "Movies: Warm and Humid." <u>The New Republic</u>.
          8.1.49.

Anne Baxter and Dan Dailey have such a good time with
their roles in <u>You're My Everything</u> that the effect on
the audience is certain to be bracing.

See: F24

B257   _____. "Theatre and Films." <u>The Nation</u>. 12.8.56.

In <u>The Ten Commandments</u>, Anne Baxter is a "Folies Bergere
Nefretiri."

See: F38

B258   Haugh, Brian. "Anne Baxter's Tragedy Robs Her of the
              Triumph of Her Own Story on Film." <u>Star</u>. 12.24.85.

        Anne Baxter returned to her one-time home in Australia
        just months before she died, to prepare for her great
        professional dream: making a movie of her life in the
        rugged outback.

B259   Hecht, Ken. <u>Who's Who in Show Business, 1969-1971</u>
              Who's Who in Show Business. New York. 1968, 1971.

        Anne Baxter is represented by Chasin Park-Citron Agency.

B260   "Here Comes Old Nick." <u>Newsweek</u>. 11.4.46.

        Anne Baxter is the secretary to the judge (Angel) and
        is properly bewildered as the victim in a two-in-one
        romance in <u>Angel on My Shoulder</u>.

        See: F16

B261   Heston, Charlton. <u>An Actor's Life: Journals, 1956-1976</u>.
              Simon and Schuster. New York. 1976.

        The following diary listings are quoted or paraphrased:
        March 27, 1956: "Spent the day dangling Anne Baxter's
        double by her heels." March 20, 1956: The love he felt
        for son, Fraser, when he took his first step was played
        between them with more love than his love scene with
        Anne Baxter. May 9, 1956: He's letting his hostility
        toward Anne Baxter rise, so he will be effective in the
        scene where he throws her off the "ranch." He felt she
        was making it easy for him to play the scene. A
        postscript mentions that he said this "as a snotty young
        actor." He also states, "Anne is a good lady and a pro."
        when he realized that personal chemistries can often
        be used by the directors in inventive ways to make the
        scenes more realistic. May 16, 1956: He likes what
        he did in the last scene with Anne Baxter in <u>Three Violent
        People</u>.

        See: F39

B262   Higham, Charles. <u>Bette: The Life of Bette Davis</u>.
              Macmillan Publishing Company, Inc. New York. 1981.

Because of the Academy's split in their voice of Davis and Anne Baxter for <u>All About Eve</u>, Davis's Oscar was canceled for probably the best performance of her career. Davis enjoyed the challenge of working with the truly remarkably well-cast performers.

See: F26

B263   Hine, Al. "SR Goes to the Movies: Lust in Germany, Crime in Miami." <u>Saturday Review</u>. 5.8.54.

In <u>Carnival Story</u>, Anne Baxter's "sensuous charms and considerable acting ability shine." "This is her picture and she deserves its top honors."

See: F33

B264   Hirschhorn, Clive. <u>The Hollywood Musical</u>. Crown Publishing, Inc. New York. 1981.

Anne Baxter was the adult voice-over for Connie Marshall in <u>Mother Wore Tights</u>. Also mentioned are the songs sung in the film <u>You're My Everything</u>.

See: F19, F24

B265   _____. <u>The Warner Bros. Story</u>. Crown Publishing, Inc. New York. 1979.

Anne Baxter's good work in <u>I Confess</u> enhanced this Alfred Hitchcock film of murder and intrigue. In <u>Chase a Crooked Shadow</u>, she is an attractive widow. <u>Chase a Crooked Shadow</u> was competently directed, and the story was later remade as a 1975 television movie titled <u>One of My Wives Is Missing</u>.

See: F32, F40

B266   Hirschhorn, Joel. <u>Rating the Movie Stars</u>. Beckman House. New York. 1983.

Anne Baxter rated 3 stars (2.98) for her "driving ambition, unlimited energy, and a competely honest if occasionally withering tongue." The bit includes her movie filmography to date.

B267   ____ . Rating the Movie Stars for Home Video, TV, Cable.
            Beckman House. New York. 1983.

Anne Baxter is most remembered for her roles as the ever-
loyal wife or woman waiting for her man. She was once
described as being known for her driving ambition,
unlimited energy, and complete honesty.

B268   Hodgens, R. M. Film Quarterly. Fall, 1966.

Anne Baxter is Nefretiri in The Ten Commandments. She
hardens the Pharaoh's (Yul Brynner) heart and together
they provide the most impressive explosion of drama,
as opposed to spectacle, in the film. "They have been
extravagant presences suggesting merely mean pride and
sexuality." When Moses (Charlton Heston) returns from
exile, they come alive.

        See: F38

B269   "Hollywood Oscar Awards." London Times. 3.15.47.

The 1946 Academy Awards were presented to the winners
for 1946 films. Anne Baxter won for her acting in a
supporting role in The Razor's Edge. Other Oscars were
given to William Wyler for directing The Best Years of
Our Lives, for which Fredric March won as Best Actor
in the same film. Olivia de Havilland won Best Actress
for her role in To Each His Own. Claude Jarman won as
Best Child Actor in The Yearling.

        See: F17

B270   "Hollywood's Ten Most Lavish Weddings." Hollywood Studio
            Magazine. May, 1977.

In the subchapter titled "Other Notable Hollywood
Weddings," a photograph of Anne Baxter and new husband
John Hodiak is shown, captioned that they were wed at
the home of her parents in Burlingame, California.

B271   Hoover, B. "Portrait: One-Woman Army of Liberation."
            Biography News. March, 1975.

This article expounds on the courage and single-handedne
with which Anne Baxter dealt with her change of lifestyl
in the Australian outback during her marriage to second
husband, Randolph Galt.

B272   "Horse Without Opera." Newsweek. 7.8.46.

Anne Baxter, Fred MacMurray, and Bruce Cabot supply the
human element in Smoky, with restraint and uncommon good
sense.

See: F15

B273   "How Top TV Shows Cope When Death or Illness Strikes
        Their Favorite Stars." Star. 1.10.84.

Bette Davis had appeared in the two-hour pilot of the
TV series Hotel then was felled by a mastectomy and
stroke. They quickly hired Anne Baxter to portray Davis'
sister-in-law, Victoria Cabot. There were frequent
conversational references made to Davis's character,
which left the door open for her return.

See: T54

B274   "Insider: Grapevine: All About Anne." TV Guide.
        3.8.86.

Plans are under way to commission a portrait of the late
actress Anne Baxter. It will be hung in the lobby of
the fictional series as long as Hotel is on the air.

See: T54

B275   "Insider: Grapevine: Room at the Top." TV Guide.
        12.28.85.

Anne Baxter unexpectedly died on December 12, 1985.
A question arose as to who would replace her. A script
was written to have Peter McDermott (James Brolin) take
Anne's position but was scratched by the producers,
leaving the question unresolved.

B276   "Interview." London Times. 12.23.84.

Visiting actress Anne Baxter is interviewed.

B277   Israel, Lee. Miss Tallulah Bankhead. G. P. Putnam's
        Sons. New York. 1972. Berkley Books. New York.
        1973.

Bankhead was extremely jealous of Baxter because of her
youth, personality, and politics.

B278   Jacobs, Herbert. Frank Lloyd Wright, America's Greatest
        Architect. Harcourt, Brace and World, Inc.
        New York. 1965.

Stage and television personality Anne Baxter was one
member of the good-sized contingent of Frank Lloyd
Wright's descendants -- his granddaughter.

B279   Jahr, C. "Great Hollywood Comebacks." Ladies Home
        Journal. June, 1985.

The terrific actress Anne Baxter makes a screen comeback
to star in the television series Hotel. She took over
the role originally slated for Bette Davis, who had within
a two-week suffered a mastectomy and stroke.

See: T54

B280   Jenkins, Stephen. Fritz Lang: The Image and the Look.
        British Film Institute. London, England. 1981.

The Blue Gardenia is given a detailed scrutiny.

See: F31

B281   Jewell, Richard B., and Harbin, Vernon. The RKO Story.
        Arlington House. New York. 1982.

The authors mention Anne Baxter's roles in The Outcasts
of Poker Flat, The Magnificent Ambersons, The North Star,
and Carnival Story.

See: F5, F9, F28, F33

B282   "John Hodiak Weds Anne Baxter." New York Times. 7.8.46

The two performers were married in a garden ceremony
at the home of her parents, Mr. and Mrs. Kenneth S.
Baxter.

B283   Johnson, Catherine. "Anne Baxter Describes Life without
        Television." TV Guide. 11.11.61.

Anne Baxter describes her life in the Australian bush
while married to rancher Randolph Galt.

B284   Jones, Dorothy B. "The Hollywood War Films: 1942-1944."
        Hollywood Quarterly. October, 1945.

Reviewed are North Star, The Eve of St. Mark, and The
Fighting Sullivans (also titled The Sullivans).

See: F9, F10, F11

B285   Joseph, Robert, "One Film Program in Germany: I. How
        Far Was It a Success?" Hollywood Quarterly. January,
        1947.

Because of the war effort and subject matter of the films
it was argued that The Sullivans would, among others,
have to reestablish balance after such films as Air Force
and Corvette K-255 were withdrawn (since Corvette K-255
showed an Allied officer in the dress of a German
soldier).

See: F11

B286   Kael, Pauline. Kiss Kiss, Bang Bang. Little Brown and
        Company. New York. 1968.

"It's hard to believe Anne Baxter would ever be a threat
to Bette Davis," in All About Eve. Yellow Sky is a remake
of The Tempest. Anne is a member of the cast of The
Magnificent Ambersons, where Agnes Moorehead's performance
"just about belts you out of the theater."

See: F5, F23, F26

B287   Kaplan, Mike. Variety International Show Business
          Reference. Garland Publishing, Inc. New York and
          London. 1981.

A brief listing of Anne Baxter's films is given. Also
mentioned is her nomination for an Emmy for her role
in "The Bobby Currier Story" episode of The Name of the
Game on NBC. The Emmy that year for Outstanding Single
Performance by an Actress in a Leading Role went to
Geraldine Page for The Thanksgiving Visitor on ABC.
The other nominee in the category was Lee Grant for her
role in "The Gates of Cerberus" episode of the series
Judd for the Defense on ABC.

See: T32

B288   _____. Variety Presents the Complete Book of Major
          U.S. Show Business Awards. Garland Publishing,
          Inc. New York and London. 1985.

Included are The Razor's Edge (Oscar), All About Eve
(Nomination), and The Name of the Game (Emmy Nomination).

See: F17, F26, T32

B289   Kass, Judith M. The Films of Montgomery Clift. The
          Citadel Press. Secaucus, New Jersey. 1979.

Anne Baxter is Ruth Grandforth in I Confess. She's
blackmailed because she still loves an ordained priest
(Clift) to whom she was engaged before he left for World
War II and later the clergy. Although Clift's mother
tried to prevent him from dating his actress co-stars
and others she considered unsuitable for him, he
occasionally saw Anne Baxter or Louisa Horton.

See: F32

B290   Kass, Robert. Catholic World. April, 1953.

Kass critiques O. Henry's Full House, observing that
the brief tale titled "The Last Leaf," with Anne Baxter,
Jean Peters, and Gregory Ratoff, was "sticky in a way
which O. Henry never intended."

See: F30

B291   _____. Catholic World. April, 1953.

In I Confess, "Anne Baxter looks too hard and steely
as the young love interest of the priest." Hitchcock's
photography does not flatter Anne.

See: F32

B292   No entry.

B293   _____. Films in Review. March, 1953.

Kass feels that the choice of a blonde Anne Baxter in
I Confess is a mistake. Her hairdo makes her appearance
hard, and there is no different in her portrayal as the
young girl in love and a married woman being blackmailed.

See: F32

B294   Katz, Ephraim. The Film Encyclopedia. Thomas Y. Crowell
         New York. 1979.

Anne Baxter was eleven years old when she began to study
acting with Maria Ouspenskaya. She made her debut in
Broadway's Seen But Not Heard, at age 13. She relied
on her natural charm more than physical beauty to
construct an interest career.

See: S1

B295   _____. "Sleepers: The Only Thing These Films Need...Is
         Audience." Video Times. August, 1985.

I Confess is a "thriller of claustrophobic proportions."
A photograph shows Anne and Montgomery Clift in a scene
in the moody and atmospheric Quebec setting.

See: F32

B296   Keen, Eleanor. "Trite Plot, Many Cliches Mark 'The Blue
         Gardenia.'" Chicago Sun Times. 3.26.53.

Anne Baxter heads the cast of The Blue Gardenia. She
is an attractive member, who gives a creditable
performance in this suspenseful murder mystery. Anne

is a young woman who thinks she has killed someone while
in a drunken stupor.

See: F31

B297   Knight, Arthur. "SR Goes to the Movies: The Women."
          Saturday Review. 2.18.61.

Anne Baxter's role as the jealous, hard, dance-hall girl
brought a spot of life and color to an otherwise drab
remake of Cimarron. However, her role was pared down
so much that nothing could save it from being an overlong,
boring story.

See: F41

B298   _____. "SR Goes to the Movies: Everybody's Talkin'
          About Heaven." Saturday Review. 11.10.56.

Anne Baxter is part of an able cast in the epic The Ten
Commandments.

See: F38

B299   Kotsilibas-Davis, James. The Barrymores: The Royal
          Family in Hollywood. Crown Publishers, Inc.
          New York. 1981.

While filming The Great Profile, John Barrymore was
exasperated with Anne's exaggerated arm movements. She
felt he was sleepwalking in his role, even though he
would quote lengthy Shakespearean passages. At the 1946
Academy Awards presentation, Lionel Barrymore presented
the Oscar for Best Supporting Actress to Anne Baxter.
That year, she defeated Ethel Barrymore, who was nominated
for her role in The Spiral Staircase.

See: F2

B300   La Guardia, Robert. Monty: A Biography of Montgomery
          Clift. Arbor House Publishing Co., Inc. New York.
          1977.

202   Anne Baxter

Anne Baxter won the part in I Confess over Olivia
de Havilland. The film took two months to film in Quebec
and Hollywood.

See: F32

B301   Lamparski, Richard. Whatever Became of...? Volume 7.
            Bantam Books, Inc. New York. 1977.

Anne Baxter is mentioned as being a personal friend of
actress Andrea King. The chapter on Barbara Bates cites
her as the girl who is discovered standing in front of
the mirror holding the award that Anne Baxter had just
won in the film All About Eve.

See: F26

B302   _____. Whatever Became of...? Volume 9.   Crown
            Publishers, Inc. New York. 1985.

Bonita Granville had wanted the part of Sophie in The
Razor's Edge, because it was predicted that the role
would give the actress who played it the Oscar.   20th
Century-Fox had neglected to pick up Anne Baxter's option
and she refused to re-sign with the studio unless she
got the role. She got the part and the Academy Award
for Best Supporting Actress.

See: F17

B303   Lanchester, Elsa. Elsa Lanchester Herself. St. Martin's
            Press. New York. 1983.

Anne Baxter replaced Judith Anderson in the 1952
successful staging of John Brown's Body, directed by
Lanchester's husband, Charles Laughton. Actually, Anne
finished the tour during the last six months on the road.
Also on the tour was Raymond Massey, Tyrone Power, and
Anne's ex-husband, John Hodiak.

See: S6

B304   Lardner, David. "The Current Cinema: Geniuses at Work."
            The New Yorker. 8.15.42.

"Anne Baxter puts in an unexpected kick in her ingenue role" in The Magnificent Ambersons.

See: F5

B305   _____. "The Current Cinema: Popular Affront." The New Yorker. 5.1.43.

It's not easy to put your finger on the good it did for Anne Baxter, Dana Andrews, James Gleason, and Dame May Whitty to have appeared in Crash Dive.

See: F7

B306   _____. "The Current Cinema: Exhibit A." The New Yorker. 6.3.44.

Anne Baxter and William Eythe know exactly what they're about in the war film The Eve of St. Mark, and they are well-supported.

See: F10

B307   _____. "The Current Cinema." The New Yorker. 6.5.43.

Anne Baxter, Franchot Tone, and Akim Tamiroff give creditable performances in the war film set in Egypt, Five Graves to Cairo.

See: F8

B308   _____. "The Current Cinema: Murder." The New Yorker. 1.27.45.

Anne Baxter is natural and effective in Sunday Dinner for a Soldier. Co-star and future real-life husband John Hodiak is nice in this engaging movie.

See: F12

B309   Lasky, Betty. RKO: The Biggest Little Major of Them All. Prentice-Hall, Inc. Englewood Cliffs, New Jersey. 1984.

RKO released Samuel Goldwyn's <u>North Star</u> on November 4, 1943.

See: F9

B310   Leaming, Barbara. <u>Orson Welles: A Biography</u>. Viking
         Penguin, Inc. New York. 1983 and 1985.

Brilliant and egocentric Orson Welles's second feature
film <u>The Magnificent Ambersons</u> featured a nice performan
by Anne Baxter, as the young love interest of the spoile
destructive son of the Ambersons, who brings about their
ruin.

See: F5

B311   Lee, Raymond. "Cecil B. DeMille's <u>The Ten Commandments</u>.
         <u>Movie Classics Magazine</u>. August, 1973.

Featured is a photograph of Nefretiri (Anne Baxter) and
Rameses the Magnificent (Yul Brynner) keeping watch over
Pharaoh Sethi (Sir Cedric Hardwicke) from the film <u>The
Ten Commandments</u>.

See: F38

B312   Leff, Leonard J. <u>Hitch with Selznick: The Rich and
         Strange Collaboration of Alfred Hitchcock and David O.
         Selznick</u>. Weidenfeld and Nicolson. New York. 1987.

Briefly noted is Anne Baxter's performance in <u>I Confess</u>.

See: F32

B313   Leiter, Samuel L. <u>Ten Seasons: Theatre in the Seventies</u>.
         Greenwood Press. Westport, Connecticut, New York,
         and London. 1966.

Noel Coward's two, one-act plays set in a Swiss hotel,
are given brief synopses. The plays were produced on
stage under the title <u>Noel Coward's in Two Keys</u>, starring
Hume Cronyn, his wife, Jessica Tandy, and Anne Baxter.

See: S10

B314   Lentz, Harris M., III. Science Fiction, Horror and
             Fantasy Film and Television Credits Supplement
             Through 1987. McFarland Publishers and Company,
             Inc. Jefferson, North Carolina, and London. 1989.

        Anne Baxter's credits include a Get Smart episode on
        April 6, 1968, and The Masks of Death, 1984 (which was
        never completed).

        See: T26

B315   Linet, Beverly. Star-Crossed: The Story of Robert
             Walker and Jennifer Jones. G. P. Putnam's Sons.
             New York. 1986.

        On December 5, 1942, Anne was tested by Henry King and
        Bill Goetz for the role of Bernadette in The Song of
        Bernadette. The part went to Jennifer Jones, who won
        an Oscar for Best Performance by an Actress.

B316   Lloyd, Ann, and Fuller, Graham. The Illustrated Who's
             Who of the Cinema. Macmillan Publishing Co., Inc.
             New York. 1983.

        Anne never quite reached the expected height of stardom
        usually associated with stage work, as well as receiving
        an Academy Award. She was tested for a role in Rebecca
        at age 16, but lost out to Joan Fontaine. However, she
        won a long-term contract with 20th Century-Fox.

B317   Lockhart, Jane. "Looking at Movies." Rotarian.
             April, 1949.

        Yellow Sky contains all of the ingredients of a
        traditional western, plus a harrowing and convincing
        picture of a desert journey that rivals that in The Three
        Godfathers.

        See: F23

B318   _____. "Looking at Movies." Rotarian. October, 1949.

        You're My Everything is a zestful, appealing musical
        made likeable and unpretentious because of the likeable

performances by Dan Dailey and Anne Baxter. Their famil
enjoyed the riches of show business and the ability to
keep their love alive after their show business life
ended.

See: F24

B319   Loney, Glenn. 20th Century Theatre, Volume 1. Facts
            on File Publications. New York. 1983.

On July 17, 1936, Anne Baxter made her Broadway debut
in Seen But Not Heard. On February 14, 1953, John Brown
Body opened on Broadway at the New Century Theatre, for
65 performances, staged by Charles Laughton. The stars
were Tyrone Power, Raymond Massey, and Judith Anderson
(later replaced by Anne Baxter).

See: S1, S6

B320   Lyon, Christopher. International Dictionary of Films
            and Filmmakers. St. James Press. New York. 1984.

Anne Baxter is mentioned for her roles in The Magnificen
Ambersons and All About Eve.

See: F5, F26

B321   "Made in Hollywood." Time. 5.5.52.

My Wife's Best Friend featured an unusual Anne Baxter:
one as an Egyptian belly dancer with a topaz in her nave
She would like to be known as a glamorous star, as well
as a straight dramatic actress.

See: F29

B322   Magill, Frank N. Magill's Annual Survey of Cinema.
            Salem Press. New York. 1983.

Included is a review of The North Star.

See: F9

B323   _____. Magill's Survey of Cinema, Series I. Salem
        Press. New York. 1981.

        Reviewed are The Magnificent Ambersons (pages 1036-1038),
        The Razor's Edge (pages 1429-1433), and All About Eve
        (pages 40-42).

        See: F5, F17, F26

B324   _____. Magill's Survey of Cinema, Series II. Salem
        Press. New York. 1983.

        Contained are reviews of Five Graves to Cairo (pages
        789-791), Mother Wore Tights (pages 1658-1660), I Confess
        (page 1080), and The Ten Commandments (pages 2430-2433).

        See: F8, F19, F32, F38

B325   "The Magnificent Ambersons, Welles's Film from Novel
        by Tarkington, Opens at Capitol." New York Times.
        8.14.42.

        The Magnificent Ambersons is a relentlessly sober drama
        on a barren theme staged by Orson Welles. The cast
        contributed fine performances in an exceptionlaly well-
        made film.

        See: F5

B326   Mandell, Paul R. "Parting the Red Sea and Other
        Miracles." American Cinematographer. April, 1983.

        Mandell provides an indepth commentary on the structuring
        and filming of The Ten Commandments..

        See: F38

B327   Mann, Roderick. "Baxter Checks in for Bette Davis on
        Hotel." San Francisco Chronicle. 9.18.83.

        Anne "filled in" for ailing Bette Davis on the TV series
        Hotel, as Davis's sister-in-law, hotel manager. The
        series premiered on September 28, 1983.

        See: T54

B328   _____. "Will Baxter Meet Davis in 'Hotel?'" Los Angele
        Times. 8.30.83.

        Shortly after visiting Anne Baxter at her home in
        Connecticut, Bette Davis suffered a stroke. She had
        been scheduled to appear as Laura Trent on the upcoming
        TV series Hotel. Anne Baxter was summoned to fill in
        as her sister-in-law. Anne looked forward to Davis
        returning to the show, since she hadn't worked with her
        since their co-starring roles in All About Eve.

        See: F26, T54

B329   Marill, Alvin H. Movies Made for Television: The
        Telefeature and the Mini-Series, 1964-1986, Vol.
        II. Zoetrope. New York. 1987.

        Anne Baxter is mentioned for her roles in Hotel, Marcus
        Welby, M.D., The Moneychangers, and Nero Wolfe.

        See: T33, T49, T51, T54

B330   "Marriage Dissolved." London Times. 1.31.70.

        American actress Anne Baxter was divorced from her secon
        husband, Randolph Galt.

B331   Marx, Kenneth S. Star Stats: Who's Whose in Hollywood.
        Price, Stern, Sloan Publishers, Inc. Los Angeles,
        California. 1979.

        Marx lists Anne Baxter's family tree.

B332   Maslin, Janet. "The Screen: 'Jane Austen.'" New York
        Times. 11.18.81.

        Anne Baxter's flair for the sweeping gesture is perfectly
        contrasted by the eerie, unnerving, calm performance
        of Robert Powell in Jane Austen in Manhattan.

        See: F50

B333   Massey, Raymond. A Hundred Different Lives. Little,
        Brown, and Company. Boston, Massachusetts. 1979.

Anne Baxter replaced Judith Anderson on the second tour of <u>John Brown's Body</u>. Massey felt that both actresses were of great accomplishment and of high, though differing, talents.

See: S6

B334   McCann, Graham. <u>Marilyn Monroe</u>. Rutgers University
            Press. New Brunswick, New Jersey. 1987.

The leading female star of a movie has the eyes of the camera. The audience will identify the reality of her projected persona by the ability to make the camera believe what it is seeing. During the "Hollywood years," conceptions of women's roles were short on substance but strong on spectacle, as confirmed by Anne Baxter's role in <u>The Ten Commandments</u> (quote from Anne: "Moses, Moses, you splendid, stubborn, adorable fool.").

See: F38

B335   McCarten, John. The Current Cinema." <u>The New Yorker</u>.
            3.15.47.

In <u>Blaze of Noon</u>, Anne Baxter is the little woman who sits nervously at home while her own true love is skittering around in the sky.

See: F18

B336   _____. "The Current Cinema." <u>The New Yorker</u>. 1.30.49.

Anne Baxter gives an engaging performance in <u>You're My Everything</u>.

See: F24

B337   _____. "The Current Cinema." <u>The New Yorker</u>. 2.12.49.

Anne Baxter shares prominence with her co-stars in <u>Yellow Sky</u>.

See: F23

B338   _____. "The Current Cinema: All Aboard for Colorado."
          The New Yorker. 5.27.50.

          A Ticket to Tomahawk features Anne Baxter as a comely,
          innocent, but dangerous character with a knife or gun.

          See: F25

B339   _____. "The Current Cinema: Bonanza for Bette."   The
          New Yorker. 10.21.50.

          In her role in All About Eve, Anne Baxter is always
          interesting to watch, even when her claws are showing
          a little too obviously.

          See: F26

B340   _____. "The Current Cinema: Darryl in a Dhoti."
          The New Yorker. 11.30.46.

          In The Razor's Edge, Anne Baxter wrestles valiantly but
          unsuccessfully as Sophie, a part in which the "most naiv
          readers of Cosmopolitan would hardly place any credence.

          See: F17

B341   _____. "The Current Cinema: DeMille at the Old Stand."
          The New Yorker. 11.17.56.

          Anne Baxter in The Ten Commandments is foolishly kitteni
          as the princess who loves Moses.

          See: F38

B342   _____. "The Current Cinema: Meandering with Alfred."
          The New Yorker. 4.4.53.

          Anne Baxter is cast as a girl so hell-bent on suffering
          in I Confess that it is "hard to imagine her as anything
          but a heroine in one of those lachrymose radio programs
          designed to keep ladies from their morning vacuuming."

          See: F32

B343   _____. "The Current Cinema: New Old Frontier." The
           New Yorker. 2.25.61.

     Anne Baxter is a member of the supporting cast of
     Cimarron, who are all admirable in their performances,
     "even though none of them will manage to interfere for
     long with the memories of the 1931 version."

     See: F41

B344   _____. "The Current Cinema: Siamese and Horses."
           The New Yorker. 7.6.46.

     Fred MacMurray, Anne Baxter, and Burl Ives support the
     horse, who has the title role in Smoky, a film as relaxing
     as a drive in the country.

     See: F15

B345   McCarthy, John, and Kelleher, Brian. Alfred Hitchcock
           Presents. St. Martin's Press. New York. 1985.

     The authors give a synopsis and air date of "A Nice
     Touch," an episode of the television series The Alfred
     Hitchcock Hour, which featured guest star Anne Baxter.

     See: T12

B346   McClelland, Doug. Eleanor Parker: Woman of a Thousand
           Faces, A Bio-Bibliography. The Scarecrow Press,
           Inc. Metuchen, New Jersey, and London. 1989.

     Anne Baxter co-starred with Miss Parker in Three Violent
     People. The film was originally titled The Maverick.

     See: F39

B347   McNeil, Alex. Total Television. Penguin Books.
           New York. 1980.

     Anne Baxter starred in "Bitter Choice" on G.E. Theater
     on April 21, 1957.

     See: T1

B348   McWilliams. <u>TV Series</u>. Perigee Books. New York. 1987

From the beginning of her career, Anne Baxter exhibited
a striking style -- heated, heavy-lidded and hard-
breathing. According to McWilliams, cult fans have
disagreed on whether she was a bad actress, a lucky lady
a gifted diva, a bit of all three, or none at all. She
is included in the chapter on "Glamorous Strangers."
Her own life reflected her role as Eve Harrington in
<u>All About Eve</u>.

See: F26

B349   Medved, Harry, and Medved, Michael. "Golden Turkey
        Awards, Part 1 of a Hilarious Star Book Extra."
        <u>Star</u>. 3.18.66.

Anne Baxter's scene with Charlton Heston in <u>The Ten
Commandments</u> is included in the authors' new book chapter
"The Most Awkward On-Screen Marriage Proposals." In
the scene, Princess Nefretiri summons Moses (Charlton
Heston) to her barge to persuade him to forsake his people
and marry her.

See: F38

B350   Menosky, Joe. "Action/Adventure." <u>Video Times</u>.
        January, 1985.

The 1943 movie <u>North Star</u> was released on video cassette
at a cost of $39.95.

See: F9

B351   Michael, Paul. <u>The Great American Movie Book</u>.
        Prentice-Hall, Inc. Englewood Cliffs, New Jersey.
        1980.

Anne's work is mentioned for her roles in the films <u>All
About Eve</u>, <u>The Pied Piper</u>, <u>The Ten Commandments</u>, and
<u>The Razor's Edge</u>, for which she won the Oscar for Best
Supporting Actress.

See: F6, F17, F26, F38

B352   "Milestones." Time. 12.16.85.

Anne Baxter suffered a stroke on December 4, 1985, while
hailing a taxi to take her to a hair appointment.

B353   _____. Time. 12.23.85.

Anne Baxter dies at age 62 in New York City, after
suffering a stroke on December 4, 1985.

B354   "Miss Anne Baxter, Hollywood Leading Lady." London Times.
         12.13.85.

This overseas publication featured a brief biography
of the later American actress Anne Baxter.

B355   Mitchell, Milo, Brooks, Chris, and Robidas, Ted. "Coming
         Attractions." Prevue. November-December, 1984.

Anne Baxter was slated to star in a new Sherlock Holmes
thriller The Masks of Death, with Ray Milland, John Mills,
and Peter Cushing. The film was never released.

B356   Montgomery, Charles, Mullins, Joe, Robin-Tani, Marianne,
         Sternig, Barbara, and Wright, David. "'Hotel' Star
         Anne Baxter -- The Untold Story of Her Roller-Coaster
         Ride to Tragedy." National Enquirer. 12.24.85.

The star of the popular TV series Hotel lived life at
a killing pace, commuting 5,000 miles every other week
to report to work in Los Angeles from her home in
Connecticut. Anne's hectic schedule and high blood
pressure pushed her to the breaking point.

B357   Morella, Joe. Films of World War II. The Citadel Press.
         Secaucus, New Jersey. 1973.

Anne Baxter is mentioned in the following film synopses:
Crash Dive, Five Graves to Cairo, North Star, The
Sullivans, and Sunday Dinner for a Soldier.

Of all the films during the war years, these covered a variety of story lines.

See: F7-9, F11, F12

B358   Moritz, Charles. "Anne Baxter." <u>Current Biography</u>
            <u>Yearbook</u>. July, 1973.

Moritz provides an up-to-date biography of Anne Baxter.

B359   Moss, Marquita. "The Late Liz: A Metamorphosis of a
            Rich Alcoholic." <u>Christianity Today</u>. 10.22.71.

Anne Baxter is the star of this "true story" based on a rich alcoholic woman's salvation via her religious convictions. <u>The Late Liz</u> delivers a message without preaching and was considered worthwhile.

See: F48

B360   "Movie Review." <u>The Green Sheet</u>. 4.15.53.

<u>The Blue Gardenia</u> is a mystery that features Anne Baxter as a young telephone operator involved in murder. Two ratings boards considered the heroine's drinking scene overlong and embarrassing.

See: F31

B361   "Movie Review." <u>Motion Picture</u>. June, 1953.

<u>The Blue Gardenia</u> is an entertaining "who-dun-it." This spine-tingler is based on a story by Vera Caspary, from <u>Today's Woman, The Magazine for Young Wives</u>.

See: F31

B362   "Movie of the Week." <u>Life</u>. 8i.10.42.

<u>The Pied Piper</u> tells of a group of refugee children escaping from Nazis in Europe. "It combines a mixture of poignance and humor and its able cast, headed by Monty Woolley, which lift it into the class of worthwhile films." Anne Baxter is the young French woman who

assists the Englishman and five children in escaping
Brest, France, for England in a fishing boat.

See: F6

B363   _____. Life. 11.1.43.

"Goldwyn makes an eloquent tone poem of a Russian town
in peace and war" in North Star. It has epic breadth
and sweep. Anne Baxter is pictured herding geese through
the street, thinking of little but love and comrades
from her local school. Another photo shows her with
blinded sweetheart Farley Granger, who was wounded after
smuggling guns and ammunition to the guerillas.

See: F9

B364   _____. Life. 11.18.46.

The Razor's Edge, by W. Somerset Maugham, makes a superb
film. The movie shows an absorbing interplay of character
among natural human adults. It is good art, as well
as entertainment.

See: F17

B365   "Movie Review." Movie Play. May, 1953.

The Blue Gardenia features a new Anne Baxter, with lovely
blonde hair, in a good follow-up to her outstanding role
in I Confess.

See: F31, F32

B366   "Movie Review." Esquire. December, 1950.

Anne Baxter gives a fine performance in All About Eve,
deemed to be a classic.

See: F26

B367   "Movie Review." New American Mercury. January, 1951.

Featured is a glowing review of All About Eve, with Anne
Baxter in the pivotal role of Eve Harrington.

See: F26

B368   "Movie Review." Photoplay. April, 1953.

The Blue Gardenia is an undistinguished mystery that
has a predictable end and some attractive performances
by Anne Baxter, Richard Conte, and Ann Sothern.

See: F31

B369   "Movie Review." Women's Home Companion. November, 1944

This article provides a review of the new release A Gues
in the House.

See: F13

B370   "Moviereel." Hollywood Studio Magazine. October, 1982.

Anne Baxter fractured her ankle and appears in a cast
for her debut as Queen Gertrude in Hamlet, staged at
the American Shakespeare Theatre in Stratford,
Connecticut.

See: S12

B371   "Movies." Newsweek. 5.31.43.

There is little or no fuss about Nazi ideology and
democratic rebuttal in the nontypical World War II film
Five Graves to Cairo, featuring Anne Baxter.

See: F8

B372   _____. Newsweek. 12.2.46.

Anne Baxter's portrayal of Sophie MacDonald in The Razor'
Edge is highlighted. In this role, she brought pathos

and drama.   The longer-than-average film was an otherwise slow-moving movie.

See: F17

B373   _____.   Newsweek.   3.17.47.

Anne Baxter handles the love interest well in Blaze of Noon.

See: F18

B374   "Movies: Much of a Muchness."   Newsweek.   8.9.48.

As the young female lawyer and love interest of the town's most promising attorney, Anne Baxter is included in scenes that are satisfying in The Walls of Jericho.

See: F21

B375   "Movies."   Newsweek.   8.1.49.

In You're My Everything, Anne Baxter, re-creates a reasonable facsimile of the ebullient Clara Bow (only better) and gets the film off to a good start.

See: F24

B376   _____.   Newsweek.   5.22.50.

Anne Baxter co-stars as rootin-tootin' tomboyish Kit Dodge, Jr., a young woman who has never been kissed and not likely to be once she's appointed deputy sheriff in A Ticket to Tomahawk.

See: F25

B377   _____.   Newsweek.   10.16.50.

Anne Baxter is quite effective in her role of Eve Harrington opposite Bette Davis (Margo Channing) in All About Eve.

See: F26

B378   _____. Newsweek. 4.16.51.

As Valerie Hogan in Follow the Sun, Anne Baxter is
steadily paced and gives a fine, convincing portrayal
of the wife of pro golfer Ben Hogan. He is the only
to person to win the U.S. Open twice (to date), which
was quite an accomplishment after a near-fatal car
accident.

See: F27

B379   _____. Newsweek. 10.6.52.

In "The Last Leaf," one of four stories in O. Henry's
Full House, Anne Baxter is introduced as a New York girl
jilted by an actor and despaired of life. The vignette
ends in a tricky O. Henry finale.

See: F30

B380   _____. Newsweek. 3.2.53.

In I Confess, Anne Baxter, Montgomery Clift, and O. E.
Hasse could scarcely be bettered in their unorthodox
roles.

See: F32

B381   _____. Newsweek. 4.5.54.

Anne Baxter is Willi, the homeless German girl in the
beautifully photographed Carnival Story.

See: F33

B382   "Moving Picture Reviews." Film Comment. Summer, 1971.

Given is a retrospective of the Orson Welles classic
The Magnificent Ambersons.

See: F5

B383   Mr. Harper. <u>Harper's Magazine</u>. January, 1951.

Anne Baxter co-stars in <u>All About Eve</u>, a talky film that
is "redolent with an up-to-date aroma while still managing
to pull at the heartstrings."

See: F26

B384   Naremore, James. <u>The Magic World of Orson Welles</u>. Oxford
        University Press. New York. 1978.

<u>The Magnificent Ambersons</u> co-starred film luminaries
Joseph Cotten, Agnes Moorehead, and ingenue Anne Baxter.

See: F5

B385   Nash, Bruce. <u>Tubeteasers</u>. A. S. Barnes and Company.
        New York. 1979.

"Prestidigitator Anne Baxter baffled Batman with her
feats of legerdemain as the magician-turned-jewel thief
Zelda the Great on the TV series <u>Batman</u>.

See: T15

B386   "New Films: Sunday Dinner." <u>Newsweek</u>. 2.5.45.

Anne Baxter is Tessa, part of the impoverished family
who invite G.I. John Hodiak home in <u>Sunday Dinner for
a Soldier</u>, a charming little World War II movie.

See: F12

B387   "New Movies." <u>Fortnight</u>. 12.30.46.

Anne Baxter contributes a memorable performance in <u>The
Razor's Edge</u>, as the degraded woman whom the hero offers
to marry but doesn't. Her dipsomania is as alarming
as Ray Milland's in <u>The Lost Weekend</u> and provides the
film's momentary spark of reality.

See: F17

B388   "New Picture." <u>Time</u>. 10.16.50.

    "<u>All About Eve</u> is the needle-sharp study of bitchery
in the Broadway theater." Anne Baxter's portrayal of
Eve Harrington makes her one of Hollywood's most versatil
performers. She makes Eve everything she should be by
playing her with sensitivity and modulation.

    See: F26

B389   Nichols, Lewis. "Theater Reviews." <u>New York Times</u>.
      3.3.38.

    Nichols reviews the stage version of <u>There's Always a
Breeze</u>, which featured a teenaged Anne Baxter.

    See: S2

B390   Nickens, Christopher. <u>Bette Davis: A Biography in
      Photographs</u>. Doubleday. New York. 1985.

    Anne Baxter shares stills with the great Davis in their
roles in <u>All About Eve</u>.

    See: F26

B391   "Obituary." <u>Variety</u>. 12.18.85.

    Although Anne Baxter never gained super-stardom, she
was a survivor and had the reputation of being a dedicate
and reliable worker.

B392   "Obituary -- Miss Anne Baxter, Hollywood Leading Lady."
      <u>London Times</u>. 12.13.85.

    The London newspaper gave an extensive obituary on the
American actress Anne Baxter.

B393   O'Donnell, Monica. <u>Contemporary Theatre, Film and
      Television</u>. Gale Research Company. Detroit,
      Michigan. 1984.

    Provided is a revealing biography and filmography of
Anne Baxter.

B394   "On a High Note." Los Angeles Times. 1.28.73.

Anne Baxter was introduced as the new president of the
Chamber Symphony Society of California at an
office-warming cocktail party. Next Sunday, she is to
host anmother party for the board of trustees at UCLA's
Recreation Center immediately following the concert at
Royce Hall.

B395   Oppenheimer, Jerry, and Vitek, Jack. Idol: Rock Hudson.
          Villard Books. New York. 1986.

Anne is mentioned in the filmography which includes her
co-starring role with Rock Hudson in One Desire.

See: F35

B396   Osborne, Jerry, and Hamilton, Bruce. Soundtracks and
          Original Cast Albums Price Guide. Carole House
          Publishers. New York. 1981.

Listings include soundtracks for A Walk on the Wild Side
and The Ten Commandments.

See: F38, F43, M1, M2

B397   Osborne, Robert. 60 Years of the Oscar. Abeeville Press
          Publishers. New York. 1989.

Anne Baxter is quoted on her dilemma when she lost her
Oscar statue while moving to a new home. She had to
buy a new one, which broke, too! Also mentioned are
her nominations and winning for The Razor's Edge.

See: F17

B398   "Oscar Costume Gallery." Daytimers Real Life Looks
          Behind the Oscars Magazine. Spring, 1983.

Included is a photograph of Anne Baxter, Bette Davis,
Marilyn Monroe, and George Sanders from All About Eve.
Costumes were by Edith Head and C. Le Maire.

See: F26

B399   "Oscar-Winner Anne Baxter Is dead at 62." San Francisco
        Chronicle. 12.13.85.

Anne Baxter's life accomplishments and list of films
and television series credits are included in the article
on the death of the actress.

B400   Ott, Frederic W. The Films of Fritz Lang. The Citadel
        Press. Secaucus, New Jersey. 1979.

The Blue Gardenia was made in 20 days. Lang used a unique
camera dolly to photograph the scenes. Anne made a
thoroughly attractive murder suspect.

See: F31

B401   "Overdone." Newsweek. 1.16.61.

Anne Baxter is Dixie, a lady in red once loved by Yancey
(Glenn Ford), who settles in Oklahoma with his new wife
(Maria Schell), in Cimarron. Under the direction of
Anthony Mann, the cast uniformly overact.

See: F41

B402   Ozer, Jerome S. Film Review Annual 1982. Film Review
        Publications. New York. 1983.

Anne Baxter's role as Lilianna Zorska in Jane Austen
in Manhattan is reviewed in Films in Review (March, 1982)
Monthly Film Bulletin (August, 1980), New Statesman (July
25, 1980), New York Post (November 18, 1981), and Sight
and Sound (Autumn, 1980).

See: F50

B403   Parish, James Robert. Actors' Television Credits, Volume
        I and II. The Scarecrow Press, Inc. Metuchen,
        New Jersey. 1973.

Listed are television episodic credits for Miss Baxter.

B404   _____. Cinema of Edward G. Robinson. A. S. Barnes.
        New York. 1972.

Parish mentions Anne Baxter in the chapter that discusses
Robinson's work in The Ten Commandments.

See: F38

B405   _____.   Fox Girls.   Arlington House.   Metuchen,
          New Jersey.   1971.

Dramatic actress Anne Baxter was one of the powerhouse
actresses at the 20th Century-Fox Studio.

B406   _____.   The Great Combat Pictures: Twentieth-Century
          Warfare on the Screen.   The Scarecrow Press, Inc.
          Metuchen, New Jersey, and London. 1990.

Crash Dive is synopsized, which starred Anne Baxter in
the soap-opera World War II film that also won two Academy
Awards (Special Effects, Sound for Ben Carter;
Photography, for Fred Sersen).

See: S7

B407   _____.   The RKO Girls.   Rainbow Books.   Carlstadt,
          New Jersey.   1974.

Anne Baxter co-stars with Ann Sothern and Farley Granger
in 1943's North Star.   Anne was considered for the title
role in Rebecca.   In the mid-1950s, Universal acquired
the performing services of Anne Baxter and Jeanne Crain.
Barbara Hale was compared to Anne Baxter and Gene Tierney.
Barbara's son, William Katt, made his movie debut with
Anne Baxter in the 1971 film The Late Liz.

See: F9, F48

B408   _____, and Stanke, Don E.   The Swashbucklers.   Rainbow
          Books.   Carlstadt, New Jersey.   1976.

In Crash Dive, too much time was devoted to the love
triangle between the submarine lieutenant (Tyrone Power)
and his commanding officer (Dana Andrews) and the
commanding officer's girlfriend (Anne Baxter).   In The
Razor's Edge, Anne is Sophie, the childhood friend of
Larry Darrell (Power), who meets a tragic death.   In
The Luck of the Irish, Power is a New York executive,

who gives up marriage to his boss's daughter (Jayne
Meadows) in order to court and marry a beguiling, plain
Irish girl (Baxter). Anne is an attractive law school
graduate in The Walls of Jericho.

See: F7, F17, F21, F22

B409   . The Tough Guys. Rainbow Books. Carlstadt,
           New Jersey. 1976.

In The Walls of Jericho, Anne Baxter is the law school
graduate who loves the married Cornel Wilde, who is
publicly smeared by his uncontrollable wife (Linda
Darnell).

See: F21

B410   , and Whitney, Steven. Vincent Price Unmasked.
           Drake Publishers, Inc. New York. 1974.

In The Eve of St. Mark, Anne Baxter was the glossy-eyed
ingenue to the handsome but bland William Eythe. Anne
was a lady-in-waiting to czarina Catherine the Great
in A Royal Scandal. She was Nefretiri in The Ten
Commandments.

See: F10, F14, F38

B411   Parsons, Louella O. "Surprise Ending." Photoplay.
           January, 1946.

Anne Baxter is slated to co-star in The Razor's Edge,
which had been turned down by Judy Garland and Betty
Grable.

See: F17

B412   Paul, E. "Anne Baxter Complex." Photoplay. October,
           1944.

No-punches-pulled young actress Anne Baxter is profiled.

B413   Peary, Danny. Close-Ups: The Movie Star Book. Workman
           Publishing. New York. 1978.

Betty Grable was offered the part of Sophie in The Razor's Edge. She turned it down because her fans would expect her to surface from her drowning scene to sing a love song. Anne Baxter went on to win an Oscar for her portrayal of the tragic Sophie.

See: F17

B414   _____. Cult Movies. Delacorte Press. New York. 1981.

In All About Eve, Anne Baxter is the consummate manipulator of everyone with whom she comes in contact. Although critics didn't laud her performance, citing a lack of depth in her shallow character, it is by design that her personality is conveyed as such. Although she was not considered a great actress, Anne Baxter's Eve was perfect: calculating, cool and controlled, and empty.

See: F26

B415   Perry, George C. Hitchcock. Doubleday. New York.
          1975.

I Confess starred a blonde Baxter in the low-key mystery filmed in Quebec, Canada.

See: F32

B416   Perry, Jeb H. Universal Television: The Study and Its
          Programs, 1950-1980. The Scarecrow Press. Metuchen,
          New Jersey, and London. 1983.

Included are listings for movies for television starring Anne Baxter: Marcus Welby, M.D. (pilot), The Challengers, Companions in Nightmare, Ritual of Evil, and Stranger on the Run.

See: T18, T29, T33, T37, T38

B417   Pickard, Roy. The Award Movies: A Complete Guide from
          A to Z. Schocken Books. New York. 1980.

Anne Baxter is listed as the winner of the Best Supporting Actress for The Razor's Edge. Anne is part of an unrepeatable cast, who fire off Mankiewicz epigrams.

This movie was a hit with all the major award boards but came in second after <u>Sunset Boulevard</u> (from the National Board of Review). The film won the following awards: American Academy Award for Best Film, the New York Critics Award for Best Film, and Britain's Academy Award for Best Film, Any Source.

See: F17

B418   Pitts, Michael R. <u>Radio Soundtracks: A Reference Guide</u>. The Scarecrow Press. Metuchen, New Jersey, and London. 1986.

Listed are Anne's appearances on <u>Lux Radio Show on the Air</u> (<u>Five Graves to Cairo</u>), December 13, 1943; <u>House of Strangers</u>, December 16, 1950; and <u>Theatre Guild on the Air</u> (<u>Dead End</u>).

See: F8, R1, R2, R23

B419   _____. <u>Western Movies</u>. McFarland and Company, Inc. Jefferson, North Carolina. 1986.

Pitts synopsizes the following films in which Anne Baxter starred: <u>Cimarron</u>, <u>Outcasts of Poker Flat</u>, <u>Smoky</u>, <u>The Spoilers</u>, <u>Stranger on the Run</u>, <u>The Tall Women</u>, <u>Three Violent People</u>, <u>A Ticket to Tomahawk</u>, <u>Twenty Mule Team</u>, and <u>Yellow Sky</u>.

See: F1, F15, F23, F25, F28, F36, F39, F41, F46, T18

B420   Pollock, L. "Between Heaven and H...." <u>Photoplay</u>. April, 1957, and May, 1957.

These two issues featured articles on Anne Baxter's career to date and her aspirations for the future.

B421   Quinlan, David. <u>The Illustrated Directory of Film Stars</u>. Hippocrene Books, Inc. New York. 1981.

Anne Baxter is particularly good at playing deceptively sweet personalities, as in <u>All About Eve</u>. She had an unsuccessful try at revising her dramatic image to pin

up girl in the fifties. Listed are her movies and
television credits, as well as a brief biography.

See: F26

B422   Quirk, Lawrence J. The Films of William Holden. The
            Citadel Press. Secaucus, New Jersey. 1973.

Anne Baxter seems ill at ease in her lightweight role
in Blaze of Noon. James Agee, of Nation magazine, says
the film gets monotonous when the little woman has to
wait out the stunts done by the brothers, which brought
brief to the family.

See: F18

B423   Ragan, David. Movie Stars of the 40's. Prentice-Hall.
            Englewood Cliffs, New Jersey. 1985.

Provided is a brief but indepth biography of actress
Anne Baxter, with a partial list of her film credits.

B424   _____. Who's Who in Hollywood, 1990-1976. Arlington
            House Publishers. New Rochelle, New York. 1976.

Ragan gives a brief listing of screen credits for Anne
Baxter, noting her Oscar award and nominations.

B425   Reid, Alexander. "Anne Baxter Is Dead at 62; Actress
            Won Oscar in 1946." New York Times. 12.13.85.

The Academy Award-winning actress, who gained wide acclaim
for her role as Eve Harrington in All About Eve, died
after suffering a stroke on December 4, 1985.

See: F26

B426   Rhodes, K. "The Hodiaks." Photoplay. September, 1946.

Young actors Anne Baxter and John Hodiak are to be married
after a two-year courtship.

B427   Ricci, Mark, and Conway, Michael. <u>The Complete Films</u>
        <u>Marilyn Monroe</u>. The Citadel Press. Secaucus,
        New Jersey. 1964.

        Anne Baxter is mentioned for her roles in Marilyn Monroe
        early films <u>A Ticket to Tomahawk</u> and <u>All About Eve</u>.

        See: F25, F26

B428   Ringgold, Gene. <u>The Films of Bette Davis</u>. The Citadel
        Press. Secaucus, New Jersey. 1966.

        Anne Baxter co-starred with Davis in <u>All About Eve</u>, which
        according to Leo Mishkin of the <u>New York Morning</u>
        <u>Telegraph</u>, was "probably the wittiest, the most
        devastating, the most adult and literate motion picture
        ever made that had anything to do with the New York
        stage."

        See: F26

B429   _____. <u>The Films of Cecil B. DeMille</u>. The Citadel Press
        Secaucus, New Jersey. 1969.

        Anne is mentioned as being a star of the film <u>The Ten</u>
        <u>Commandments</u>.

        See: F38

B430   Roberts, John. "Jeff Chandler: Rugged Star of the 50's."
        <u>Hollywood Studio Magazine</u>. December, 1977

        United International cast Chandler in the remake of <u>The</u>
        <u>Spoilers</u>, with a rather tepid cast, including Anne Baxter
        and Rory Calhoun.

        See: F36

B431   _____. "Steve Cochran: A Tough Guy's Bizarre Movie Life.
        <u>Hollywood Studio Magazine</u>. August, 1983.

        Steve Cochran returned to RKO Studios, in pursuit of
        Anne Baxter as the high-diving circus performer in
        <u>Carnival Story</u>. The article told of Cochran's other
        film roles that brought him attention as a touch guy.

He was known to be as tough in real life as he was on
the screen. He was a hard-driving, hard-drinking man
who loved the ladies.

See: F33

B432   Robinson, D., and Kobal, John. Marilyn Monroe: A Life
           on Film. Hamlyn Books. New York. 1974.

        Anne Baxter is included in the synopses of movies A Ticket
        to Tomahawk and All About Eve, which featured a very
        young Marilyn Monroe in minor parts.

        See: F25, F26

B433   Robinson, Jeffrey. Bette Davis: Her Films and Stage
           Career. Scribner. New York. 1982.

        Bette Davis co-starred with acting competitor Anne Baxter.

B434   Rogow, Lee. "SR Goes to the Movies: Put Out that Damn
           Light." Saturday Review. 4.23.55.

        Anne Baxter is "flavorsome" as the singer being chased
        by a gang of Parisians because she shot the brother of
        an influential man in Bedevilled.

        See: F34

B435   Rohmer, Eric. Hitchcock: The First 44 Films. F. Ungar
           Books. New York. 1979.,

        Anne Baxter provided competent acting in I Confess,
        directed by the dean of mystery, Alfred Hitchcock.

        See: F32

B436   Rosen, Marjorie. Popcorn Venus. Avon Books and Coward,
           McMann and Geoghegan. New York. 1973.

        The 1950s provided a panoply of biblical sagas that
        allowed sex without censure, such as portrayed by Anne
        Baxter in The Ten Commandments. The actresses were tended

to by scantily clad handmaidens that provided many
subliminal messages.

See: F38

B437   Rosenblum, Constance. "Video Recording Review."
       New York Times. 4.26.87.

Rosenblum reviews Jane Austen in Manhattan. She
particularly liked Anne Baxter's performance.

See: F50

B438   Rovin, Jeff. The Fabulous Fantasy Films. A. S. Barnes
       and Company. New York. 1977m

Anne Baxter is the heroine in the film Angel on My
Shoulder, which co-starred Paul Muni and Claude Rains.

See: F16

B439   _____. The Films of Charlton Heston. The Citadel Press.
       Secaucus, New Jersey. 1977m

In The Ten Commandments, Nefretiri is confronted with
a piece of Hebrew cloth that is the key to Moses's origin
Her love for him is so strong she lies, betrays, and
kills. "Anne Baxter is an overripe plum picked from
the 'DeMille School of Public Sensuality.'" She is
convincingly conniving in the role that lacked depth.
In Three Violent People, Anne's overacting plays well
against Heston's inflexible bearing.

See: F38, F39

B440   _____. The Signet Book of TV Lists. New American
       Library. New York. 1982.

In a bit of "Holy Malfeasance!" Anne Baxter is one of
the actors who succeeded in portraying an enemy of Batman
and Robin on the popular prime time series from 1966-
1968. She was Zelda. Other characters who were enemies
of the Dynamic Duo are listed.

See: T14-T16, T19

B441   "Saddle Soap Opera." Newsweek. 1.28.57.

Fresh from her role in The Ten Commandments, Anne Baxter
again co-stars with Charlton Heston in Three Violent
People, a "period western spiced with a dash of
fashionable psychology."

See: T38, T39

B442   Samudio, Josephine. Book Review Digest, 1976. H. W.
           Wilson Company. New York. 1977.

In Intermission: A True Story, Anne describes her
experiences with husband and children in Giro, the 37,000-
acre cattle ranch north of Sydney, Australia, from 1959-
1963. The book was reviewed by the Library Journal on
June 15, 1976, and the New York Times Book Review on
September 10, 1976.

B443   Schallert, Edwin. Los Angeles Times. 3.28.53.

Because of Fritz Lang's direction of The Blue Gardenia,
"there is rare atmosphere, plenty of neat touches to
augment interest."

See: F31

B444   _____. "Cast, Language Give Bloom to Thriller."
           Los Angeles Times. 5.10.53.

Anne Baxter is the telephone operator who suspects herself
of being a murderess in The Blue Gardenia. The strong
cast and direction give qualities that make this film
a cut above the routine murder thriller.

See: F31

B445   Schanke, Robert. Eva Le Gallienne: A Bio-Bibliography.
           Greenwood Press. Westport, Connecticut. 1989.

Anne Baxter portrayed Rosalie in Madame Capet on Broadway.

See: S3

B446   Scheuer, Steven H. <u>TV: The Television Annual, 1978-1979</u>
        Macmillan Publishing Co., Inc. New York. 1979.

        Anne Baxter is effective in <u>Little Mo</u>, an above-average
        television movie depicting the life of Maureen Connolly,
        the first woman to win the Grand Slam of tennis.

        See: T50

B447   "The Screen." <u>New York Times</u>. 8.21.47.

        Although none of the songs is particularly tuneful and
        the dance numbers are routine, Dan Dailey shines in the
        musical <u>Mother Wore Tights</u>, narrated by Anne Baxter.

        See: F19

B448   _____. <u>New York Times</u>. 8.5.48.

        <u>The Walls of Jericho</u> is "a lengthy, leisurely, and often
        none too well-defined portrait of sacred and profane
        love, politics, and murder in a sleepy town."

        See: F21

B449   _____. <u>New York Times</u>. 4.26.51.

        <u>Follow the Sun</u> is a story of courage that is inspiring
        and should enlighten the hearts of all who are weighted
        with adversities."

        See: F27

B450   _____. <u>New York Times</u>. 9.3.55.

        <u>One Desire</u> is nothing more than a plodding, soap opera
        about a love triangle: a big handsome bloke (Rock Hudson)
        a slightly shady lady (Anne Baxter) "with a heart as
        big as turn-of-the-century Oklahoma," and a cold, schemin
        younger woman (Julie Adams). All three rate credit for
        pluck and perseverance as the script focuses on his iron-
        jawed commuting between Adams's meanness and Baxter's
        agonized nobility.

        See: F35

B451   Seiler, Michael. "Anne Baxter Dies at 62 -- 50 Years
        of It as Star in Films, Stage and TV." <u>Los Angeles</u>
        <u>Times</u>. 12.13.85.

The naturally glamorous actress's 50 years in the
entertainment business were forever stilled when she
succumbed Thursday morning, December 12, 1985, in
New York City. Her life and career are highlighted.
<u>Times</u> staff writer Judith Michaelson contributed to this
article on the risk-taker Anne Baxter.

B452   Selby, Spencer. <u>Dark City: The Film Noir</u>. McFarland.
        Jefferson, North Carolina, and London. 1984.

Included in this book are <u>The Gardenia</u>, <u>The Come On</u>,
<u>A Guest in the House</u>, and <u>I Confess</u>.

See: F13, F31, F32, F37

B453   Sennett, Ted. <u>Great Hollywood Movies</u>. Harry N. Abrams,
        Inc., Publishers. New York. 1983.

Anne Baxter is the scheming minx Eve Harrington, who
makes Margo Channing (Bette Davis) the target of her
ambition in <u>All About Eve</u>.

See: F26

B454   Shale, Richard. <u>Academy Awards</u>. Frederick Ungar
        Publishing Co. New York. 1978, 1982.

Anne Baxter was nominated for an Academy Award for Best
Supporting Actress on February 10, 1947. The ceremony
took place on March 13, 1947, at the Shrine Auditorium,
with emcee Jack Benny. She was nominated for Best Actress
for <u>All About Eve</u> on February 12, 1951. The ceremony
took place on March 29, 1951, at the RKO Pantages Theatre,
with emcee Fred Astaire. She lost to Judy Holliday.

See: F26

B455   Shepard, Richard F. "Serban in Film Debut, Meets Jane
        Austen." <u>New York Times</u>. 1.28.80.

Katrina Hodiak, the 28-year-old singer-songwriter daught
of actress Anne Baxter, co-stars with her mother in the
90-minute, made-in-America production for British
television, Jane Austen in Manhattan. The film will
be broadcast in England in May, and released to theaters
thereafter. Anne found the experience of working with
her daughter "peculiar," because she had nothing to draw
from. She did not consider herself a a typical stage
mother.

See: T50

B456   Sheppard, Dick. Elizabeth: The Life and Career of
        Elizabeth Taylor. Warner Books. New York. 1975.

Hedda Hopper, in essence, slandered Elizabeth Taylor
in her book The Whole Truth and Nothing But by claiming
she and Taylor had made up after Hopper's vicious commen
regarding the scene in All About Eve, where Anne Baxter'
character sends a note to the playwright's wife requesti
a meeting. Only 11 times in the history of the Academy
Awards (to date) had more than one performer from the
same film been nominated in a major competition. Bette
Davis and Anne Baxter battled over All About Eve. The
others were Bing Crosby and Barry Fitzgerald (Going My
Way), Maximilian Schell and Spencer Tracy (Judgment at
Nuremberg), Clark Gable, Charles Laughton, and Franchot
Tone (Mutiny on the Bounty), Burt Lancaster and Montgome
Clift (From Here to Eternity), James Dean and Rock Hudso
(Giant), Tony Curtis and Sidney Poitier (The Defiant
Ones), Richard Burton and Peter O'Toole (Becket), Dustin
Hoffman and Jon Voight (Midnight Cowboy), and Laurence
Olivier and Michael Caine (Sleuth).

See: F26

B457   Shevey, Sandra. The Marilyn Scandal. William Morrow
        and Company. New York. 1987.

Marilyn Monroe had difficulty working with stage actresse
Anne Baxter and Bette Davis in All About Eve.

See: F26

B458   "Since the Tragic Death."   Examiner.   4.8.86.

Producers of the TV series Hotel have decided not to
replace Anne Baxter's role in the series following her
death. They are considering having Bette Davis make
occasional guest appearances in her role of the hotel
owner.

See: T54

B459   "Sleeper." Newsweek. 1.8.62.

Season of Passion stars Anne Baxter as Olive -- a happy-
go-lucky mistress of "Roo." a cutter who, with pal Barney
(John Mills), spends off-seasons with their girlfriends.
The film is honest, compassionate, and enlightening.

See: F42

B460   Slide, Anthony. Selected Film Criticisms, 1941-1950.
            The Scarecrow Press. Metuchen, New Jersey. 1982.

Slide critiques The Magnificent Ambersons, Five Graves
to Cairo, The Razor's Edge, and All About Eve.

See: F5, F8, F17, F26

B461   Smith, Ella. Starring Miss Barbara Stanwyck. Crown
            Publishers. New York. 1974, 1985.

Anne Baxter co-starred with Miss Stanwyck in A Walk on
the Wild Side.

See: F43

B462   Spoto, Donald. The Art of Alfred Hitchcock: Fifty Years
            of His Motion Pictures. Doubleday. New York.
            1976, 1979.

Spoto's commentary includes I Confess.

See: F32

B463   _____. The Dark Side of Genius: The Life of Alfred
          Hitchcock. Little, Brown and Company. New York.
          1983.

          Anne Baxter and John Hodiak attended a dinner party at
          Bellagio Road, along with Ingrid Bergman and Peter
          Lindstrom, Cary Grant, and Teresa Wright and her husband
          During filming of I Confess, Hitchcock insisted that
          Anne bleach her hair a light blonde. Anne found him
          to be very quiet yet commanding a great deal of respect.
          She felt he would do anything to avoid people overreacti
          to him. Her scenes with Montgomery Clift were difficult
          and trying because of his drinking problems. Her poodle
          Petunia, adored Hitch. Anne attended the ceremony where
          Hitchcock was awarded the French Arts and Letters Award,
          making him an Officer des Arts et des Lettres, on
          September 5, 1969.

          See: F32

B464   Springer, John. Forgotten Films to Remember. The Citad
          Press. Secaucus, New Jersey. 1980.

          Anne made her film acting debut in 1940, along with the
          other newcomers Arthur Kennedy, Judith Anderson, Ruth
          Gordon, Gene Tierney, Dan Dailey, Mary Martin, Glenn
          Ford, Carmen Miranda, Victor Mature, and Carole Landis.
          In 1941, Charley's Aunt was an unforgettable film. Amon
          Anne Baxter's other motion pictures that fit this catego
          were: The Magnificent Ambersons, The Pied Piper, Five
          Graves to Cairo, North Star, The Eve of St. Mark, The
          Sullivans, A Royal Scandal, The Razor's Edge, Mother
          Wore Tights, Blaze of Noon, Yellow Sky, You're My
          Everything, All About Eve, Follow the Sun, I Confess,
          and The Ten Commandments.

          See: F5, F6, F8-11, F14, F17-19, F23-24, F26-27, F32,
               F38

B465   Stallings, Penny, with Mandelbaum, Howard. Flesh and
          Fantasy. St. Martin's Press. New York. 1978.

          In the chapter titled "Four Views of Womanhood," Anne
          Baxter is featured in a photograph from The Ten
          Commandments, in a costume by Edith Head. She is in
          Egyptian garb as Nefretiri. The amalgams of style
          resulted in a distracting strangeness. According to

Joseph Mankiewicz, Margo Channing's character in <u>All About Eve</u> is based on stage and screen actress Elizabeth Bergner. A movie still from <u>You're My Everything</u> is included in the chapter titled "Purely Coincidental," about screen characters based on real people.

See: F24, F38

B466   "Star People." <u>Star</u>. 10.25.83.

Anne Baxter's second autobiography is due to be published in the spring.

B467   Stine, Whitney, with Davis, Bette. <u>Bette Davis: Mother Goddam</u>. Hawthorn Books, Inc. New York. 1974.

Anne Baxter, one of Hollywood's most versatile performers, gives a sensitively modulated performance in <u>All About Eve</u>. Davis felt Anne had a diabolically hard job. Baxter gave a tremendous performance in <u>Applause</u>. Davis saw Anne on Broadway in the role and exclaimed, "You <u>were</u> Margo.!"

See: F26, S9

B468   Strauss, Theodore. "Hitched to a Star." <u>New York Times</u>. 8.15.43.

Coming from a Welsh heritage, Anne Baxter is a young woman of depth and character, even at the age of 20.

B469   _____. <u>New York Times</u>. 5.10.40.

<u>Twenty Mule Team</u> is a desultory drama set in Furnace Flat. Anne Baxter is the tavern mistress's daughter with "a hankering for a sweet-mannered feller."

See: F1

B470   _____. <u>New York Times</u>. 8.2.41.

<u>Charley's Aunt</u> was an occasionally chuckling charade with comic situations obviously plotted. Although

breezily played, it had the gaiety of "an old gentleman cutting a caper."

See: F3

B471   _____. New York Times. 11.17.41.

"Some first-rate talents have disappeared over their ears in Swamp Water."

See: F4

B472   _____. New York Times. 8.13.42.

The Pied Piper is a warm, winning, and altogether delightful film, wherein the producers had the good judgment not to allow the harsh tragedy of Nazi war atrocities to overwhelm its light and pathetic story.

See: F6

B473   Strick, Philip. Great Movie Actresses. William Morrow. New York. 1982.

Anne Baxter was the intriguing Oscar winner in The Razor Edge, who worked with Orson Welles, Alfred Hitchcock, and Billy Wilder. She gave up her career for sheep farming then returned in the 1970s.

See: F17

B474   Sullivan, Dan. "Cause Celebre at Ahmanson." Los Angele Times. 10.13.79.

In Cause Celebre, a Terrence Rattigan play staged at the Ahmanson Theater in Los Angeles, Anne Baxter looks wonderful in the costumes without losing touch with her character, and she "twinkles her legs" in the bedroom scene.

See: S11

B475   _____. "Two Toasts to Coward." Los Angeles Times. 7.2.75.

Anne Baxter's throaty voice and well-preserved, handsome
beauty assist the performances of Hume Cronyn and Jessica
Tandy in the superbly acted Noel Coward plays, "Come
into the Garden, Maude" and "A Song of Twilight," billed
as Noel Coward's In Two Keys.

See: S10

B476   Swanson, Gloria. Swanson on Swanson. Simon and Schuster.
            New York. 1980.

Anne was nominated for an Oscar in the company of Gloria
Swanson, Bette Davis, Judy Holliday, and Eleanor Parker
in 1950. Holliday won for her role in Born Yesterday.
Anne was dubbed a dark horse because of her adept
portrayal of a stage aspirant.

B477   Taubman, Howard. New York Times. 4.23.56.

In Bedevilled, Anne Baxter is the slightly scarlet lady
who mysteriously flees from the gendarmes and hoods in
Paris, France. Taubman felt the story was mildly
compelling.

See: F34

B478   Taylor, John Russell. Hitch: The Life and Times of Alfred
            Hitchcock. Pantheon Books. New York. 1978.

Anne Baxter, Margaret Sullavan, and Joan Fontaine were
considered for the title role in Rebecca. Fontaine beat
out the 16-year-old Anne. Later, Hitchcock unhappily
settled for Anne Baxter to star in I Confess.

See: F32

B479   _____. Hollywood Musicals. McGraw-Hill Book Co.
            New York. 1971.

Anne Baxter is mentioned for her role as the voice-over
in Mother Wore Tights.

See: F19

B480   _____. Orson Welles: A Celebration. Little, Brown.
            Boston, Massachusets. 1986.

            Anne is mentioned for her role as Lucy Morgan in The
            Magnificent Ambersons.

            See: F5

B481   Thomas, Kevin. "DeMille's Re-Released
                'Commandments' -- Better Than Ever." Los Angeles
                Times. 5.16.90.

            Anne Baxter's heavy vamping in The Ten Commandments could
            have used the light touch Claudette Colbert brought to
            her role of Poppaea in Cecil B. DeMille's The Sign of
            the Cross.

            See: F38

B482   Thomas, Tony. The Films of the Forties. The Citadel
                Press. Secaucus, New Jersey. 1975.

            Acting honors go to Anne Baxter for her tragic Sophie
            and Clifton Webb for his prissy aristocrat in The Razor's
            Edge, a film about an idealistic man, who returns from
            World War I to find the sources of wisdom.

            See: F17

B483   _____, and Solomon, Aubrey. The Films of 20th Century
                Fox. The Citadel Press. Secaucus, New Jersey.
                1979, 1988.

            See FILMOGRAPHY for films produced by 20th Century-Fox
            Studio that featured or starred Anne Baxter.

B484   Thompson, Howard. New York Times. 2.5.62.

            Anne Baxter is first-rate but a bit strident in Season
            of Passion, a sterling film set in the cane fields of
            Down Under. It is a funny, tender, and disturbing film
            about some lusty cane-cutters, their traditional vacation

with two cooperative city belles, and the abrupt collapse of their long idyll.

See: F42

B485   _____. New York Times. 6.8.67.

The Busy Body is a film of the macabre played for laughs, replete with cameos that work well in this who-dun-it.

See: F47

B486   _____. "Video Tape Review." New York Times. 1.12.86.

Thompson reviews the 1946 film The Razor's Edge, starring Tyrone Power, Gene Tierney, and Anne Baxter.

See: F17

B487   Thomson, David. A Biographical Dictionary of Film.
        William Morrow and Company, Inc. New York. 1976.

The author provides a brief biography that includes Anne Baxter's filmography. He mentions that she later made fewer films and "too many wasteful TV appearances," until she appeared in Applause ("one of life's braver attempts to match wit").

See: S9

B488   Tierney, Gene, with Herskowitz, Mickey. Self-Portrait.
        Wyden and Berkley Books. New York. 1979, 1980.

Anne Baxter showed she was a fine actress in The Razor's Edge. Anne replaced Gene Tierney in The Walls of Jericho.

See: F17, F21

B489   Tinney, Steve. "Anne Baxter's Ghost Haunts Hotel Set."
        Globe. 1.9.86.

Some of the crew members of the TV series Hotel reportedly received visitations from the popular Anne Baxter --

after her death! Her ghost was seen wearing her raincoat
and green scarf (that she had worn before makeup
sessions), wrestling the wardrobe rack. Another person
saw her Limoges china cup with warm milk turn up near
the phone on her desk. Someone else had a "run-in" with
her tan canvas-backed chair.

See: T54

B490   Torme, Mel. <u>It Wasn't All Velvet</u>. Kensington Publishers
        New York. 1988.

Torme was surprised that Anne Baxter even knew who he
was when they first met.

B491   "TV -- Behind the Scenes." <u>National Enquirer</u>. 5.22.84.

Anne Baxter was seen about town with a new date, interior
decorator Hal Broderick.

B492   _____. <u>National Enquirer</u>. 1.21.86.

Anne Baxter had filmed 20 episodes of the new season
of <u>Hotel</u> before her untimely death. The executives
decided that her character would also die, but hadn't
decided how. The new owner of the hotel will be Peter;
the new manager will be Christine.

See: T54

B493   _____. <u>National Enquirer</u>. 1.28.86.

A photograph is shown of Anne in her last episode on
the TV series <u>Hotel</u>, which aired January 29, 1986. She
is seen dancing with an old flame, played by Robert
Lansing.

See: T54

B494   Vance, Malcolm. <u>The Movie Ad Book</u>. Control Data
        Publishing. Minneapolis, Minnesota. 1981.

<u>Crash Dive</u> was the Tyrone Power "farewell role for the
duration of World War II." In the film, he leads a
reckless crew on the war's most dangerous mission,
battling death in a submarine. He finds romance in stolen
moments with lovely Anne Baxter. Power and Baxter are
shown in an embrace. The film enjoyed moderate box office
success.

See: F7

B495   _____. <u>Tara Revisited</u>. Award Books. New York. 1976.

Anne Baxter and husband John Hodiak co-starred with Clark
Gable and Lana Turner in the successful wartime film
<u>Homecoming</u>.

See: F20

B496   Vermilye, Jerry. <u>Bette Davis</u>. Galahad Books. New York.
         1973. Pyramid Books. New York. 1973, 1974.

As Eve Harrington, "Anne Baxter is so quietly accurate
that one tends almost to overlook her next to the
astringent perfection that Bette Davis brings to Margo."
Her understated performance made her deceptive character
even more detestable, yet certainly the most watchable.

See: F26

B497   "Video Flicks." <u>Video Review</u>. February, 1982.

<u>Yellow Sky</u> is a solid, entertaining western drama about
a motley crew of bandits, who take refuge in a ghost
town. There they find unexpected opposition in the person
of Anne Baxter, who lives there with her grandfather.
"The casting is offbeat and might not have worked in
directorial hands other than those of William Wellman."

See: F23

B498   Voyeur. "The New Films." <u>Theatre Arts</u>. December, 1949.

Anne does a commendable job in <u>You're My Everything</u>.

See: F24

B499   _____. "The New Films." <u>Theatre Arts</u>. December, 1950.

In <u>All About Eve</u>, Anne Baxter plays the insistent theme
of Eve Harrington with commendable intensity. In the
scene where the critic savagely exposes her, she creates
a character of some emotional depth.

See: F26

B500   Walsh, Moira. <u>America</u>. 3.28.53.

Although <u>I Confess</u> was absorbing, it was less than
satisfactory in its portrayal of the girl (Anne Baxter)
who was being blackmailed by the murdered man.

See: F32

B501   _____. <u>America</u>. 5.15.54.

Anne Baxter's performance in <u>Carnival Story</u> is honest
and intelligent, as the girl whose sins are humanly
understandable. Her decent instincts evenly triumph.

See: F33

B502   _____. <u>America</u>. 5.14.55.

Anne Baxter is an American girl in <u>Bedevilled</u>, fleeing
from the private vengeance of a prominent citizen. She
knows she is in need of spiritual rehabilitation.

See: F34

B503   _____. <u>America</u>. 9.3.55.

<u>One Desire</u> is a western soap opera that features Anne
Baxter as a reformed dance hall girl, who tries to settle
into respectability and domesticity after adopting a
pair of orphans (one is the 15-year-old Natalie Wood).
She is "driven" out of town, taking the children with
her. She returns years later to be with the man she
loves.

See: F35

B504   _____. America. 12.1.56.

In The Ten Commandments, Anne Baxter plays the tiger-
kittenish hereditary princess whose hand was to be given
to Moses by the Pharaoh's court, inciting jealousy from
the Pharaoh's son (Yul Brynner), after Moses's true birth
story is discovered.

See: F38

B505   _____. America. 4.5.58.

Chase a Crooked Shadow is a fairly interesting tale
starring Anne Baxter as a bereaved heiress who lives
on Spain's Costa Brava and is confronted by a strange
young man who claims to be a brother presumed long-dead.

See: F40

B506   _____. America. 3.11.61.

Anne Baxter's role of a shady lady with a heart of gold
makes little sense in the remake of Edna Ferber's classic
Cimarron.

See: F41

B507   _____. America. 6.2.62.

Anne Baxter co-stars in A Walk on the Wild Side, a lurid,
sometimes comic melodrama set in a New Orleans bordello.

See: F43

B508   _____. America. 10.2.71.

Anne Baxter has a small role in Fool's Parade, set in
the Depression era.

See: F49

B509   Warner, Alan. Who Sang What on the Screen. Angus and
            Robertson Publishers. London. 1984.

Anne Baxter is seen in a poster ad for The Razor's Edge.
"Mam'selle," sung by Art Lund for the film, became a
hit. Nat "King" Cole sang the title song in The Blue
Gardenia. Brook Benton sang the title song in A Walk
on the Wild Side. Dan Dailey sang "Chattanooga Choo-
Choo" in You're My Everything.

See: F17, F24, F31, F43

B510   Warner, Karen, and Iapoce, Michael. The Ultimate Trivia
          Quiz. 101 Productions. San Francisco. 1986.

The questions were: Who was the granddaughter of
architect Frank Lloyd Wright who won an Oscar for Best
Supporting Actress in The Razor's Edge, and who were
the two female leads that received Oscar nominations
for Best Actress for the 1950 film All About Eve. The
answers: Anne Baxter.

See: F17, F26

B511   Warren, Doug. Betty Grable. St. Martin's Press.
          New York. 1974.

Anne Baxter provided the off-camera voice of the grown-
up daughter in Mother Wore Tights.

See: F19

B512   Warrick, Ruth, with Preston, Don. The Confessions of
          Phoebe Tyler. Prentice Hall, Inc. Englewood
          Cliffs, New Jersey. 1980.

Ruth Warrick co-starred with Anne Baxter in A Guest in
the House, with Anne as the neurotically predatory guest
in Ruth's home. She sets out to drive everyone crazy
but finds her nemesis in the form of Ruth's aunt.

See: F13

B513   Waterbury, Ruth. Los Angeles Examiner. 3.28.53.

The Blue Gardenia had fine performances by all.

See: F31

B514   Weber, Louis. <u>All-Time Favorite Movies</u>. Publications
           International Ltd. New York. 1986.

        Anne Baxter is cited for her roles in <u>All About Eve</u>,
        <u>The Magnificent Ambersons</u>, and <u>The Ten Commandments</u>.

        See: F5, F26, F38

B515   Westmore, Frank, and Davidson, Muriel. <u>The Westmores</u>
           <u>of Hollywood</u>. J. B. Lippincott Company. New York.
           1976.

        While filming <u>The Ten Commandments</u>, the cameraman became
        ill with the flu and had an assistant take over. He
        was so entranced with the love scene between Charlton
        Heston and Anne Baxter that he managed to knock
        Cecil B. DeMille off his chair. Frank Westmore did the
        makeup on <u>The Fool's Parade</u>.

        See: F38, F49

B516   "What They Said About Marilyn," <u>Hollywood Studio</u>
           <u>Magazine</u>. August, 1987.

        In the article "Star Speak, Hollywood on Everything,"
        by Doug McClelland, Anne Baxter is quoted about Marilyn
        Monroe: "The final straw for me at 20th Century-Fox
        came when they would not let me test for <u>How to Marry</u>
        <u>a Millionaire</u>. I'd watched Marilyn Monroe come up from
        an extra and how she seemed to represent the wave of
        the future. I knew her first as a grubby sort of thing,
        very frightened, and now she was going to replace (Betty)
        Grable and all I knew was I wanted out."

B517   "Movies: What They Said About Eve Ain't So." <u>Life</u>.
           10.30.50.

        The article features a picture essay from <u>All About Eve</u>.
        Eve Harrington (Anne Baxter) is shown trying on Margo
        Channing's mantle; then her own upstart is also doing
        the same. Margo Channing (Bette Davis), angry with Eve
        at a birthday party for Bill, coldly implores Eve to
        "please stop acting as if I were the queen mother."

        See: F26

B518   "Where the Yellow Begins." <u>Newsweek</u>. 12.20.48.

In <u>Yellow Sky</u>, Anne Baxter is clad in a woman's shirt, jeans, and gun belt. She is very pleasant to look at.

See: F23

B519   Wiley, Mason, and Bona, Damien. <u>Inside Oscar</u>. Ballantin
        Books. New York. 1986.

Anne Baxter won the Best Supporting Actress Oscar for <u>The Razor's Edge</u> in 1946, the year of the feud between acting sisters Joan Fontaine and Olivia de Havilland. Joan won as Best Actress for her role in <u>Rebecca</u>, for which Anne had auditioned. Anne Baxter and John Hodiak presented the Oscar to the winner for Best Cartoon in 1949. In 1949, Anne Baxter was nominated for Best Actress, along with Bette Davis, for their roles in <u>All About Eve</u>. At the Academy Awards presentation telecast in 1964, Anne Baxter presented the Oscar to the winner for Best Art Direction.

See: F17, F26

B520   Willis, John. <u>Screen World 1986</u>. Crown Publishers,
        Inc. New York. 1986.

Anne Baxter's obituary states that she died of a cerebral hemorrhage on December 4, 1985, after suffering a major stroke in New York City.

B521   Winnington, Richard. <u>Film Criticism and Caricatures,</u>
        <u>1943-1953</u>. Barnes and Noble Books. New York.
        1976.

Anne Baxter is mentioned for her portrayal of Eve Harrington in <u>All About Eve</u>.

See: F26

B522   Wlaschlin, Ken. <u>The Illustrated Encyclopedia of the</u>
        <u>World's Great Movie Stars</u>. Harmony Books.
        New York. 1979.

The book gives a brief biography and list of her best
films. The author felt that she should have been a major
star but she wasn't, primarily because she never developed
the smiling schemer into the screen persona that would
have fit so well. She worked with top directors and
appeared in excellent films. She is quoted, "I am an
actress, not a personality."

B523   Wood, Michael. "Parade's End: The Past in Movies."
        American Film. March, 1976.

"Movies preserve the past so well for us by preserving
what is, for them, the present. They are perfect,
animated picture albums." For example, Anne Baxter
dressed impeccably as the Egyptian princess and acted
fairly well in The Commandments, but she remained as
"All-American" as Roy Rogers. Being Anne Baxter means
"carrying all kinds of traces of your time."

See: F38

B524   Wood, Robin. Alfred Hitchcock Films. A. S. Barnes.
        New York. 1977.

I Confess featured Anne Baxter in a role that found her
in a rather unusual Hitchcock mystery.

See: F32

B525   Yost, Elwy. Magic Moments from the Movies. Doubleday.
        New York. 1978.

Anne Baxter is mentioned in the reviews of her films
The Pied Piper and The Magnificent Ambersons.

See: F5, F6

        The following are unannotated bibliographic sources
wherein Anne Baxter's name was mentioned but she was not written
about. Other titles include sources that were unavailable for
review in this author's research.

UB1   Agee, James. "Films: So Proudly We Fail." The Nation.
        10.30.43.

250　　Anne Baxter

UB2　　_____.　"Films."　The Nation.　4.7.45.

UB3　　_____.　"Films."　The Nation.　3.22.47.

UB4　　Agin, Patrick.　Is That Who I Think It Is?　Ace Books.
　　　　New York.　1975.

UB5　　American Cinematographer.　January, 1951.

UB6　　_____.　April, 1983.

UB7　　American Film.　July-August, 1983.

UB8　　American Photographer.　July, 1953.

UB9　　Andersen, Christopher.　Citizen Jane: The Turbulent Life
　　　　of Jane Fonda.　Henry Holt and Company.　New York.
　　　　1990.

UB10　　Anderson, J.　Marilyn Monroe.　Crescent Books.　New York.
　　　　1983.

UB11　　"Anne Baxter to Narrate Film About Her Grandfather's
　　　　Life."　London Times.　11.13.83.

UB12　　Bazin, Andre.　Jean Renoir.　Simon and Schuster.
　　　　New York.　1973.

UB13　　Bellamy, Ralph.　When the Smoke Hit the Fan.　Doubleday
　　　　and Company, Inc.　New York.　1979.

UB14　　Bessy, Maurice.　Orson Welles.　Crown Publishers.
　　　　New York.　1971.

UB15　　Blum, Daniel, and Kobal, John.　A New Pictorial History
　　　　of the Talkies.　G. P. Putnam's Sons.　New York.
　　　　1958, 1968, 1973, 1982.

UB16　　Blum, Daniel.　A Pictorial History of the American
　　　　Theatre, 1860-1976.　Crown Publishers.　New York.
　　　　1977.

UB17　　Blum, Daniel.　Screen World 1951.　Biblio and Tannen.
　　　　New York.　1951.

UB18　　Blum, Daniel.　Screen World 1953.　Biblio and Tannen.
　　　　New York.　1953.

UB19   Blum, Daniel. Screen World 1958. Biblio and Tannen.
        New York. 1959.

UB20   Brady, Frank. Citizen Welles: A Biography of Orson
        Welles. Scribner. New York. 1989.

UB21   Brokaw, Bob, Jamieson, Bill, and Russell, Jo. What's
        Playing at the Movies? Pisani Printing Company.
        San Francisco, California. 1965.

UB22   Bronaugh, Robert Brett. The Celebrity Birthday Book.
        Jonathan David Publishers, Inc. New York. 1981.

UB23   Canby, Vincent. "For DeMille, Moses' Egypt Was Really
        America." New York Times. 3.25.84.

UB24   "Cinema." The London Times. 3.5.43.

UB25   "Cinema." Time. 7.20.42.

UB26   _____. Time. 10.14.46.

UB27   _____. Time. 9.8.47.

UB28   _____. Time. 4.30.51.

UB29   _____. Time. 9.22.52.

UB30   _____. Time. 11.12.56.

UB31   _____. Time. 2.24.61.

UB32   Comito, Terry. Touch of Evil: Orson Welles, Director.
        Rutgers University Press. New Brunswick, New Jersey.
        1985.

UB33   Corliss, Richard. Talking Pictures: Screenwriters in
        the American Cinema, 1927-1974. Overlook Press.
        New York. 1974.

UB34   Cowie, Peter. Ribbon of Dreams: The Cinema of Orson
        Welles. A. S. Barnes. New York. 1973.

UB35   Crichton, K. "Lady with a Zip." Colliers. 12.12.42.

UB36   David, Nina. TV Season, 1976-1977. Oryx Press.
        New York. 1978.

UB37   Dick, Bernard F. _Billy Wilder_. Twayne Publishers.
        New York. 1980.

UB38   _____. _Joseph L. Mankiewicz_. Twayne Publishers.
        New York. 1983.

UB39   "Drama." _Video Times_. May, 1986.

UB40   Durgnat, Raymond. _Jean Renoir_. University of California
        Press. San Francisco, California. 1974.

UB41   _____. _Films and Feelings_. Faber and Faber. London.
        1967.

UB42   _____. _The Strange Case of Alfred Hitchcock or the Plain
        Man's Hitchcock_. University of California Press.
        San Francisco, California. 1974.

UB43   Dyer, R. _Stars_. British Film Institute. London. 1982.

UB44   Edwards, Anne. _The DeMilles: An American Family_.
        H. N. Abrams. New York. 1988.

UB45   Ellis, Jack, Derry, Charles, and Kerns, Sharon. _The
        Film Book Bibliography, 1940-1975_. The Scarecrow
        Press. Metuchen, New Jersey, and London. 1979.

UB46   Everett, Robert. "Films: There Was a Young Fellow
        from Goshen." _The New Republic_. 12.10.56.

UB47   Fontaine, Joan. _No Bed of Roses_. William Morrow and
        Company. New York. 1978.

UB48   Fordin, Hugh. _Film TV Daily, 1970 Yearbook of Motion
        Pictures and Television_. Arno Press. New York.
        1970.

UB49   France, Richard. _The Theatre of Orson Welles_.
        Bucknell University Press. New York. 1977m

UB50   Frank, Gerold. _Judy_. Dell Publishing Co. Inc.
        New York. 1975.

UB51   Freeman, David. _The Last Days of Alfred Hitchcock: A
        Memoir_. Overlook Press. New York. 1984.

UB52   Gianakos, Larry James. <u>Television Dramatic Series Programming: A Comprehensive Chronicle, 1947-1959</u>. The Scarecrow Press. Metuchen, New Jersey and London. 1981.

UB53   _____. <u>Television Dramatic Series Programming: A Comprehensive Chronicle, 1975-1980</u>. The Scarecrow Press. Metuchen, New Jersey and London. 1981.

UB54   _____. <u>Television Dramatic Series Programming: A Comprehensive Chronicle, 1980-1982</u>. The Scarecrow Press. Metuchen, New Jersey and London. 1983.

UB55   Goldberg, Lee. <u>Unsold Television Pilots, 1955 Through 1988</u>. McFarland and Company, Inc. Jefferson, North Carolina, and London. 1990.

UB56   Griffith, R. <u>The Talkies</u>. Dover Publications. New York. 1971.

UB57   Guernsey, Otis L. <u>Curtain Times: The New York Theater, 1965-1987</u>. Applause Theatre Book Publishers. New York. 1987.

UB58   Guiles, Fred Lawrence. "Marilyn Monroe." <u>This Week</u>. 3.2.69.

UB59   _____. <u>Tyrone Power: The Last Idol</u>. Doubleday. New York. 1979.

UB60   Handel, L. A. <u>Hollywood Looks at Its Audience</u>. University of Illinois Press. Urbana, Illinois. 1950.

UB61   Higashi, Sumiko. <u>Cecil B. DeMille: A Guide to References and Resources</u>. H. K. Hall. Boston, Massachusetts. 1985.

UB62   Higham, Charles. <u>Cecil B. DeMille</u>. Scribner. New York. 1973.

UB63   _____. <u>Charles Laughton: An Intimate Biography</u>. Doubleday. New York. 1976.

UB64   _____. <u>The Films of Orson Welles</u>. University of California Press. Berkeley, California. 1970.

UB65   _____. <u>Orson Welles: The Rise and Fall of an American Genius</u>. St. Martin's Press. New York. 1985.

UB66   _____. Sisters: The Story of Olivia de Havilland and
        Joan Fontaine. G. P. Putnam's Sons. New York.
        1984.

UB67   Huston, John. An Open Book. Ballantine Books.
        New York. 1981.

UB68   Johnson, Catherine. TV Guide: 25 Year Index, April 3,
        1953 - December 31, 1977. Triangle Publications,
        Inc. New York. 1979.

UB69   Kanin, Garson. Hollywood. Hart Davis Books. London.
        1975.

UB70   Kowalski, Rosemary Rebich. Women and Film: A
        Bibliography. The Scarecrow Press. New Jersey.
        1976.

UB71   Leff, Leonard J., and Simmons, Jerold L. The Dame in
        the Kimono. Grove Weidenfeld. New York. 1990.

UB72   Levin, M. Hollywood and the Great Fun Magazines. Ian
        Allen. London. 1976.

UB73   Literature/Film Quarterly. Summer, 1974.

UB74   "The Little Known Phrases." London Times. 7.13.85.

UB75   Logan, Joshua. "A Grief Observed." Show. September,
        1972.

UB76   Magill, Frank N. Magill's Annual Survey of Cinema.
        Salem Press. New York. 1982.

UB77   Marx, S. Mayer and Thalberg. Random House. New York.
        1975.

UB78   McBride, Joseph. Orson Welles. Viking Press. New York.
        1972.

UB79   McCarten, John. "The Current Cinema." The New Yorker.
        10.19.46.

UB80   _____. "The Current Cinema." The New Yorker. 5.8.48.

UB81   _____. "The Current Cinema." The New Yorker. 5.24.54.

UB82   _____. "The Current Cinema: Battle for Undersea." The
        New Yorker. 5.24.52.

UB83   McClelland, Douglas. Hollywood on Hollywood. Faber
        Faber. London. 1985.

UB84   McCreadie, M. The American Movie Goddess. Lilly Boks.
        New York. 1973.

UB85   "Medieval to Modern Evil." Newsweek. 3.5.62.

UB86   Morella, Joe, and Epstein, Edward Z. Lana: The Public
        and Private Lives of Miss Turner. Lyle Stuart,
        Inc. New York. 1971, 1972.

UB87   Myers, Hortense, and Burnet, Ruth. Cecil B. DeMille:
        Young Dramatist. Bobbs-Merrill. New York. 1963.

UB88   Oppenheimer, Jerry. Barbara Walters: An Unauthorized
        Biography. St. Martin's Press. New York. 1990.

UB89   Parish, James Robert. The Complete Actors' Television
        Credits, 1948-1988. Volume 1, Actors. The Scarecrow
        Press. Metuchen, New Jersey, and London. 1989.

UB90   Pepitone, Lena, and Stadlem, William. Marilyn Monroe
        Confidential. Simon and Schuster. New York. 1979.

UB91   Phillips, Gene D. Alfred Hitchcock. Twayne. New York.
        1984.

UB92   Pitts, Michael R. Radio Soundtracks: A Reference Guide.
        The Scarecrow Press. Metuchen, New Jersey, and
        London. 1986.

UB93   _____. Western Movies. McFarland and Company, Inc.
        Jefferson, North Carolina. 1986.

UB94   Poteet, G. Howard. Published Radio, Television and
        Film Scripts: A Bibliography. The Whitson
        Publishing Company. Troy, New York. 1975.

UB95   Powdermaker, H. Hollywood: The Dream Factory. Little,
        Brown. Boston, Massachusetts. 1950.

UB96   Reed, Rex. Conversations in the Raw. American Library,
        Inc. New York. 1969.

UB97   _____. People Are Crazy Here. Dell Publishing Co.,
        Inc. New York. 1974.

UB98   Rehrauer, George. <u>Cinema Booklist, Supplement One</u>.
        The Scarecrow Press, Inc. Metuchen, New Jersey.
        1974.

UB99   Renoir, Jean. <u>My Life and My Films</u>. Atheneum Books.
        1974.

UB100   "Review." <u>American Film</u>. March, 1976.

UB101   Robinson, Edward G., with Spigelgass, Leonard. <u>All My
        Yesterdays</u>. Hawthorn Books, Inc. New York. 1973.

UB102   Robinson, Jeffrey. <u>Bette Davis: Her Films and Stage
        Career</u>. Scribner. New York. 1982.

UB103   Rosenblum, Constance. "Video Recording Review."
        <u>New York Times</u>. 4.26.87.

UB104   Rothman, William. <u>Hitchcock: The Murderous Gaze</u>.
        Harvard University Press. New York. 1982.

UB105   Russell, Jane. <u>An Autobiography</u>. Sidgwick and
        Jackson. London. 1986.

UB106   Sadoul, George. <u>Dictionary of Films</u>. University of
        California Press. Los Angeles, California. 1972.

UB107   Sayre, Nora. <u>Running Time: Films of the Cold War</u>. Dial
        Press. New York. 1982.

UB108   Schickel, Richard. "Black Daubs on a Green Landscape."
        <u>Life</u>. 6.11.71.

UB109   _____. <u>The Stars</u>. Dial Press. New York. 1974.

UB110   Schultz, Margie. <u>Ann Sothern: A Bio-Bibliography</u>.
        Greenwood Press. Westport, Connecticut, New York,
        and London. 1990.

UB111   Schuster, Mel. <u>Motion Picture Performers: A Bibliography
        of Magazine and Periodical Articles, 1900-1969</u>.
        The Scarecrow Press. Metuchen, New Jersey. 1971.

UB112   "Screen." <u>Village Voice</u>. 2.1.62.

UB113   <u>Scribner's Commentator</u>. October, 1941.

UB114   Seidman, Steve. <u>Film Career of Billy Wilder</u>. G. K.
        Hall. New York. 1977.

UB115   Sesonske, Alexander. Jean Renoir: The French Films.
         The Harvard University Press. Trenton, New Jersey.
         1980.

UB116   Shipman, David. Great Movie Stars. A&W Visual Library.
         New York. 1976.

UB117   Smith, M. Marilyn. Barven Public. New York. 1971.

UB118   Spada, James, and Zeno, G. Marilyn: Her Life in Pictures.
         Sidgwick and Jackson. London. 1982.

UB119   Steinberg, C. Reel Facts: The Movie Book of Records.
         Vintage Books. New York. 1982.

UB120   Steinberg, Corbett. TV Facts. Facts on File, Inc.
         New York. 1980.

UB121   Steinem, Gloria, with Barris, George. Marilyn. Henry
         Holt Books. New York. 1986.

UB122   Strasberg, Susan. Bittersweet. G. P. Putnam's Sons.
         New York. 1980.

UB123   Taylor, R. G. Marilyn on Marilyn. Omnibus Press.
         London. 1983.

UB124   "A Tearful Bride on the Frontier." Life. 2.10.61.

UB125   Terrace, Vincent. Encyclopedia of Television Series,
         Pilots, and Specials, 1937-1973. Volumes 1 and
         2. Zoetrope. New York. 1986.

UB126   _____. Encyclopedia of Television Series, Pilots, and
         Specials, 1937-1984. Volume 3. Zoetrope.
         New York. 1986.

UB127   _____. Television 1970-1980. A. S. Barnes and Company,
         Inc. San Diego, California. 1981.

UB128   Thomas, Tony. The Films of Kirk Douglas. The Citadel
         Press. Secaucus, New Jersey. 1972.

UB129   Walker, Alexander. Bette Davis: A Celebration. Little,
         Brown. Boston, Massachusetts. 1986.

UB130   Welsch, J. R. Film Archetypes: Sisters, Mistresses,
         Mothers and Daughters. Arno Press. New York.
         1978.

UB131 Willis, John. <u>Screen World</u>. Crown Publishers, Inc.
       New York. <u>1960</u>-1990.

Awards Conferred

This chapter presents awards, offices, and memberships bestowed upon Anne Baxter for her work in film and personal endeavors. Films in which she starred or appeared that received nominations and/or awards are also listed.

A1   THE PIED PIPER
      Oscar Nomination: Best Picture; Actor; Photography (B&W)

      See: F6

A2   THE MAGNIFICENT AMBERSONS
      Oscar Nomination: Best Picture; Supporting Actress (Agnes Moorehead); Photography (B&W); Art Direction (B&W); Set Decoration (B&W)

      See: F5

A3   CRASH DIVE
      Oscar Nomination: Special Effects (Won)

      See: F7

A4   FIVE GRAVES TO CAIRO
      Oscar Nomination: Photography (B&W); Art Direction (B&W); Set Decoration (B&W); Editing

      See: F8

A5   NORTH STAR
      Oscar Nomination: Screenplay (Lillian Hellmann); Photography (B&W); Art Direction (B&W); Set Decoration (B&W); Music Score; Special Effects; Sound

      See: F9

A6   THE SULLIVANS
        Oscar Nomination: Screenplay (Edward Doherty and Jules
        Schermer)

        See: F11

A7   A GUEST IN THE HOUSE
        Oscar Nomination: Music Score

        See: F13

A8   THE RAZOR'S EDGE
        Oscar Nomination: Supporting Actress (Anne Baxter) (Won
        Best Picture; Supporting Actor (Clifton Webb); Art
        Direction (B&W); Set Decoration (B&W)

        Foreign Press Award (Golden Globe) Nomination: Supporti
        Actress (Anne Baxter) (Won)

        Golden Apple Award Nomination: Best Supporting Actress
        (Anne Baxter) (Won)

        See: F17

A9   MOTHER WORE TIGHTS
        Oscar Nomination: Music Score (Won); Photography (Color
        Song

        See: F19

A10   THE LUCK OF THE IRISH
        Oscar Nomination: Supporting Actor (Cecil Kellaway)

        See: F22

A11   ALL ABOUT EVE
        Oscar Nomination: Best Picture (Won); Supporting Actor
        (George Sanders) (Won); Director (Joseph Mankiewicz)
        (Won); Screenplay (Joseph Mankiewicz) (Won); Costumes
        (B&W) (Won); Sound (Won); Actress (Anne Baxter); Actress
        (Bette Davis); Supporting Actress (Celeste Holm);
        Supporting Actress (Thelma Ritter); Photography (B&W);
        Editing; Art Direction (B&W); Set Decoration (B&W); Music
        Score

        See: F26

A12   THE TEN COMMANDMENTS
       Oscar Nomination: Special Effects (Won); Best Picture;
       Photography (Color); Editing; Art Direction (Color);
       Set Decoration (Color); Costumes (Color); Sound

       See: F38

A13   CIMARRON
       Oscar Nomination: Art Direction (Color); Set Decoration
       (Color); Sound

       See: F41

A14   A WALK ON THE WILD SIDE
       Oscar Nomination: Title Song

       See: F43

A15   President, Chamber Symphony Society of California

Index

Numbers without a prefix refer to pages in the "Biography," numbers preceded by an "F" to the "Filmography," numbers preceded by a "T" to "Television Productions," numbers preceded by "R" to "Radio Productions," numbers preceded by "M" to "Musical Recordings/Soundtracks," numbers preceded by "S" to "Stage Plays," numbers preceded by "B" to "Annotated Bibliography," numbers preceded by "UB" to "Unannotated Bibliography," and numbers preceded by "A" to "Awards" section.

Burgess, Patricia, B59
Burke, Alfred, F44
Burke, Walter, T18
Burks, Robert, F32
Burnet, Ruth, UB87
Burnet, W. R., F7, F23
Burns, Catherine, T42
Burns, Elizabeth, 26, 41,
  F48
Burns, Ernest D., B60
Burns, Michael, T18
Burns, Paul, F4
Burr, Ann, F27
Burr, Raymond, 13, 25,
  F31, T27, T34, B101
Burrows, John H., F37
Burton, Jay, T53
Burton, Richard, B456
Bussieres, Raymond, F34
Busy Body, The, 24, 41, F47,
  B485
Butterworth, Donna, F45
Buttolph, David, F4, F7
Buttons, Red, T53

Cabot, Bruce, F15, B272
Cabot, Sebastian, 20, F45,
  T8
Caesar, Sid, 24, F47
Caffey, Richard, F39
Caged, 11
Cahoon, Herbert, B187, B188
Caillou, Alan, T37
Cain, Arthur, F49
Caine, Michael, B456
Calhoun, Rory, 9, 15, 16,
  F25, F36, B430
Calkins, Johnny, F11
Callow, Simon, B61
Cambridge, Godfrey, F47
Camel Screen Guild Theatre,
  38, R20
Campanella, Frank, T51
Campbell, John, F11
Campbell, Kippy, S7
Campbell, Richard H., B62
Campbell, Robert, B63
Canby, Vincent, UB23

Cannon, 41, T44
Cannon, Kathy, F49
Canty, Marietta, F12
Cape Playhouse, S4, S5
Capote, Truman, 25
Capucine, 21, F43, B51
Card, Kathryn, F34
Cardwell, James, F11
Carey, Gary, B64, B65
Carey, Macdonald, 12, F29,
  B242
Carey, Timothy Agoglia,
  T52
Carl, Richard, F49
Carlin, Chet, S12
Carlson, Timothy, B66
Carmichael, Ralph, F48
Carnival Story, 14, 39,
  B33, B38, B92, B128,
  B204, B244, B263, B281,
  B381, B431, B501
Carradine, John, F4, F38
Carricart, Robert, T36
Carrillo, Leo, F1
Carruth, Milton, F35
Carter, Ben, F7, B406
Carter, Harry, F15, F23,
  F25, F38
Case, Allen, T51
Casey, Lawrence, T47
Cason, John, F41
Caspary, Vera, F31, B361
Cass, Maurice, F3, F16
Cassel, Seymour, F16
Cassell, Walter, F37
Cassini, Oleg, B67
Castle, Nick, F24
Castle, William, F47
Castleman, Harry, B68
Castillo, Leo, F39
Catcher, The, 27, 41, T42
Caulfield, Edward, S2
Cause Celebre, 30, 42,
  S11
Cavalcade of America, 38,
  R7, R17
Cerf, Bennett, 28
Chad Hanna, 3
Challengers, The, 41, T37

About the Author

KARIN J. FOWLER is the author of *Ava Gardner: A Bio-Bibliography* (Greenwood, 1990), and has published children's stories.